C000219606

BACK FROM TI

By

JAMIE WEBSTER

and

RUSSELL WALKER

GLASGOW
BROWN, SON & FERGUSON, LTD.
4-10 DARNLEY STREET, G41 2SD

First Edition - 2008

ISBN 978-0-85174-808-5

© 2008 Brown, Son & Ferguson, Ltd., Glasgow G41 2SD
Printed and made in Great Britain

The Authors

Jamie Webster was born in Glasgow in 1951 and became an apprentice at the Fairfield shipyard in Govan in 1968. He was inspired to become active in trade unionism by the famous Upper Clyde Shipyard work-in of 1971 which was led by Jimmy Reid and Jimmy Airlie. Jamie became a union official at Govan in 1982 and yard convenor in 1998. He was awarded the MBE for services to industrial relations in 2004. Jamie lives in Glasgow with wife Isabel. They have three children, three grandchildren and a dog called Lambie, after legendary Partick Thistle manager John Lambie.

Russell Walker is an award winning television and radio producer and director. He has worked for *Radio Clyde, Granada Television* and was MD of an independent production company in the north west of England. In 1998 Russell took a year out to run a bar on Barbados. He returned to journalism and met Jamie Webster at the start of the campaign to save the Govan yard. Russell now works as a freelance producer and director.

ACKNOWLEDGEMENTS

The authors are indebted to *Radio Clyde* for permission to transcribe the contents of interviews and to the *Evening Times* for the use of their photo library; Jim McNeish was an ace archivist. We would like to thank the people who appear in the book, without whom there would have been no story. But, we are especially grateful to the twelve hundred or so workers at Govan in 1999. They cannot all be mentioned by name, but their spirit and determination not to waver in the face of adversity was an inspiration. Finally we wish to thank Nigel Brown, managing director of Brown, Son & Ferguson, Ltd., for the faith he showed in publishing this book.

This book grew from the detailed diaries kept by Jamie Webster and interviews conducted by Russell Walker from January to July 1999. Much of the narrative depends on Jamie's opinion of events and people. We are confident in the integrity of the information contained, although we do accept there might be minor discrepancies when it comes to exact times and dates.

DEDICATED TO THE MEMORY OF EDDIE URIE

FOR ISABEL, JULIE, FRASER AND AMANDA
AND FOR AUDREY

CONTENTS

LIST OF ILLUSTRATIONS
Page 306 on

1. An inspirational Jimmy Reid leading the '70s UCS work-in
2. Govan Shipyard, 1977
3. Portrait of the Author as a Young Man
4. Gunnar, Sir Gavin, & Lord Gus tour the yard
5. Kjell Almskog–CEO Kvaerner
6. Unopened redundancy letters *en route* to Kvaerner HQ
7. Celebrate good times, come on!
8. Our proudest moment. Our jobs were safe… or so we thought
9. Celebrating our success with Lord Macdonald
10. Joe Brown, Jamie's oldest friend in the yard
11. All smiles: Jamie with John Reid and Mohammad Sarwar
12. Happy days. Jamie's grand-daughter Robyn arrives
13. The Webster family
14. Jamie and 'My Rock', Isabel
15. Jamie Webster MBE: *'an acknowledgment of the ordinary people in our industry of whom I was just one'*

All photographs courtesy Newsquest (Herald & Times) Ltd. except No. 5: courtesy UPPA/Photoshot.

APPENDICES

Transcriptions of interviews by Russell Walker from March–July 1999

"I fully understand the strains and pressure you and all the workers at Govan have been under. If you feel it's all too much and want to call an end to it, then perhaps it's for the best."

Donald Dewar, Scotland's First Minister, Friday 9 July 1999.

FRIDAY
9 JULY 1999

Donald Dewar throws in the towel...

1

I ARRIVED early for the Task Force meeting in an agitated state. I was struggling to cope with the pressure and weight of expectation of my shop stewards and the workforce.

It had been six months since Norwegian multinational Kvaerner announced it was reviewing its interests in global shipbuilding. Since then the fate of twelve hundred workers at its Glasgow Govan yard on the River Clyde had been far from certain. In Glasgow parlance, 'oor jaikits were on a shoogly nail'.

The meeting was at the Scottish Office building in the city centre. A sixth floor meeting room had been reserved for us. After the full time union officials arrived the usual small talk began but this time it passed me by. I'm not great on aimless chit-chat and, not for the first time, I felt isolated and detached from the union hierarchy. We should have been walking a common road, but where they appeared to be striding along in stout shoes on even tarmac, I felt as if I were barefoot, gingerly picking my way across a 'C' road strewn with rocks and nettles.

Some of them appeared edgy. That worried me because often the union hierarchy knows the script of the meeting beforehand. On this occasion I hoped I was wrong.

Just before we began, I heard the chairman of the Task Force, Gavin Laird, had suffered a family bereavement. His brother had passed away only days before and when he opened the meeting the strain was visible. Momentarily I forgot about our problems in the yard and I felt genuine and deep sympathy for him.

I always respected the fact he showed such commitment and fortitude in turning up for that meeting at such a difficult personal time.

To compound this, the Task Force members were displaying body language that said to me all was not well and it was quite apparent they were suffering acute frustration.

After several minutes senior civil servant John Mason left the room and returned soon after, accompanied by Scotland's First Minister Donald Dewar and Scottish Secretary John Reid.

For an instant I deluded myself that their joint presence could herald the news that a deal had been done.

Within seconds of Dewar's opening remark I realised I was wrong as he indicated that the situation was extremely grave and that no breakthrough had been achieved in the negotiations between GEC and Kvaerner. GEC owned the big naval yard at Barrow-in-Furness in the northwest of England and the company had appeared to be in the box seat to buy us.

I could see the First Minister was very much ill at ease and I was firmly of the belief that the two things uppermost on his mind were:

1. He wished he was not at the meeting.
2. He was more concerned with what I would say to the media afterwards.

I was totally unable at that stage to control my emotions, and lost my composure.

"The outrageous conduct of both these companies recently beggars belief. They've taken the workers on a nightmare ride, on an emotional roller coaster and if the situation is now that GEC don't want to purchase Govan, tell them to come clean and at least let me get back to my workmates with the truth and allow us to get on with our lives."

The First Minister's response sent a shockwave through me.

"I fully understand the strains and pressure you and all the workers at Govan have been under. If you feel it's all too much and want to call an end to it, then perhaps it's for the best."

I couldn't believe what I was hearing. Donald Dewar, the so-called Father of the Nation, rather than lift my sunken spirits, was displaying serious signs of defeatism.

SIX MONTHS EARLIER

TUESDAY
12 JANUARY 1999

The fight begins…

2

THERE WAS a serious situation developing in the yard. The alarm bells were ringing loud, as strong rumours circulated that Norwegian heavy industry giant Kvaerner was considering pulling out of shipbuilding worldwide.

The company had a proud heritage. It was founded in 1853 in Oslo and just under a century and a half later it had assembled a collection of engineering and industrial businesses. These included shipbuilding, the operation of a shipping fleet, construction of offshore oil and gas platforms and production of pulp and paper manufacturing equipment.

Govan shipyard came under Kvaerner's wing in 1988. We'd been put up for sale after the former British Shipbuilders Corporation was privatised and the assets sold off.

In 1996, Kvaerner bought the British conglomerate Trafalgar House for £904 million pounds and moved its corporate headquarters from Oslo to London. Trafalgar House had interests in property, property development, construction, passenger shipping and engineering. It also owned John Brown Engineering in Clydebank, which as a shipyard had built famous vessels like The *Lusitania* and the *QE2*. This business was renamed Kvaerner Energy.

Maybe the Norwegians had bitten off more than they could chew. Trafalgar House became a millstone and coupled with a downturn in manufacturing and the shipping industry, Kvaerner faced severe financial problems.

The Chief Executive was replaced by 60-year-old Kjell Almskog who had previously worked with oil, gas and petrochemical company ABB. Officially, he'd been appointed to execute a major turnaround in the business. Word had come to us from our local Kvaerner directors that his nickname was 'The Iceman', and it was widely feared at Govan that he had been appointed as a hatchet man.

With the world commercial shipbuilding market in recession, the shipbuilding sector of the group appeared to be the most vulnerable. The order book at Govan was almost empty, an added cause for concern. Everyone in the yard realised we needed new contracts, and we needed them now. We were bidding for a Ministry of Defence (MoD) contract for six roll-on/roll-off ferries. However, with no decision imminent we were relying on winning an order to build an Antarctic survey vessel.

The shop stewards committee which I led decided to write to all the Labour MPs in Glasgow, west and central Scotland, asking for their support in securing the survey ship as it was government linked. I drafted the letter which outlined the gravity of the situation, emphasising that the future of the yard and more than one thousand jobs were at stake.

Over the next couple of weeks the tension grew, as stories that a mass cull of administration staff had taken place at Kvaerner HQ in London, on the orders of Almskog. In the yard I detected an increasing nervousness from our Managing Director, Gunnar Skjelbred, and other members of the board. They were getting bad vibes about our bid for the survey vessel, and they knew that with no new contracts our hopes for survival would be very slim. By now, it was early February and we would have virtually no work by summer.

Gunnar had arrived in Govan only months previously and had quickly gained the respect of the workforce. He was very down to earth, approachable, and had come through the ranks of the shop floor in his native Norway. In my fourteen years as a shop steward he was the most decent boss I had worked with. We had mutual respect for each other and that relationship was to prove vital over the next year or so. Throughout early February I went to see him on an almost daily basis to see if there was any news on our bid for the survey vessel. There wasn't.

TUESDAY
9 FEBRUARY 1999

Naming and shaming...

3

THE TELEPHONE rang in the shop stewards office and I answered. It was Christine, Gunnar's secretary, informing me that he wanted to see the convenors at ten thirty that morning in his office. I contacted three of the other convenors, Joe Brown, John Johnson and Davie Torrance. Minutes before we went in to see Gunnar, we all felt he was going to tell us the decision on the survey vessel contract.

To this day I have never asked Joe, John or Davie how they felt as they walked along the corridor to that meeting. My heart was racing and my stomach was churning with nerves. It was an experience that I would encounter many times over the next couple of years.

As we entered the office and saw Gunnar my heart sank. His facial expression and body language said it all. He told us we'd lost out in our bid for the survey vessel. He continued for a couple of more minutes, but to be perfectly honest I didn't listen to a word. My head was spinning because I knew we were in a perilous position.

We walked back to the shop steward's office without saying a word to each other. After composing myself I discussed with them the gravity of the situation and we agreed to call a shop stewards meeting early the next morning.

That afternoon I decided to take a course of action that would springboard our campaign to the forefront of the media for the first time. Almost three weeks later, we'd had at best a moderate response from the Labour MPs we'd sent letters to.

I sat in the office angry and disillusioned at such apparent apathy. I felt isolated and sorely let down.

The phone rang, and it was a reporter from *Radio Clyde*, Scotland's largest commercial station. Their news team had always had an excellent reputation for sniffing out stories and breaking exclusives so I felt confident that when their chief reporter Russell Walker called asking me to confirm we had lost out on the contract I could trust him.

I also told him about my disgust at the lack of response from the Labour MPs.

He asked,

"Jamie, would you name them? The ones that didn't get back to you."

I hesitated for a moment, then said,

"It's the truth, why shouldn't people know?"

Russell came down to the yard and I did my first radio interview.

Immediately after *Radio Clyde* used the story in their mid-day news naming and shaming the thirteen MPs who hadn't responded, the phone rang again.

It was *The Daily Record*. They wanted to follow up the story and I agreed to be interviewed. It was front page in the following day's paper. They used the headlines *"Silence of the Damned"*, and *"Betrayed by MPs"*, alongside the names and photos of the MPs. George Robertson, Robin Cook, Henry McLeish, Sam Galbraith, John McFall, Jimmy Hood, Rosemary McKenna, Jimmy Wray, John Maxton, George Galloway, Des Browne, Irene Adams and Douglas Alexander.

Some pretty high profile names, some of whom like Des Browne and Douglas Alexander went on to become Cabinet Ministers. The late Robin Cook of course was Foreign Secretary and George Robertson was promoted to Defence Secretary and, later, Secretary General of NATO. Henry McLeish was Scotland's second First Minister before resigning after a "muddle not a fuddle" issue about his office expenses.

At the shop stewards meeting that morning the yard officials supported my action. The vast majority of workers also supported me, apart from a very small minority who claimed as trade unionists we should not have done anything to embarrass Labour. My response was that all MPs are accountable to the electorate, and the public were entitled to know the truth. Later that morning the phone rang, and Jim McFall, another of the stewards, answered it.

I could see he was uneasy and I was curious to find out who the caller was. Jim handed the phone over and told me it was someone from Labour headquarters in Glasgow, enquiring about the article in *The Daily Record.*

I realised early on in the conversation that there was an assumption I was a member of the Labour party. I told them I was a trade unionist and attached to no political party and emphasised my loyalty and commitment to the workers in the Govan shipyard who had elected me to represent them along with the other shop stewards.

The spokeswoman claimed some of the thirteen hadn't received the letter. She pointed out that Scottish Business and Industry Minister Lord Gus Macdonald was working hard to help and the government had played a key role in winning a contract for an ice-breaker to safeguard jobs at the yard over the next few months. I was certain Lord Macdonald was doing all he could, but I was cynical about MPs not receiving the letter. It smacked to me of the apathy that I felt was prevalent in certain quarters of our elected representatives.

In the following two years, I met most of the thirteen. Some became allies in our long campaign, others were 'reluctant conscripts', and a small number, in Glasgow terminology, 'went off in the huff'.

Later I was told the convenors were to meet Lord Macdonald at his office in Glasgow the following day, along with full time officials from the various unions involved. I had met the minister on several previous occasions, including once when he visited the yard. Gus had left school at fifteen and started his working life as a fitter in the Glasgow shipyards. He'd then gone into politics of a sort, working on the left leaning journal *Tribune*. A career in broadcasting had seen him rise to the top at *Channel 4* and *Scottish Television*. He struck me as being up-front and direct. Generally speaking, that is the kind of person I like to do business with. However, due to the front-page article in *The Daily Record* I was somewhat wary as to how my co-convenors and I would be received by him.

WEDNESDAY
10 FEBRUARY 1999

Deciding strategy…

4

THE DAY began normally with me reporting for work at Govan. A phone call from a secretary at the AEEU (Amalgamated Engineering and Electrical Union) head-quarters in Glasgow swiftly changed all that.

I was told that the full time officials wanted to speak to me and my convenors prior to the talks with Gus Macdonald. There was a frostiness to the tone of that call and I reckoned I was going to get my knuckles rapped for the article in *The Daily Record*. I forewarned Joe, Johnny and Davie what I envisaged happening just before we left Govan for that meeting. I told them,

"I won't be bullied or gagged by full time officers. Remember, our direct accountability is to the workers in the yard. They'll be the judges of whatever decisions we make."

On arriving at AEEU Head Office we weren't long in finding out that we were not flavour of the month with the union hierarchy. Within minutes, John Quigley, a national officer launched a scathing attack on my leadership style and political incorrectness. He also criticised the fact that I had named the thirteen Labour MPs in the media, hinting darkly that I had probably now made enemies in the political arena.

I responded by telling him that without a high media profile our campaign message would go out to one man and a dog. I also said that I had no interest in being politically correct. I just wanted to be politically effective and the public had the right to know which MPs had not supported our fight for jobs.

I believed then as I believe now that it was thinly veiled bully boy tactics, to remove control of our campaign away from the union reps at the yard into the hands of the local and national full time officials. During a particularly heated exchange of views, Jim Moohan (GMB full time official) and Tracey White (STUC) arrived and were taken aback by the fierce exchanges between John Quigley and myself.

The convenors made it abundantly clear that we would run the campaign and we would be accountable to our members for its success or failure. We stood our ground, put our marker down. The campaign would be run from the grassroots.

Joe Brown has often told me that doing this was a landmark event in the campaign. But, as we all walked the short distance from the AEEU building to the Scottish Office my head was in turmoil about what lay ahead and what we had taken on. One thing was clear. We were going into uncharted territory. Gut reaction and intuition would be our guide.

I couldn't help but think,

"Will we be up for it"?

As I found out during the campaign, much of the opposition to my style of leadership was coming from national AEEU officials like Quigley and Alan Robson, who was now chairman of the Confederation of Shipbuilding and Engineering Unions. I always felt my own union, the GMB, was either prepared to give me free rein and trust my judgement or were wary of criticising one of their own grass root convenors in public.

On reaching the Scottish Office I was very apprehensive about the reception we would get. My fears were totally unfounded as we were greeted warmly by senior civil servant John Mason, and Gus Macdonald. I knew John relatively well from previous dealings with him. He was so different from the pinstriped, staid stereotypical image most people have of these men and women. I developed the highest respect not only for

John, but many of the Scottish Office civil servants I met. They were very committed, helpful and sympathetic to our plight.

Gus Macdonald gave me a warm handshake and never even mentioned our controversial article in *The Daily Record*. He suggested that he arrange a meeting with Chief Executive Kjell Almskog in London as soon as possible. I must admit, the thought of meeting 'The Iceman' filled me with both curiosity and a fair degree of apprehension.

The end of the meeting resulted in a joint news conference with me, John Quigley and Lord Macdonald. There was a large presence of TV, radio and newspapers. We all emphasised the gravity of the situation but felt that, until we met Almskog, the position would remain unclear.

The following morning we held a joint shop stewards meeting. I was very direct with them and told them that our position was perilous. I made it clear that if we were to have any chance of saving the yard and our jobs, we must develop a strategy and be prepared for a very difficult struggle. I had learnt in the past that although we did not always agree unanimously on some issues, we had a track record of sticking together when the going got tough. I detected a general unity of thought and purpose, and trusted that I could rely on them through the challenges that lay ahead. We exchanged views on our campaign strategy, and ultimately decided on a three -pronged approach.

We would have a political campaign.

We would have a media campaign.

We would have a public campaign.

We set ground rules that we would not waver from. If something had to be said, we would say it. If something had to be done, we would do it. Time would tell if our strategy would work. We all agreed that if we were to fail in our quest to save the yard, and our jobs, it would not be through lack of effort. We also didn't want to think in future years, "I wish we had said that," or, "I wish we had done that."

A phone call later that day invited us up to the City Chambers to meet Group Leader Frank McAveety, and his deputy Charlie Gordon. The convenors agreed that although we knew City Councils are limited in the political muscle they have, it would have been rude to refuse the offer to discuss the difficulties in a yard that had been one of the symbols in Glasgow's role as second city of The Empire.

When we arrived at the City Chambers we were conscious of staring eyes as we walked along the corridor to the meeting room. It was abundantly clear that we were, as is known in Glasgow, 'the talk of the steamie'. The article in the *Record* had stirred a hornet's nest and we were, whether we liked it or not, in the public eye.

We got a very cordial greeting from Councillor McAveety and his colleagues, and they asked if there was anything that they could do to help. They acknowledged the strong links that our industry had with the city, and how it had a place close to the hearts of many working class people, not only in Glasgow but throughout Scotland. We informed them that after losing the contract for the survey vessel, the company was now trying for steel sub-contract work from Harland and Wolff in Belfast. That would tide us over to the summer and give us some breathing space.

Several weeks later, we did get the work from Harlands. I never found out the specific involvement of the City Council, however, I do know they put forward a package that assisted us in securing that vital contract. There was little said about it at the time, but we were and always will be indebted to the Council for that gesture. Who knows where fate could have led us if the gap-plugging work had not been won.

On 15 February Nicola Sturgeon, SNP candidate for Govan and party leader Alex Salmond visited the yard. Nicola was well known in Govan. She was well respected by the unions and the workforce in the yard and regarded as a loyal ally who had always spoken up for us. Throughout our campaign, many political opponents were to deride her for the active role she played in trying to save our yard. On a personal note, I had the greatest respect for her. I thought of her as 'a nippy sweetie'. This was meant as a compliment. My view was that she was very much in your face and to the point, and was a capable politician. She's now Deputy Leader of the SNP.

It was the first time I had met Alex Salmond. I explained to him that the unions in the yard would appreciate support given by any political party in our struggle. I emphasised that a fight for jobs was a social issue that all politicians worth their salt would support. Scotland's first Parliamentary election was looming in May and I told Salmond we would not take kindly to any political party that tried to use us as a political football. He assured us that would not happen and the following week he wrote a very passionate and purposeful case for our campaign in the *Scottish News of the World*.

TUESDAY
16 FEBRUARY 1999

The Iceman and the Hood…

5

OUR VISIT to London for the meeting with Kjell Almskog at the Scottish Office included a union delegation of the Govan convenors, a couple of full time officers, and Tracey White, Assistant Secretary of the STUC. We also expected Kvaerner Govan's Managing Director Gunnar Skjelbred to be there as a matter of protocol for the company.

We arrived half an hour before the talks were due to start and were met by John Mason and Gus Macdonald. We had an informal chat for about fifteen minutes and set our stall out to try and smoke out Almskog's true intentions for Kvaerner. He arrived at the meeting accompanied by Gunnar and another Kvaerner senior executive. There were no signs The Iceman was nervous at meeting us on our turf. Although small in physical stature, he had a presence about him. Gunnar sat next to me and I detected he was ill at ease.

Lord Macdonald opened the dialogue, trying valiantly to get Almskog to open up and show his hand. Gus tried to be optimistic in respect of Govan's bid for the Ro-Ro ferry contract, and the general merits of the Govan yard. I followed Gus with an impassioned plea in respect of the excellent industrial relations in the yard, our wide-ranging flexible working practices, and the commitment of the workforce.

We had history on our side. In 1971 Upper Clyde Shipbuilders had gone into receivership. Further government support in the form of a £6 million loan had been refused by the Conservative government under Edward Heath. Instead of striking, the unions decided to complete the current orders of the shipyard demonstrating that the labour force was not 'work-shy' and illustrating the long-term viability of the yard. This was successful to a degree. Govan was sold off in 1973 as Govan Shipbuilders.

Gunnar, to his credit, willingly supported my views. But, his input was met with a glare from Almskog. It was clear our Managing Director has overstepped the mark and his boss was not amused. Although Almskog listened courteously to our points, he was clinical in his response and remained impassive. I could see Gus become exasperated at his inability to get Almskog to open up, and that we were flogging a dead horse.

Almskog persistently reiterated that a corporate review of the company was underway, and that until it was completed all assumptions of the company's intentions were speculation.

After Almskog left I was despondent and slumped into a large sofa at the corner of the room on a complete downer. Gus came over and immediately saw how concerned and frustrated I was. He asked the convenors out on to a balcony adjoining the office, and put his cards on the table. Both Gus and John Mason spelled it out that they were firmly of the view that Kvaerner was intending to pull out of shipbuilding worldwide. There was only one option. We had better start looking for a new owner.

All of us on that balcony knew that was a tall order. In layman's terms, who would want to buy a shipyard with no work? Yet, despite the enormity of the task, I was reassured by the fact that Gus and John promised full commitment to that challenge.

I attempted to get chirpy again, and left to head for a hastily arranged meeting with MPs at the nearby House of Commons. As we left the Scottish Office we were swamped by the media who were waiting for the result of our talks with Almskog. Usually I had felt quite at ease giving interviews to TV, radio and newspapers, however on this occasion I was caught off-guard and ill-prepared. This was not *Radio Clyde*, *BBC Scotland* or *STV* doing an interview in my local territory. It was Whitehall in London, and *BBC* Political Reporter David Porter wanted to do a live interview. I must admit, I felt out of place and overawed.

My immediate thought was had I coped okay? I turned for reassurance and saw Tracey White and the convenors having a right good laugh. Tracy consoled me by telling me that I had handled a tricky interview very well and their laughter wasn't directed at me, but at the comments of passers-by that had stopped out of curiosity to witness the interview.

From inside the crowd that had gathered, two old ladies had asked,

"Is that anybody famous?"

Tracy had replied,

"No, just a working class hero."

The old ladies shrugged their shoulders and trudged off, somewhat disappointed. We all burst into fits of laughter. It brought us all down to earth and lightened the atmosphere as we headed for the House of Commons.

A committee room had been set aside for the convenors to give an update on the situation in the yard to a considerable number of Scottish Labour MPs. It only then dawned on me that there was a distinct possibility that some of the MPs I had shamed in the media could be present. As we approached the room I could feel my throat going dry and the adrenaline pumping. If I was going to get a roasting, I was going to defend our corner. MPs or not, we had to show our mettle. Again I prayed I would be up to it.

Maria Fyfe, MP for Maryhill, my home constituency, was the first to arrive. With a friendly arm around me she introduced me around as the Govan yard convenor, and a member of her constituency. Without even thinking about it, and in an attempt to break the ice, I replied,

"Yes, Maria, I am in your constituency, and don't ever forget it!"

It was said tongue-in-cheek, and most MPs laughed.

What followed, however, was less amusing when Jimmy Hood, the MP for Clydesdale rose to speak. He spent most of his speech in a tirade against our naming MPs in *The Daily Record*, including himself. That was followed by a lecture on how we should learn to be politically correct. He was very hostile and aggressive and I couldn't help wondering how an MP who portrayed himself as working class could have a go at a union man just trying to save the jobs of Clyde shipbuilders.

I got the feeling he was ready for me and had nominated himself as the one to 'sort me out' and put me in my place. I did feel somewhat isolated and under the microscope of the MPs and union officials, but I was in no mood to be chastised for telling the truth, and for asking MPs to be accountable.

At the end of Hood's rant, my gut reaction was to embark on a head-on slanging match with him, but I got the impression that's exactly what he wanted. I looked around the room and I could sense that all the other MPs and union officials were waiting to see how I responded or coped with his fierce verbal attack. I bit my tongue and responded by asking the other MPs if they had any "relevant" questions they wanted to ask me.

I hadn't taken the bait. I'd kept my cool and gave the MPs a report of the meeting that had taken place between Almskog, Gus Macdonald and us and how the unions saw the current situation. I felt sure leaving the Commons that day that the MPs now realised that we were not the naïve, loudmouthed buffoons perhaps some of them had originally thought.

As we flew home that night I gave serious thought to a hastily arranged mass meeting of workers we had called for the following day. Reflecting on the meeting we had with the MPs, I felt reasonably confident that we had presented a clear and concise case to them, and could at least be assured of some of them being firm allies in the months ahead.

17 February 1999 was the day the fight to save the yard really began. I knew before I addressed the mass meeting that the reaction of the workers to our current serious plight would determine if we could muster the resolve for a monumental struggle.

WEDNESDAY
17 FEBRUARY 1999

Support from the workers...

6

I HAVE never been one for preparing speeches. Generally speaking, I have always believed that if you know the subject matter, and tell the truth, it will come across okay. As I stood up to speak I hoped my intuition and passion would be my guide. The shop stewards were prepared to lead the struggle, but would the masses support us?

I said what my inner feelings told me. I will never forget the sentiments that I expressed. They are etched in my memory forever.

"If we're committed to saving our yard and jobs, we must be prepared to go on a long and arduous journey. There may well be many obstacles, and twists and turns on that journey. However, if we stay united, display determination, resilience and keep focused, we can do it. The shop stewards will lead that fight, and come to you when we need your active support."

I asked them if they were up for it. Having spent virtually my whole working life in the yard, I knew Govan body language. They were up for it. Now the real struggle began.

I had realised that our local Directors were shell-shocked, and incapable of lifting or motivating the workforce at this difficult time. With the exception of Gunnar they were all worried about how they'd be seen at Kvaerner corporate level and I believe were determined not to do or say anything that their bosses wouldn't like. However, they were prepared to sit back and let the unions take the lead in trying to save their jobs. It was then clear that our yard and jobs would be saved by a campaign by the unions or it would surely close.

As I returned to the shop stewards office after the meeting, I was well satisfied by the positive support from the workers. That was counter-balanced by the fact that it was finally dawning on me what a weight of responsibility I had with the rest of the shop stewards to provide real leadership. I realised it was a daunting task, but we would give it one hundred per cent effort.

Over the next couple of days there were continuing communications from, or on behalf of many of the thirteen MPs that hadn't replied to our letter asking for their support. George Galloway, then Labour MP for Glasgow Kelvin was less than amused when I was quoted in the local *Evening Times* newspaper as saying that he should spend more of his time fighting for the sixty or so workers in Govan who lived in his constituency.

I was fierce in my criticism of Paisley North MP Irene Adams, who also had many Govan workers living there. (Adams subsequently left Parliament in 2005 and was made a life peer, Baroness Adams of Cragielea.)

As I said earlier, the Labour party had put it about that perhaps some of the MPs hadn't received the letter, but even if that was the case, once they were identified as having not replied you have thought they'd have made it their business to get on board, even at that late stage.

There was great anger in the yard at the apparent lack of interest being displayed by those MPs. We were also suffering from the fact that we had no direct contact at that time from Govan MP Mohammad Sarwar, due to his involvement in a legal case. On the other hand we were getting good support from MPs such as Ian Davidson, and, much to their credit, considerable support from MPs whose constituencies were geographically a fair distance from Govan.

Des Browne (Kilmarnock), Norman Godman (Greenock & Inverclyde) and Sandra Osborne (Ayr) are three that readily spring to mind, all of whom contacted us to find out what practical support they could give us. I reckoned Browne had been smart enough to realise he should be seen to be with us and it would soon be forgotten that he'd been one of the original thirteen missing MPs. Further down the line in the campaign they were always on hand at the Commons to offer help, which is more than can be said for a number of Glasgow MPs who were notable by their absence.

22 February was a day when we perked up somewhat. We heard that it looked likely we would secure the vital sub-contract steelwork from Harland and Wolff in Belfast. Later that day we were told we were on the shortlist of three for the contract to build four Roll on Roll off (Ro-Ro) ferries for the Ministry of Defence. The Harlands work would take us through until the summer, and perhaps we could use the possibility of winning the Ro-Ro contract to entice Almskog into a more positive frame of mind about keeping our Govan yard as part of the Kvaerner Empire.

I told all the shop stewards to get about the workforce and emphasise that the securing of the Harlands work in conjunction with us being short-listed for the Ro-Ro's was good news and a step forward. We had to keep morale up and remain focused on any positive developments that arose.

We maintained a high profile in the media, most of whom I suspect believed they would soon be witnessing the end of commercial shipbuilding on the upper Clyde at Govan. We kept the pressure on the politicians, and after a meeting in the yard on 25 February with Ian Davidson and Norman Godman it was agreed a delegation of MPs would meet the convenors and directors.

Despite some nudge-nudge hints at times, we emphasised our political campaign would be cross party. While appreciating the heavy involvement on our behalf by some Labour MPs, we wanted to keep a good working relationship with all sides of the political spectrum. The date was fixed for Monday 8 March.

Labour was holding a conference, on Saturday 6 March at the Royal Concert Hall in Glasgow. George Robertson, the Defence Secretary, was giving a speech so we discussed the idea of lobbying the conference. It would let him see at first hand the importance we placed on winning the order for the Ro-Ro ferries.

Members of the shop stewards committee were apprehensive about what kind of support we would get from the workers in asking them to give up their Saturday morning. I reminded the stewards that when I addressed the mass meeting I told the workers that we would lead and drive the campaign, but there would be times when a 'call to arms' would be needed to support us. This was to be the first test of their commitment and resolve.

We held a short, ten minute meeting a couple of days before the conference, and told the workers,

"We need you that day, to stand beside our shipyard trade union banner. To show the politicians, the media, and the public that we won't just talk a fight, we will fight that fight."

After the meeting there were differing views in the shop stewards committee as to the turnout we would get. Some, expecting only a token response, listed all the reasons why many would not turn up. Living too far away, transport problems, domestic reasons, Saturday football, golf, pub and bookies. The list was endless.

I listened, but something about that meeting in February had told me that we had signed a verbal covenant with the workers. They would fight. They did care. They would turn up. I had belief in them.

In my home the night before the rally I asked my wife Isabel, son Fraser and daughters Julie and Amanda to come along for moral support. They agreed without hesitation. It was the first of many sacrifices they were to make for me over the next two years.

SATURDAY
6 MARCH 1999

Rallying the troops...

7

THE MORNING of the rally had me in my usual state when I'm anxious. Butterflies in the stomach, unable to eat breakfast, and very irritable. When we left the house it was an overcast morning. I said a little prayer to myself as we made our way there.

"Please don't rain, and show my belief in my workmates is justified by delivering a good turnout."

Not a lot was said on our way to the Royal Concert Hall. Isabel knew me well enough not to disturb my thoughts and for Julie, Fraser and Amanda, it was a whole new experience. I think they were too nervous to say anything to me. We arrived about twenty minutes early and I was heartened to see a crowd of around a hundred was there before us. Isabel looked at me and said,

"Don't worry Jamie, they'll come."

I began to feel a bit more confident she was right. The shop stewards were already there to assemble the banner, and there was a very positive buzz about the place. We were on the opposite side of the road from the Concert Hall where the police erected barriers that we were to congregate behind. We saw quite clearly that many of the delegates entering the Hall had seen us, and we got many encouraging shouts of support. That was uplifting, and I saw how it boosted the spirits of my workmates.

Our numbers increased significantly over the next fifteen to twenty minutes, to well in excess of four hundred. Obviously I wanted even more, but as some of my colleagues reminded me, I am an idealist, and a demanding bugger. As I looked around, I felt a surge of pride in them all. They had made the effort. It was not to be the last time that I would experience that emotion. I also noticed that there was a wide cross-section of the workforce present. Shop floor manual workers, office staff, technical staff, line management, and even some senior management. As we all stood around chatting there was a great feeling about our gathering. It was positive and it was purposeful. It's often been remarked to me by many present that day that it brought us all closer together. It was unity at work.

And, it must have impressed, or perhaps alarmed, some of the Labour party high-ups in the Hall. Ian Davidson appeared from the conference and stated that George Robertson would like to meet the convenors to discuss our position. It was too good an opportunity to miss. Instinctively, I jumped on to a higher level of concrete steps at a sculpture situated near to where we were all standing. I told them we were getting this opportunity to personally put our case to the Defence Secretary.

I asked them to give us a Clyde cheer as we entered the Hall. Boy, did they let rip. They nearly blew the roof off the building. The four hundred present seemed more like four thousand. As we walked up the stairs to the main foyer, we saw many of the delegates rush to the main windows to see what the commotion was outside. We heard a few comment,

"It's the Govan shipyard workers giving their shop stewards a send off."

We felt ten feet tall as we reached the top of the stairs. I thought to myself,

"Everyone in this hall knows we mean business. Our fight for our jobs will be driven wherever and whenever it is necessary."

The meeting with George Robertson was informal, with the convenors, Jim Moohan the GMB full time official, and a couple of senior civil servants present. It was an open and frank exchange of views on our current position, and how vital it was that we secured the Ro-Ro ferry contract.

Under European law, the building of all non-combatant ships must be open to worldwide tender. We argued strongly against the MoD designating the contract as a semi-commercial order which meant it could be awarded to a foreign yard. I felt that by minor modification to the specification of the vessels, they could be reclassified meaning they could legitimately be built in the UK. In conjunction with the vast majority of people I believed no other European country would ever allow such a major contract in defence to leave their shores.

But there you have it. The good old United Kingdom. Honest to a fault in playing by the Queensbury rules, while many in Europe blatantly flaunted them. The Defence Secretary put up a case for the necessity to open them to foreign tender. He was not convincing and we were not convinced. It was hard not to blame the government for allowing the possibility to arise where a £240 million contract could go overseas.

It was the sort of thing we could have expected from the Tories, but not from Labour. Robertson, I believe, showed a lack of foresight and concern at the implications losing such a contract would have for the Clyde. Just five months after our meeting, Robertson was made a life peer, Baron Robertson of Port Ellen and then in October, he was appointed Secretary General of NATO. I think that he was a career politician who lost touch with his Labour roots.

During our talks, we also urged a review of the current building programme of two Auxiliary oil support vessels, again for the MoD, that were under construction at the GEC yard in Barrow. Our information was that the programme was at least one year behind schedule. We pushed for one of the ships to be transferred to Govan, to get the programme back on track. Robertson seemed taken aback by our revelation and he committed to look into our information on the contract. History was to prove our information was accurate.

We left the meeting and returned to our workmates who were waiting patiently outside. Perched once more next to the statue I brought them up to speed with the discussions we'd had with the Defence Secretary. I explained that while we'd received no guarantees about the Ro-Ro contract, we had put our arguments well and it was now up to George Robertson to make his decision. It had, I said, "... been a good day at the office. Now go and enjoy the rest of the day."

After the euphoria of Saturday, it was back to the daily grind on Monday. Surprise, surprise, all the talk was about the lobby on Saturday. Everybody who was there commented on how good a day it had been. I could detect a mixture of guilt and envy from those that hadn't shown up. I wound some of them up by saying that I would book them in for our next crusade.

Monday was also the day the MPs had been asked to come in and meet the convenors. At our insistence, it was a cross-party delegation with representatives of all the four main parties.

The two leaders of the delegation at that time were Ian Davidson and Norman Godman. David Marshall (Glasgow Shettleston), John Maxton (Glasgow Cathcart)—who stood down from Parliament in 2001 and was made Baron Maxton in 2004—and Jimmy Wray (Glasgow Baillieston) were also there. In my view, Wray proved to be as much use later on in the campaign as a chocolate fireguard in front of a furnace. He turned up, late, for one meeting I held in the yard with other MPs and didn't convince me that he'd done his homework on the issues. After that, it seemed to me that he disappeared off the radar.

The meeting was a forum for us to persuade them how important it was to pursue the MoD on the oiler contract and the Ro-Ro's. So, this was upping the ante and stating quite clearly that the oiler had to be there to secure the yard's short term future and the ferry order was vital for our future in the long term. At this point we were still trying to convince Kvaerner that there could be big contract in the offing which would make it more attractive to keep Govan open.

Either out of genuine support for our campaign or for their own survival it now appeared we were enlisting considerable political support. We were beginning to get a solid base of MPs across all of the main parties which I think was mainly down to the fact that they realised we weren't going away and we were serious.

On Wednesday we got information that Ian Davidson and Norman Godman had asked questions in Parliament regarding the oiler contract at GEC Barrow. They were both working hard to keep the profile high. Securing the second of those oilers was our best chance of getting significant work into Govan at short notice. As expected, the MoD issued a wishy-washy answer relating to the lateness of the order. 'There is a degree of slippage in timescale' was exactly the answer we expected. In reality the contract was significantly late and was becoming a source of major concern for the MoD.

It was frustrating and becoming a worry that no-one in the department could see the best solution all round was to send one of the ships up to Govan. The contract would be finished on time and we would have work to tide us over until Kvaerner made up its mind what it was doing long term.

The camaraderie among shipyard workers was highlighted a couple of days later when the owner of Farstad Shipping, a Norwegian company we had built a support vessel for, gave me a cheque for £1,500 as a token of appreciation for the effort the workforce had shown in delivering his order on time. He insisted on speaking to the media, to praise the workers for maintaining such a high level of commitment and pride in their work during a very testing time. It was a great personal touch that was very much appreciated by everyone in the yard.

The shop stewards decided to put the names of all the employees in a prize draw, to split up the £1,500. Fifteen workers got a hundred pounds each. I went home that Friday quite happy and chuffed. That human gesture had brightened up our day. However, I couldn't escape the fact that completion of that ship focused us more on the ever decreasing volume of work at the yard.

All workers are an inter-related team at a yard. From naval architects to welders, painters, accountants, secretaries or receptionists, there's a joint pride in the launch of a ship. You can point and say,

"That was my wee bit."

"I helped with that on the launch day."

Office staff play their part in winning and designing the order and they also appreciate how tough it is to get a ship built. They only have to look out of their window in the middle of winter to notice construction workers beavering away in sub-zero temperatures. Sometimes it's so cold on the scaffolding welders have to use their blow torches to melt the icicles on the end of their noses. Well, perhaps that's a bit of shipyard licence, but you get the picture.

It's a long hard slog to build a ship and everyone in a yard has their role. The gesture from the owner of Farstad showed that shipyard workers the world over belong to a kind of brotherhood, and let's not forget the sisters, that allows each and every one of us to understand and sympathise with colleagues whose backs are against the wall. And believe me, at that time I felt our backs were well and truly up against it.

It was still all systems go on the political trail. Letters, letters and more letters to Gus Macdonald and all Scottish MPs. Jan, Jean and Christine, three of the secretaries in the company must have been sick of the sight of me. Type, photocopy, post. Type, photocopy, post. There was no idle time for any of them.

I was still keeping in touch on a daily basis with my Managing Director Gunnar Skjelbred. He kept me abreast of any information he got from Head Office in London, although even at this stage Gunnar was looking like a very small fish in a very big pond. Kvaerner corporate was in reality almost certainly keeping him in the dark. To his credit, Gunnar was still out and about in the yard facing the workers. Always approachable, even at a time when the company was low in the popularity stakes, he still commanded great respect.

Later that week we started getting delivery of the first batch of steel for the Harlands contract. That perked us all up a bit, as we knew it would give us at least three to four months respite from the chronic lack of work. However, as is often the case there was a sting in the tail. The yard directors sent for the convenors and emphasised that the contract had been taken on at a tight cost and delivery schedule. It would need one hundred and forty steelworkers to work the one-week Easter holiday. This was a tricky situation as I knew that most workers were looking forward to a short break from the pressure and the stress.

Nevertheless we agreed to go back to the steelworker section, my home base, and try to get volunteers. I discussed it with my co-steelwork convenor, Johnny Johnson, and we decided that both of us would volunteer to work the holiday to set an example.

There was nothing unique in Johnny working on the shop floor during the holidays. But it was different for me because I was the full time convenor and away from the sharp end. In fact, I knew I would have to go to the training school for a one-day welding refresher test. Ironically, it worked in our favour, as at the meeting when I emphasised we needed one hundred and forty volunteers, the main joke was that people were prepared to do it just to see me working. On the day we got one hundred and eighty, a remarkable response. The company was even taken aback. On reflection I wasn't really surprised, because in a way we had 'called them to arms' again.

The following week the convenors and I met Gus Macdonald and John Mason once more at the Scottish Office. We reiterated how vital it was that we secured the oiler contract for the second ship to be transferred from GEC Barrow to Govan. Gus reaffirmed they were still following a twin-track strategy:

1. Trying to convince Kvaerner to stay at Govan
2. Looking for any potential buyer for the yard.

That same evening of Friday 26 March, the *Sunday Mail* newspaper was holding a 'Voice of Scotland' forum. The leaders of the four main political parties were on the platform answering questions from the audience. The convenors were invited along and it was intended that we raise the issue of shipbuilding in Scotland and our fight for jobs.

We invited Alistair Goss, our industrial padre along for moral support and spiritual guidance. Well, we actually invited him because he was a great sounding board for us to bounce ideas off and he was always positive minded. As the question and answer session got underway Donald Dewar (Labour), Alex Salmond (Scottish National Party), David McLetchie (Conservative) and Jim Wallace (Liberal Democrat) were grilled on the health service and student tuition fees.

I waited patiently for our opportunity to raise our campaign for shipbuilding on the Clyde. Finally, I got in and asked all of them if they were supportive of our fight for jobs. I asked them to remember that this was a social issue that all political parties should unite on. My question got a very warm response from the audience. In fact the level of support seemed to surprise all of the party leaders.

As expected, they all gave verbal assurances of support. However, I was looking for an extra degree of commitment from Donald Dewar, as I knew he would most certainly be elected First Minister in the new Scottish Parliament after the election in May. Sadly, it was not forthcoming. He was not inspiring, and did not seem to think there was much hope of our campaign being successful. Dewar left us somewhat depressed, bringing us down to earth with a bump. The *Sunday Mail* gave extensive coverage to the road show and reported the rather pessimistic tones of Donald Dewar and our disappointment at his views.

The following day at work was a black day. Heads were down, and the general talk was that if the future First Minister was not optimistic of us securing a future for the yard then all was not well. I called a meeting of the shop stewards later that morning and told them we must get out and about the yard and get the heads back up. There was no room for feeling sorry for ourselves. We would have to learn to overcome any negativity that threw itself at us. We all worked hard that day to get a spring back into the step of the workers step. By cajoling and humouring them and by using positive propaganda I think we did it.

It was off to Manchester with the other convenors for the national shipbuilding forum on 29 and 30 March. John Battle, a junior government Minister with a remit for shipbuilding was present. I was informed that we would get about twenty minutes in private with him to put our case in relation to the Ro-Ro ferry contract, and the possibility of getting the second Auxiliary Oiler transferred from Barrow to Govan. Some of the various national union officers were there as I put my case. My adrenaline was flowing, and I felt hyper.

That didn't worry me because usually I am at my best when I feel that way. I was aware, however, that I was under the closest scrutiny from some of the national officials to see how I coped.

Media sources at *The Daily Telegraph* and the *Observer* in London had told me that various senior officials they'd spoken to believed the convenors at Govan would soon be out of their depth in the political arena. Some were saying that when we were found out, the national officers would come in and pick up the pieces and take control of the campaign. I was determined that we would prove to be up to the task.

The presentation went well. I could tell from the body language from Battle and his civil servants that we fought our corner well. I was relieved, because the view was that he would have further discussions later with the Trade and Industry Secretary Stephen Byers, Defence Secretary George Robertson, Scottish Office Minister Gus Macdonald and First Minister-in -waiting Donald Dewar, about our situation.

The anticipated Kvaerner corporate review was expected any time now, and the tension in the yard was increasing. The daily walkabouts I had were dominated by the same repetitive question,

"What's happening, Jamie?"

I would then spend a few minutes relating the endless meetings that were going on. In essence, I always tried to use the chats as an opportunity to keep everybody upbeat and optimistic. Although there was always a minority of 'doomsters', the vast majority of workers were relatively upbeat and supportive of our ongoing efforts.

MONDAY
12 APRIL 1999

Jobs on the line...

8

GUNNAR SUMMONED the convenors to his office. He had an agitated look on his face. He was edgy and ill at ease and I knew we were going to get bad news.

He informed us that Kvaerner had issued an HR1 redundancy notice. Because more than a hundred workers would be affected consultations had to start ninety days in advance of the proposed date of redundancy. Individual workers would have to be spoken to as well as the unions at the yard. Among other things, Kvaerner had to make clear the reasons for the lay-offs, the number and categories of employees involved, how they planned to select workers and how they would work out redundancy payments.

He tried to reassure us that it was only a precautionary move. However, he could see that we were unconvinced. He told us we were to meet him again the following day when the formal corporate decision from the company would be announced. As we left the meeting, a quick calculation of the dates meant that the redundancy notice would run out at the beginning of the Glasgow Fair holidays which were in mid-July. Although I pretended outwardly to everyone that the HR1 announcement was a technicality and not unexpected, deep down I knew it was bad news and I was gutted.

It would be fair to say that the announcement of the HR1 had caused a mixture of gloom and alarm. I found it a very difficult day to get through. It was hard to focus properly on anything. Like all my workmates I was irritable and nervous, as we waited for the corporate announcement due the next day.

When it was made, it was devastating. Kvaerner were to withdraw from shipbuilding. Their thirteen yards worldwide were to be sold or shut down. Although our main focus was on how the news affected Govan, we also had to spare a thought for the seven hundred or so workers at Kvaerner Energy in Clydebank. They made industrial gas turbines for the energy industry and were also to be sold off or shut down. I wondered briefly if the two facilities could fight this together.

Gunnar consulted the convenors, and we decided to call a joint mass meeting of all workers in the canteen. He knew, and we knew, that he was going into a lion's den. We all admired him for having the guts to personally address the workers. They listened intently and courteously as he read the announcement. His closing remarks were that he was totally committed to trying to secure a new owner for the yard. He also said he deeply regretted the decision made by the company. However, as we were all aware, it was part of a corporate worldwide strategy.

We had received a major body blow to securing our future. After Gunnar left, I knew I had to speak to the workforce. Most looked numb and the very few who were talking among themselves did so in whispers. This was the biggest challenge I'd had to face in my fourteen years as a union official.

As I rose to address the workers my mind flashed back to February's first mass meeting. I reminded them of that, and my warnings that we would have to undertake a long arduous journey with many obstacles in front of us if we were to save the yard and our jobs. I wound up by telling them that there was a massive media presence in the yard and the convenors would be holding a news conference very soon. Our message to the world outside is simple.

"This yard is not closing. The media will be doing a walkabout after the press conference to speak to you. I know it's hard, but I want you to echo the views of your shop stewards. Two hundred years of shipbuilding at Govan on the Clyde will not end now. We will secure work and a new owner. That is our challenge, and we will succeed."

After the mass meeting the convenors headed for the boardroom where the news conference was to be held. What awaited us was like something out of Hollywood. Flashing cameras, microphones pushed in front of my face, and questions coming from every direction. Astonishingly, I felt quite composed as I sat down. My head was clear, as was our message.

There were countless questions from TV, radio and newspapers, all rotating around one general theme,

"Is this the end of shipbuilding at Govan?"

With total conviction and belief, I told them emphatically,

"This yard will not close."

Making my way out of the door a newspaper reporter stopped me.

"Jamie, do you really believe you can save the yard?"

I replied,

"Yes, I do. Do you believe we can?"

"It doesn't matter if I believe it Jamie, as long as you do. Best of luck."

A couple of hours later a reporter from the Scotsman newspaper had just completed the walkabout. He asked me if I had brainwashed the workers at the mass meeting. He told me that they virtually all reciprocated the views that I gave at the news conference. I laughed.

"Do you honestly think twelve hundred shipyard workers would ever allow anyone to dictate to them? Maybe it's genuinely the case that we have unity of cause and belief."

As he closed his notebook he remarked,

"Jamie, you know, I think you could be right about that."

It was a long, stressful day for us all. There would be many more.

I went along to Gunnar's office to thank him for the speech he'd made and, to be honest, to find out how he was coping. Not well would be an understatement. But, he assured me that he would do all he could to assist in keeping the yard open. He admitted that in the long term he probably would not survive with the new owner, if we got one. He seemed relatively philosophical about the situation.

Back in the convenor's room, Johnny Johnson thrust a fax into my hand that had come in from the Scottish Office.

 THE SCOTTISH OFFICE

SIR GAVIN LAIRD TO HEAD TASK FORCE IN RESPONSE TO KVAERNER ANNOUNCEMENT

Scottish Business and Industry Minister Lord Macdonald today appointed Sir Gavin Laird to head a Task Force charged with the task of identifying potential purchasers of the shipyard at Govan, the engineering business in Clydebank, and for any other facilities subsequently identified for sale in Scotland. Lord Macdonald's move followed today's announcement by Kvaerner Group to seek purchasers for some of its operations including the Kvaerner Govan shipyard in Glasgow and Kvaerner Energy engineering business in Clydebank.

Lord Macdonald said:

"It is my view that both the Govan shipyard and Clydebank engineering operations can be viable businesses with considerable potential under new ownership.

"I have therefore set up a Task Force comprising a small number of highly experienced businessmen to identify, if possible, potential purchasers of the shipyard and engineering operation, and any other facilities identified for disposal by Kvaerner in Scotland, and advise on strategies to retain these key manufacturing facilities and workforces for the Scottish economy.

"Kvaerner have welcomed this initiative by The Scottish Office and have offered full co-operation in working with us to secure a positive outcome for their workforce. The shipyard has benefited greatly from its period of ownership by Kvaerner. It is now a modern, productive shipyard capable of building ships to the highest technical specification. It has good labour relations and modern working practices. That progress was not achieved without some pain, but equally was only achievable with the wholehearted support of the entire workforce.

"The Scottish Office has engaged with both company and unions in recent months in anticipation of a radical restructuring of Kvaerner's international operations. It is with great regret that we hear of their intention to sell all of their shipyards and some other assets worldwide. In Scotland our Task Force led by Sir Gavin will have the full backing of Scottish Office resources and access to whatever expert advice is required to achieve a positive outcome for Govan and Clydebank.

"In the meantime I have asked the appropriate Local Enterprise Companies, along with the Employment Service, to approach the companies with a view to making available the full range of services to those individuals who may lose their jobs as a result of this announcement. This will include help in identifying new jobs or training opportunities. The Local Enterprise Companies will also be working with the companies with a view to identifying local businesses dependant on them so that they can put in place appropriate measures to help these suppliers find new customers.

"Kvaerner's announcement is unwelcome, if not unexpected news. The challenge now is for all concerned to focus on the shared goal of ensuring a productive future for the workforces of Kvaerner in Scotland."

Sir Gavin Laird said that the Taskforce would start work immediately. He said:

"Our priorities are to have an early meeting with senior Kvaerner management and unions to identify the details of the assets for sale. We will also be seeking an early meeting with the Ministry of Defence.

"The Task Force will be employing specialist consultants who will be charged with identifying potential purchasers and advising on terms of sale as appropriate.

"The members of the Task Force are committed to finding new owners who will retain employment and keep the businesses viable. We will be working flat out to achieve this aim."

Reading this gave me a bit of a lift. Perhaps this was the political impetus our campaign needed. I got a phone call later in the day, asking me to come to the Scottish Office in Glasgow the following evening at 7 p.m. Gus Macdonald had called the meeting and, as expected, it was to meet the newly appointed Task Force.

WEDNESDAY
14 APRIL 1999

The Task Force...

9

WE WERE ushered into a room to meet Gus and the members. As I went in I got an immediate surprise to see a familiar face in David Smith. David was a very well known figure in the Govan yard. He had worked there for twenty-two years, including a distinguished period as head of the commercial department. He was widely regarded across the UK as one of the most knowledgeable experts in his field having also established and managed an international engineering company for eight years. He knew everybody that was worth knowing in the shipbuilding/ship-owner arena. He was also a Govan-ite through and through. I was delighted he was a part of the team.

Sir Gavin Laird was to head the taskforce. His knowledge of shipbuilding and broad industrial contacts would surely be invaluable. At the time he was a non-executive director on a number of boards including Scottish Media Group and Britannia Asset Management. Sir Gavin had been a leading figure in the Trade Union movement for almost twenty-five years and headed the AEU section of the Amalgamated Engineering and Electrical Union from 1992-1995.

The other two Task Force members were Bill Scott and Malcolm Clark. I didn't know either of them personally, although I knew of Bill through the UK shipbuilding network. He'd served his apprenticeship at Govan when it was known as Fairfields before embarking on a lifetime's career in shipbuilding and marine engineering. He'd been Managing Director of Kincaid's in Greenock, a non-executive director of Ailsa Troon Shipbuilders and, most importantly for me, led the revival of Ferguson Shipbuilders in Port Glasgow. He was one hundred per cent shipbuilder.

Malcolm Clark was an industry heavyweight. He served his engineering apprenticeship with Howden in Glasgow and then worked for the Ford Motor Company. He then ran the Scottish plant of US engineers Keystone International. After moving to America, Malcolm became President of the Houston-based multinational overseeing a workforce of four thousand and manufacturing operations in twenty-eight countries. He was to be the financial cog in the wheel.

I was very happy with the make-up of the Task Force. There was vast experience and knowledge among them. Equally important, they were all Clyde men, born and bred. I knew there would be no short-changing in the commitment stakes. Furthermore, with the expert back up of Scottish Office civil servants John Mason and Ben McGuire we were in good hands.

The convenor of Kvaerner Energy Clydebank, Robbie Robertson, was also at the meeting. I felt his approach was complacent. He had the belief that everything would just fall into place. I said to Robbie that Kvaerner Govan and Kvaerner Clydebank should fight for jobs and against closure together but he decided a low profile and, crucially, no media profile would be the best approach. I heard later from one reporter that Robbie refused him an interview saying he wouldn't run a campaign to save Clydebank through the media. (Months later he told the same reporter he regretted the decision).

Full time GMB officer, Jim Moohan and old ally Tracey White of the STUC made up the trade union delegation.

We discussed the task in hand in finding a new owner, and from the outset Sir Gavin emphasised that this would not be an easy task. He also reminded us that time was against us. We had three months to secure a new owner. As all the members of the Task Force emphasised, this was a very, very tight schedule for what would be a complex takeover.

Sir Gavin concluded the meeting by uttering the words that always impress me. He assured us that despite the enormity of the task they would give it one hundred per cent. I could ask for no more.

A few days later a negative story started to leak into the yard that the Task Force had been set up as a government front to appease the workforce and media. It was suggested that they would go through the motions for a few weeks until after the election of the new Scottish Parliament and then their interest would wane. Surprisingly, and much to my disappointment, ex-Clyde union stalwart of the '60s and '70s Jimmy Reid put forward the scenario in a national newspaper.

I was an apprentice on the Clyde at the time of the legendary UCS work-in. I greatly admired Reid and Jimmy Airlie for the magnificent campaign they led in 1971. However, I was well at odds with his view of the Task Force. I refuted Jimmy's analysis of the situation. The men on the Task Force were men of integrity. They had given their word to deliver maximum commitment.

I trusted them implicitly. Jimmy's view was the first public negative statement that had surfaced in our campaign. Despite this we would continue our campaign as we had started, positive and optimistic.

We were still getting extensive media coverage and we knew that a profile in the media was essential to keep the politicians on their toes. We knew that when we got an invitation to bring our banner along to the STUC conference on 20 April at the City Halls in Glasgow, our campaign would be at the forefront.

We had heard Donald Dewar would be making a speech at the conference and we wanted to show him we meant business. So, a few of the lads set up a couple of banners outside the entrance to the Halls.

It wasn't until we were contacted by *Radio Clyde News* that we realised instead of going in the front of the building where he would have seen us, the Scottish Secretary had used a back door. You can draw your own conclusions about why he did this, but, a source in Dewar's inner circle has since admitted to me that had *Radio Clyde* not run the story about the First Minister-in-waiting using the back door, he wouldn't even have commented on our plight. As it was he made a statement about how he would do everything he could to help us stay open. I felt at the time those were bland words.

A special motion on our campaign was on the conference agenda. Various local and national union officers made speeches. Disappointingly, the convenors were not given the opportunity to put our own case. We were told that it was not procedural protocol. More like the Labour party and union high heid-yins were unwilling to give us a platform because of our outspoken views about some of them. We more than made up for that by giving interviews to TV, radio and newspapers.

Even at the early stages of our campaign many people were commenting on not only the significant media coverage we were attracting but also that in general it was very supportive. That was apart from one very prominent journalist at *The Herald* in Glasgow, Alf Young. He was fast becoming our arch-enemy with constant sniping at our industry in general. He perpetuated the myth that shipbuilding had no future. He was negative about our campaign to secure a new owner. In layman's terms we should be put to rest. I consistently contradicted him reminding everyone that shipbuilding was in fact a high-tech industry and not as some portrayed it, a relic from the past.

Alf once responded by saying he was a journalist and not a PR officer for shipbuilding. I gave him several invitations to come and see for himself how advanced shipbuilding was nowadays. Alas, he never ever accepted the invitation.

On 23 April, a delegation of west of Scotland Labour MPs came into the yard to meet the directors and the convenors. I could sense a much more helpful and conciliatory attitude from them. Most of the animosity since we named the thirteen was waning, although as I expected, one of the MPs, Jimmy Hood, was never to be seen again throughout our campaign. In my view, he had gone into the huff big-time with us.

Later that day we got another visit from Nicola Sturgeon and Alex Salmond of the SNP. It was obvious there was no way they were going to get left playing second fiddle to the Labour party. They went on a walkabout and it would have to be said that Salmond got on very well with the men on the shop floor and Nicola's reputation in the yard preceded her. The shop stewards maintained their stand that all political parties would be shown courtesy and appreciation if they supported the fight for Scottish jobs.

That evening was the first update meeting of the Task Force, and I was anxious to see if any progress had been made since we first met. I was not to be disappointed. Sir Gavin reported that he had met both Defence Secretary George Robertson and Trade and Industry Secretary Stephen Byers to discuss the situation at Govan.

He said there were parties interested in buying the yard. I was well satisfied that my confidence in the Task Force and the Scottish Office civil servants has been vindicated. They were all working hard. Gradually, I began to see a very different side of the often much maligned civil servants. Perhaps we were lucky, but the ones I dealt with were hard working and purposeful, with a very humane side. They were major players in our quest to find a new owner. I left that meeting convinced we had taken the first tentative step forward towards success.

The shop stewards decided to take the campaign on to the streets of Glasgow. We got leaflets printed and met at Govan Cross, near the market. It was always busy, with many people travelling in from places like Pollok, Ibrox, Mosspark and other surrounding areas. We forgot that with the election for the new Scottish Parliament only a couple of weeks away the candidates and supporters would be out in force.

The political parties were thick on the ground all around the entrance to the Govan shopping centre and we were across the road near the outdoor market with our banner. We noticed immediately that a lot of the local people were not interested in taking the leaflets with the usual political propaganda. As we set about giving ours out we were worried in case we got the same response. Our fears were totally unfounded. We were deluged with support and best wishes from nearly everyone. Some even stopped to ask for an update on our campaign. Others offered a donation for a worker's fund.

Significantly, two common themes emerged. Firstly, that it was good to see workers actually fighting hard for their jobs. And secondly, the importance of the shipyard to the local community. It was their shipyard. It belonged to Govan.

I remember vividly approaching a group of elderly women, with the intention of giving them our leaflet. One obviously recognised me and said,

"Are you that union boy from the yard?"

I remember thinking how I enjoyed being called a boy. Then they all joined in, saying what a good job we were doing in fighting to keep the yard open. One of them, a typical Govan-wifie, looked across the road and shouted to the politicians,

"Why not get off your fat arses, and do something positive for a change?"

That Glasgow banter caused huge hilarity among passers-by, but the political brigade could only look on sheepishly.

As I made my way home, I was clear about one thing. Govan was that yard. That yard was Govan.

The beginning of the following week the shop stewards committee decided to hold another mass meeting to give the workers an update. It was vital to keep them informed and tell them of the progress of the Task Force, and our leafleting. However, I had a much more important item on the agenda. The Glasgow May Day annual rally. We had been invited to lead the procession with our banner. And, I had been asked to be one of the guest speakers. I regarded both of these invitations to be an honour.

I told the joint stewards meeting that I was going to ask for a massive response from the workforce and their families to attend that rally and once again publicly display our unity and determination. One of the stewards reminded me that on May Day Sunday, Celtic and Rangers were playing each other at Parkhead. Of all the events I could have chosen to compete with it would not have been an Old Firm match, especially one where Rangers could win the SPL title. (They did, in a 3-0 victory which went down in history for the shameful scenes in which referee Hugh Dallas was led bloodied from the pitch after being hit by a coin). However, I quickly came to my senses and told the stewards our jobs were more important than any football match and that would be tested at the mass meeting.

I gave the workers the general information and then came the crunch. I told them,

"We've been chosen to lead the annual May Day rally. It's not only a great honour, but also a great opportunity to show the public, politicians and media our campaign is on full throttle. Turn out. Let Glasgow, let Scotland see we are fighting for our jobs, for Scottish jobs. Nothing is more important that day. So forget football, the golf, the telly, the pub or long lies in bed. Be there, and bring your family, friends, and anybody that'll come and stand beside us. I'll be there with my family, will you?"

I had put it as bluntly as that to them. We would see what Sunday brought.

Later that day, I was reflecting on whether or not I'd been too dictatorial at the mass meeting. Maybe I was over abrasive about the rally. Perhaps that was because one middle manager in the technical department was overheard saying that he was giving his game of golf up for nobody.

In the administration offices I stopped to speak to the receptionist at the main switchboard, and one of the secretaries. I knew them very well and respected their views. I asked them if I had been autocratic at the meeting. Their response was,

"You were what you always are. To the point and truthful, and most people respect that."

Those words were reassuring, because they were not females of the shrinking violet type.

The following day, Swan Hunter based at Tyneside in the northeast of England, went public in expressing confirmation that they were potential buyers of the yard. Our initial upbeat mood on hearing that was quickly dampened as details of what they wanted for Govan emerged. They would turn us into a steel preparation and fabrication yard only. That type of structure would be our last option for survival. We were a shipyard and we wanted to build total ships.

The media asked for our views on the proposals put forward by Swan Hunter. My initial reaction was to be less that supportive of it. However, on reflection, I decided to keep my powder dry. They could be the new owners after all. I welcomed the interest shown and tried to be at my diplomatic best in public statements. Privately, we were apprehensive about Swan Hunter and their plans. Even more importantly, we were also hearing there could be two other interested parties.

At the next meeting of the Task Force the identities of the other new potential owners were becoming clearer. Hard on the heels of Swan Hunter's interest, the grapevine was leaking Ferguson's of Port Glasgow, and GEC Marconi. I was taken aback on hearing of the interest shown by Ferguson's. It had an unrealistic ring to it. Without intending to be rude towards them, it was the equivalent of the corner shop taking over the supermarket.

Ferguson's was a first-class small yard, second to none in the range of small to medium size ships it built. Several years previously I had worked there on a temporary transfer. It was compact and efficient. Nevertheless, I could not help but believe that they were out of their depth and did not regard them as serious players. However, the more interest that was stimulated, the more our chances increased of finding a buyer.

The other party in the frame was much more realistic. GEC Marconi was a large company that currently owned the other shipyard on the upper Clyde at Scotstoun, the famous Yarrows. They also owned the old VSEL yard in Barrow, principally known as submarine builders, whereas Scotstoun specialised in surface warships, frigates and the like.

Our keenness in GEC possibly taking over Govan was further fuelled by the fact that the second oiler we had been arguing for to be built on the Clyde was the contract currently based at Barrow. So, GEC fitted the bill perfectly. They were a large company and potentially could put work into Govan immediately.

And, there was another vital factor in the equation. British Aerospace was in the process of purchasing GEC, and there were strong rumours emanating from ministerial level in government, that talks had taken place with BAE in relation to them supporting the purchase of our yard. It was clear progress was being made and I was confident there was light at the end of the tunnel.

Despite my increasing optimism, Sir Gavin Laird and the rest of the Task Force brought me firmly down to earth by reminding me that negotiations were at an early stage. There were numerous complex problems to be solved before we could be remotely confident.

The same day witnessed a visit to the yard by Swan Hunter directors. Their Managing Director Jaap Kroese was known for being outspoken and abrasive, and when I met him he lived up to his reputation. I had a brief discussion with him and his colleagues, and they seemed very impressed by the yard. Nevertheless, there was amazement the following day when Kroese appeared to be giving the impression to the media that he was almost already in possession of the yard. He even gave a newspaper his detailed blueprint for Govan's future under his company.

I was seriously concerned about his proposals. Swan's would not see us as a shipbuilding yard but more of a fabrication site and I feared the company envisaged a core workforce of only around three hundred. But once again I displayed a diplomatic silence, something I was not known for.

SUNDAY
2 MAY 1999

A lifeline…

10

I AWOKE to glorious sunshine. It was almost time for the Glasgow May Day rally. I had never been so happy to see the sun in the sky. I was a bag of nerves, as I thought ahead to us leading the rally. What kind of turnout would we get from the workers and their families? I prayed that I had got the message across at the mass meeting earlier in the week. Funnily enough, I was less nervous at the thought of being a guest speaker at the rally at Glasgow Green at the end of the procession.

Isabel, Julie, Amanda, and Fraser were getting dressed as I fidgeted about the house, like a cat on a hot tin roof. Then the home was instantly in uproar. Isabel's elderly dad Johnny had recently come to stay with us due to his deteriorating health. She'd been caring virtually full time for both her elderly mum and dad for about two years. Her mother's health had also been getting significantly worse. Reluctantly, Isabel had to have her admitted to a local nursing home.

Johnny took ill about thirty minutes before we were due to leave for the rally. He was not one for complaining, and urged us all to go and he would be fine. Isabel, Julie and Amanda all wanted to stay with him as we called an ambulance. But, Johnny was adamant that I get family support at the rally. He was a firm supporter of our campaign, and always asked me for a daily update when I got home from work. At his insistence only Isabel stayed, and Julie, Amanda and Fraser came with me.

We arrived at George Square about 11 a.m., which was approximately half an hour before the procession set off. There were crowds of the usual annual marchers.

What a colourful scene. The sunshine really set off all the reds, blues, greens and other shades in the banners.

I didn't have to look far to spot workers from the yard. They were everywhere. I could see our colours had already been unfurled, and crowds were gathering around it. My eyes scanned the endless flow of more arrivals. Everywhere I turned I recognised colleagues from every section of the workforce. Many of them had brought their families as I had asked. Mums, dads, grannies and prams – they were a wonderful combination.

I was bombarded with the same comments from all my workmates.

"Jamie, great turnout, are you happy?"

"Jamie, I missed the pub to be here."

"Jamie, can I sign on here to prove I turned up for the rally?"

The banter was jovial and good-hearted. As we started to assemble at the head of the procession, Alex Mosson the Lord Provost approached. He told me that he had never seen such a turnout from a workplace. I turned round, and our contingent was massed about six-deep, to the end of City Chambers and right around the corner. I overheard a senior police officer comment that our part of the procession was a thousand plus. The next banner behind us seemed miles away, on the horizon.

All of the shop stewards were overjoyed at the turnout. As we stood there we knew we had called them to arms again, and they had responded. I found their unity and loyalty inspiring, and once again I felt that tingling surge of pride go through me. It was a similar feeling to the one I had when my son graduated from University and at the birth of my first granddaughter Emma.

As we marched through the city centre the bands that were accompanying the procession added to the noise and spectacle of the march. Large crowds stopped to watch, and we got lots of words of encouragement from them as we passed. In the crowd I saw several elderly retired workers. Some of them shouted that they would have walked in the procession with us if their legs had been up to it.

It's one of the unique aspects of our industry on the Clyde. If you have spent a significant part of your working life in it, an imprint is made forever. The renowned adage, 'you can take the man out of the Clyde but you cannot take the Clyde out of the man' is well justified. We arrived at Glasgow Green around 12.30 p.m., and I geared myself up to address the rally.

I followed my normal format, no notes, and no script. I simply must bank on the fact that I know the subject matter and I believed in what I am saying.

I spoke of the defeatist attitude that had prevailed about manufacturing industries since Thatcher's days. Closure is inevitable, resistance is futile. It had almost brain-washed us all. That included the public, the unions and Labour politicians. We at Govan wanted to change that philosophy. Our view was that closure was unacceptable, resistance was imperative and defeat was unthinkable.

I told the rally we must reverse Thatcher's dogma that there is no such thing as society. I stated we would win our struggle and avoid closure and told them to watch this space. I got an excellent reception from the audience. The message was getting across, our campaign was not waning. It was full steam ahead. After I'd finished I walked through the crowds to meet Julie, Amanda and Fraser. I received many pats on the back from colleagues at the yard and people I'd never even seen before.

The family were chuffed too. They couldn't believe the turnout from Govan and they were all thrilled at the response my words had received and said how well they thought I'd done. Praise is great, but I was more concerned that what I'd said had struck a chord and made people think about what we were fighting for. After all, they could find themselves in exactly the same situation in the future.

We left the rally early and headed home to see how Johnny was. I hoped I had not lost sight of the fact that, despite the importance of the campaign, family comes first.

A few days later, we heard through the grapevine that national union officers had met Almskog in London. Their aim had obviously been to make an impact on him and attempt to get him to open up and declare his intentions. Surprise, surprise they soon found out like us that The Iceman was not for melting. I was also hearing from media contacts in London that in certain union arenas I was still not flavour of the month. The media told me that some of the hierarchy still expected our campaign to fall apart at the seams. They would then come in and pick up the pieces.

There was never a dull day, and on reading *Lloyd's List* on 6 May, I had steam coming out of my ears.

Lloyd's List is the bible for shipbuilding and ship-owners. It's the daily newspaper the whole industry reads. It contained an article from my friend Almskog portraying doom and gloom regarding the future for Govan. His theme was that time was running out to find a buyer and that there were numerous obstacles to overcome if one was to be found for Govan within the appropriate timescale.

To put it mildly, he was not optimistic. Instantly, I phoned *Lloyd's List* in London to speak to the journalist who had written the article. I asked if I could have the opportunity to respond, expecting the answer would be no. Surprisingly, they told me to fax it down and they would print it the following day. I wrote the article criticising Almskog for his negative approach to securing a new owner and his lack of sensitivity towards his Govan employees.

Almskog had stated that he was a Chief Executive, not a social worker. I responded that any company that had no social conscience towards its employees could never expect commitment or loyalty. I reminded him that Kvaerner employees across the total corporate group would be watching his treatment of the Govan workers. Was he happy sending out a message that the employees were insignificant, and could be disposed of without any sensitivity?

I know he read my response. At a future meeting with him I found out his view on it and another lengthy article I wrote for a national Norwegian newspaper. Despite Almskog's negativity, I continued to base my optimism that we would get a new owner on a three-point evaluation.

1   Kvaerner would surely have preferred to sell the yard rather than close it down as they would have to pick up a significant bill for redundancy payments. It was also becoming apparent that should Kvaerner close the yard they would be required to decontaminate large areas on the site at a cost of several million pounds.

2.   GEC, our preferred new owner almost certainly saw Govan as their best option to build the second of two Auxiliary Oilers for the Ministry of Defence. It was well known that they had no chance of completing that contract within the scheduled delivery dates.

3.   It would have been politically damaging for the government to let us close.

So, I was not flying a kite. I believed that it was a balanced evaluation of the situation.

By mid-May it was abundantly clear that GEC were formally in discussion about purchasing the yard. We were now seeing a physical presence of many of their representatives at Govan as they went through all areas of our business with a fine-tooth comb. Poor Gunnar looked mystified as he witnessed an invasion of GEC high fliers. To his credit, he tried hard to encourage everyone to keep in the 'business as usual' mode and across the yard everyone seemed to be rallying round and supporting him.

As the GEC reps swarmed about, I was quite relaxed about it all. I had total confidence that they would like what they saw in Govan. We were a relatively modern yard with a flexible and committed work force. We had much to offer and I had no doubt they would like us.

At the same time a story was circulating that there was the possibility of a twelve ship contract from Cuba. The story had emerged from Scottish MP and government industry minister Brian Wilson. Reluctantly I dismissed it instantly to both the media and the workforce. This so-called potential contract had been the cause of discussion the year before and was pie in the sky. With the weakness of the economy in Cuba, somebody was kidding somebody on.

I was proved right. It soon became clear that the financial structure was not in place for Cuba to pay for it. There would be more strings attached to winning this contract than you would have seen at a puppet show.

Privately, I was also suspicious of the timing of this news. It came just before the Scottish Parliamentary election. I found it hard to believe an experienced Minister like Wilson would not have been aware of how unlikely this Cuban contract would be to materialise and so I dismissed it inwardly as pre-election spin and a political smoke and mirrors exercise.

At a mass meeting of the workers on 18 May, I gave them an updated report on how things were progressing. As was always the case, even at times of crisis, the humour in the shipyard still shone through. A wag reminded me that I kept telling them that matters would be concluded in about two weeks. He was right. Generally speaking I had consistently being doing that. Somebody else chimed in,

"Yes, you are now known as Jamie-two-weeks."

There was spontaneous laughter around the hall and it eased the tension. The meeting closed with everybody in an upbeat frame of mind. On the other hand I hadn't forgotten that the redundancy clock was ticking towards our D-Day, Friday 16 July.

One issue that we had managed to totally suppress at the meetings was any dialogue on redundancy payments getting enhanced. I knew that if dialogue on this matter was forced on to the agenda by anyone it would have distracted us from our singular aim, to save the yard. Previous industrial closure campaigns had failed because the lure of a redundancy sweetener had resulted in divisions in the workforce followed ultimately by the collapse of campaign unity.

Later that day I heard from Gunnar that there was a board meeting of GEC and that Govan was the main item on the agenda. There were conflicting views about GEC taking us over. With the current state of the market, why would they want another shipyard? The vibes I was getting also suggested the board was split on the wisdom of putting in an offer although the chairman Lord Simpson was in favour.

A few days later I got a phone call from Elspeth Atwool, an active member of the Liberal Democrats. She told me that party leader Paddy Ashdown wanted to visit the yard and meet the trade unions. The shop stewards had no objection to that as we maintained our stance in seeking support from all political parties.

When Ashdown arrived, Gunnar gave him an update on the current situation and later the convenors had an informal chat with him. He insisted on going on a walkabout and his antics caused lots of banter and laughter. He was a real action man.

In the steel fabrication shed he climbed a ladder to speak to a couple of steelworkers. Not content with that, he then climbed inside one of the units and disappeared temporarily from sight. This resulted in a group of workers congregating to witness what happened next. Many workers were aware of his armed forces background and when his head eventually surfaced back into the daylight he was met with loud cheers.

The media interviewed him after the visit and he expressed the view that he had been very impressed by the quality of ships being built and the positive attitude being displayed by the workforce at a very difficult time.

The visits of politicians helped boost morale, so it was a worthwhile venture. It was, however, being commented on by workers that up until now we had hosted visits from senior politicians from the SNP (Alex Salmond twice) and the Lib Dems, (Paddy Ashdown).

We were increasingly noticing the absence of prominent Labour politicians. Apart from Gus Macdonald, Scottish industry minister, we had not seen any of Labour's big players. Even more of a disappointment was the fact that Tony Blair had visited the GEC Scotstoun yard the previous week. We indicated to the media that a visit from the Prime Minister would have been a tremendous morale booster to Govan. When the Prime Minister was challenged on this issue he was somewhat offhand with the media. I believe that he didn't take kindly to my comment, that in the world I come from, leaders lead from the front and go where the flak is flying. We were fighting for survival, and a few words of support during his visit were the least we could have expected. Sadly, it was not forthcoming.

Around this time, there was another interesting development on the GEC front. Our technical and planning department were now visiting Barrow to discuss the possibility of transferring the building of the second MoD Auxiliary Oiler up to Govan. This was a very important development for me as it fitted perfectly into my assessment of why GEC saw us as the solution to the problem of meeting the delivery dates for the two ships.

However, not everyone shared my opinion that being taken over by GEC would turn out to be our passport to long-term security. A small minority of cynics were putting forward the view that if GEC did purchase Govan, they would only stay until the oiler contract was completed and then close the yard. Thank God, I didn't drive this campaign with such negative thoughts. I genuinely hate negativity. It's what losers are made of.

It was Task Force time again, and I noticed a marked degree of increased optimism from Sir Gavin Laird as he gave an update. Although they were not stating it publicly, I strongly suspected that the Task Force clearly had GEC firmly in mind as the preferred new owner of Govan. Officially Swan Hunter and Ferguson's were still in the ball game but realistically they were long outsiders in a three horse race.

Ironically, within days of the Task Force meeting we got another visit from Swan Hunter's management. It had emerged that they were basically a front for a Dutch company called Centre Staal, who were major players in the steelwork preparation/fabrication arena in Europe. I had still not changed my mind. This would be a poor second option for the Govan yard. However, once again I didn't dismiss their interest or criticise them, as there still remained the possibility that they could have become the new owners.

Edginess was now clearly visible in the yard. It was early June, and we were six weeks away from the date when we would be on an irreversible rundown towards closure. My daily walkabouts were stressful as countless workers stopped me to ask what was happening.

I had an obligation to keep morale high and maintain stability in the yard. All the shop stewards were aware that we had to work hard at this on a daily basis. It used to be that I was stressed out at the end of the day. Now I was stressed out before I went into work. I also had become aware that my body language was being used as a barometer by many of the workers to assess how things were going in the campaign.

If I looked chirpy and bouncy they assumed everything was going well, whereas if I looked po-faced and stressed it was assumed that there were problems. Some mornings I had to force myself into doing the daily walkabouts, while on many other occasions I had to fake an optimistic face.

Back at home I had been an utter pain in the neck to my family. Agitated, irritable and without a shadow of a doubt, ignoring their needs. I was constantly feeling guilty about this.

Often I found myself lying awake for hours in bed, head pounding with endless thoughts. What happened today? What will happen tomorrow? On many occasions I went to bed at 10 p.m. and lay awake until 2 a.m., or later, unable to sleep. This resulted in me often being snappy and short-tempered at shop steward's meetings and then regretting it afterwards. My fellow stewards, I am sure, must have wanted to throttle me on occasions but for whatever reason and to their credit they put up with it.

Despite the complexities and pressures of running the campaign we couldn't forget we were still building ships. Productivity levels were being maintained and I knew everyone was commenting on how remarkable that was considering the uncertainty that surrounded us.

However, the company came to the shop stewards on 3 June with a request that would test to the limit the influence that we had with the workers. Kvaerner had requested volunteers to work the three weeks of the Glasgow Fair which ran from mid-July until early August. This put us in an extremely delicate situation.

The HR1 redundancy notice expired on 16 July, Fair Friday, allowing the company to legally make employees compulsorily redundant from that date. I knew there would be a reaction by the workforce to this request. It would, in some quarters, be regarded as totally unacceptable and lacking in sensitivity.

However, balanced against that was the fact we had always worked normally throughout the campaign. It was essential we maintained that stance.

I went back to a mass meeting and advised the workforce that we should co-operate with the request for holiday working and follow the normal procedure for volunteering. I reminded them that we would get an owner, whether it was tomorrow, next week, or next month. We would succeed. There were murmurs of discontent and opposition from a very small minority, but our recommendation was overwhelmingly accepted. Once again, pragmatism and responsible thinking from the workforce had won the day. It was on such days that I recharged my batteries. I knew I was being biased, but I had such admiration for those men and women and their continual efforts to be helpful and responsible.

At this period our involvement with all areas of the media was at a peak. Hardly a day went by without some enquiry for information from TV, radio or newspapers. Back in February the shop stewards and workforce had sanctioned the making of a documentary by the *BBC* of our campaign. The reporter was the journalist and author Fergal Keane.

We were now just over four weeks away from the end of the legal consultation period with the HR1 redundancy notice. The nerves of everyone in the yard, including myself, were on edge. I even noticed that I was getting very narky with Gunnar on my daily visits. It was becoming very frustrating as it was clear that he was being kept out the loop. But, whenever I pressed him he said he was still optimistic a deal would be done.

Regardless of this I couldn't really be critical of him as he has been more than fair and helpful to the unions in the yard. I knew that behind the scenes he was on the phone constantly to the Kvaerner Head Office in London for an update. However, he was continually being ignored or by-passed. It must have been frustrating for him too.

Around the same time, there were speculative reports that the proposed take-over by British Aerospace of GEC could be referred to the Monopolies Commission. Should that have happened there would have been serious implications for GEC continuing with the proposed purchase of Govan shipyard. This was a potential difficulty that we could well have done without as it could have scuppered the whole deal.

Media interest was still intense and in mid-June I did lengthy interviews for Norwegian, Italian and German newspapers. Kvaerner had shipyards in both countries and the papers were intrigued about the level of political involvement in our campaign. They explained that in both Norway and Germany yard closures would usually have been accepted as inevitable.

Gunnar sent for the convenors on 24 June. The personnel manager, Davie Wilson, was also present. Gunnar had that nervous, strained look on his face as he informed us that due to the fact that the HR1 had only three weeks to run, the company were legally obliged to furnish us with a more detailed and specific breakdown of the redundancies. They wanted to tell us, department by department, the number of employees that would go in the first batch in July.

I was absolutely loathe to accept that specific information, or for the company to have released it throughout the yard. I knew it would cause alarm, depression and also badly affect morale.

The personnel manager agreed that providing the convenors formally recognised that we had been offered the details, he would not issue them publicly across the yard.

To this day I freely admit the workers had the right to know but I and the rest of the shop stewards balanced that with the negative impact the news would have had and decided not to tell them. Rightly or wrongly we regarded maintaining unity was more important than anything else.

To complete the formal legal process he handed me the information and I automatically handed them back to him without even looking at the redundancy breakdown. All the convenors agreed that it was best we did not know those details. We knew that the company would be compelled to release them soon if we didn't get a new owner within the next three weeks.

I went to the Task Force meeting the following day totally stressed out. Many people had commented that I was showing signs of wear and tear. Some of my workmates told me their wives had remarked that in recent TV interviews I had looked unwell. I must admit that in one the previous week I had looked like 'death warmed up'. What I encountered at the Task Force meeting did little to improve my state of mind as I quickly detected a high degree of frustration in the report given by the members.

The impetus appeared to have gone out of the take-over talks between GEC and Kvaerner. It was clear that a game of industrial brinkmanship continued between them. It had been reported on a couple of occasions that proposed meetings between both parties had been cancelled at short notice. The combatants were playing a game of cat-and-mouse and unfortunately, the workers remained pigs-in-the-middle as the mind games continued against one another. I got the strong impression the Task Force view was that corporate egos were getting in the way and could result in Govan closing as both GEC and Kvaerner flexed their negotiating muscles.

I found myself becoming angry towards both companies. It appeared to be that the last thing on their minds was the welfare of the twelve hundred workers in the Govan yard. After the meeting, I did interviews for *STV*, the *BBC* and *Radio Clyde*. I was on a definite downer, but again I knew I must put a face on. I was fully aware that it was Friday. Knowing that my workmates and their families would be watching my body language I decided there was no way was I going to let them suffer another weekend of increased stress and depression. I gritted my teeth and remained consistent to the theme that a deal would still be done.

At home over the weekend, I reflected on the current situation. I had left that Task Force meeting seriously worried at the apparent impasse between Kvaerner and GEC. We'd all worked tirelessly to pull the deal together, nevertheless, at this stage time was running out quickly and I was concerned that when push came to shove the Task Force would prove to be rather lightweight. I felt that if the significant and much appreciated groundwork that they had done was not to be wasted, high-level political muscle would now be needed to go that final mile.

Two days later, fate took a hand as I geared myself up for the beginning of another week at work on the emotional roller coaster. On the evening of Sunday 27 June I was speaking to a journalist from the *Press Association* who had phoned from London. I heard my mobile ring, and Isabel answered as I continued my call. When I'd finished, Isabel said,

"A guy called John Reid phoned. He'll call back in fifteen minutes."

Isabel's knowledge of who's who in the political arena wasn't the best.

"Isabel, that 'guy' John Reid is the Secretary of State for Scotland," I replied.

"Oh, I thought it was another reporter, or somebody from work. He said he'd phone back."

I had never met or spoken to John Reid. However, I was very anxious to hear what he had to say. As promised he called shortly afterwards and we discussed the seriousness and delicacy of the situation, and the way forward. He told me,

"I know how difficult and tense the situation is in the yard. I depend on you and the shop stewards to hold things together. I can assure you that I am now personally involved with Gus in trying to get both Kvaerner and GEC together for serious discussions. At this time we can both promise you nothing apart from the fact that we will give it a hundred per cent effort. Time is against us, and there are some very complex and difficult issues to resolve."

Reid also emphasised how difficult it would be to cut a deal in such a short period of time and re-iterated the problems both companies faced as they jockeyed for the best position and most favourable terms. I thought he hinted then that the process might involve a banging together of heads.

I was happy with his openness and could only ask that they do their very best. He told me that he would personally keep in touch with me regarding any developments that arose. As I had felt it was essential to get some political muscle moving I was relieved at the Scottish Secretary's involvement. He was regarded as a Rottweiler amongst politicians, a man who wouldn't be pushed around by corporate officials.

I went into work on Monday significantly more buoyant than when I had left the Task Force on the previous Friday. Early that morning the personnel manager sent for the convenors again and put us under pressure to accept more information on the redundancies. He indicated that the company proposed to bring in employment advisors since the first batch of proposed redundancies was only two weeks away. There was now a view that Almskog and co. had been prompting our local management to up the temperature in the yard in order to make sure that the unions kept the pressure on the government.

It was a disgusting tactic, but no less than we had come to expect. We responded by telling him we would not co-operate in the bringing in of those support agencies. The stewards were of the unanimous view that if we accepted their presence it would be regarded by the workforce as an acknowledgement that closure was inevitable. It would only have put more pressure on them. On a more positive note, there were vibes that GEC were about to table a bid for the yard within the next couple of days.

2 July arrived and there was still no official bid. What the hell was going on? The brinkmanship between the two companies was even more intense. The pressure was now really getting to me, as we were now only two weeks away from a certain rundown leading to complete closure by October.

It was probably no coincidence that during that period several workmates said,

"Even if we don't get a deal it won't have been the fault of the shop stewards. We've all given it everything."

Many said that the campaign strategy had been excellent. I knew many of them were trying to take the pressure off me and make me feel better. It didn't work. We had to get a deal.

A few days later I was at home in the evening when the phone rang. It was my older brother Ronald, phoning from New York. It was his fiftieth birthday and as a celebration he had gone to the Big Apple for a seven day break with two friends. I was slightly surprised that he was phoning, but was to be even more amazed at what he told me.

"James, I'm sitting in a pub with my two mates, and the *CNN* news came on. Then on the screen there's a reporter talking about the crisis on the Clyde in Scotland."

Ronald said that the three of them all looked at each other and said,

"Any bets Jamie is on in a minute?"

Low and behold, yours truly appeared, and apparently they were dumbstruck. Ronald tried to convince a couple of locals in the bar that I was his brother. He said that he finally convinced them when he showed them the name on his passport.

"Three thousand miles to get away from you and your ugly face still gets shoved in front of me!"

The following morning Gunnar sent for the convenors and informed us that the company would be sending letters out immediately to all employees asking if they wished to volunteer for redundancy. This was a serious development. If workers began to volunteer, it would all begin to run away from us. We knew we had to get them to stand firm and ensure that nobody walked across the line. Our unity had been our main asset and it had to remain intact.

I called the shop stewards together and it was decided that it was essential we hold a mass meeting the following day and ask the workers to stand firm. We also decided that we would ask them to return all the redundancy letters to us, unopened. We would treat the letters with contempt. They would be taken the following day to Kvaerner Head Office in London and dumped on the doorstep. The message would be clear. We didn't want redundancy cheques–we wanted to keep our jobs.

Incidentally, the strategy to return the letters to London did not come from either me or the shop stewards but from Thomas Brady, a welder on the back shift. It proved that good, innovative ideas could come from anywhere in the yard.

The mass meeting was tense. We had just over a week to save the yard and we realised that we had to take any appropriate step regardless of how desperate the action would appear to the public. I banked on the workforce going all the way. Encouragingly, I got solid support for the suggestion of returning the redundancy letters to Kvaerner headquarters in London.

I also emphasised that nobody should volunteer. I fully understood that for some of our older employee, those in the sixty-two-plus bracket, it would have been advantageous for them to take a package and leave right away. But, I knew from the response I received at the meeting that nobody would break ranks. I detected the workers buzzing about our plans to dump the notices at Kvaerner HQ. It was radical and direct and it sent a clear message that no worker in Govan would willingly be laid off.

We emphasised that all the shift workers must hand their unopened letters in to the gatehouse. Day-shift workers were to give them to shop stewards first thing in the morning. It was agreed that Davie Torrance, the MSF convenor, and myself would go to London to hand them in. The meeting ended on an amusing note, when one wag shouted,

"Hey, Jamie-two-weeks. You'll have to change your name now, because there are only ten days left!"

I replied, "Two weeks, two days or two hours, as long as we get a new owner, I don't care."

As the workers trudged back to work I was in a positive frame of mind for the trip to London.

The media soon switched on to our plan, and it was clear that we would get a high profile for this aspect of our campaign. Later that afternoon, Gunnar informed me that the Head Office in London had been told of our intentions. Much to my astonishment, Almskog had intimated that he was very keen to speak to Davie and myself when we came down the next day. That was a surprising response. I expected that if Head Office had heard of our plan they would have been more likely to have increased their main door security and stopped us getting in.

As I left work that evening of 6 July I was totally preoccupied about what lay ahead tomorrow in London. Little did I realise that in a few hours, events would take place that would almost break my resolve and destroy our whole campaign.

Mohammad Sarwar, MP for Glasgow Govan, phoned me on my way home. Sarwar had only recently resurfaced after his involvement in a prolonged and complex legal case. He informed me that he had arranged for Davie and me to meet a delegation of Labour MPs at Parliament after our talks with Almskog. Following that we were to have a private discussion with Secretary of State John Reid. It was apparent that tomorrow would be a very eventful day.

As I sat down to supper about 5 p.m. the phone rang. It was Russell Walker, the chief reporter from *Radio Clyde*. I had got to know Russell very well over the previous few months and he was well versed on our campaign and all the goings on around it. He informed me that an announcement was imminent from GEC and Kvaerner relating to the proposed take-over.

He asked me to go to *Radio Clyde* as soon as possible, so I could give an instant response. Still in my working clothes and with my dinner uneaten, it was off in a taxi to the station. My younger daughter Amanda had insisted on accompanying me, telling me that I couldn't be trusted to act rationally when I was hyper.

Russell met us at reception and went to the newsroom to await the announcement.

Then it broke.

"GEC today have tabled an offer for the Kvaerner Govan shipyard that is believed to form the basis of an agreement."

I remember ecstasy, total joy. We had done it. I believed I physically could have leapt over a tenement building I was on such a high. I hugged Russell with delight as Amanda looked on in amazement before chirping in,

"Dad, calm down, calm down. It's only an offer. Nothing's definite yet."

But, I was jubilant.

"Amanda, it's only the technicalities that have to be ironed out. A deal will be done."

My mind was racing again. Brilliant! All my workmates would hear the great news with their families tonight. I was so happy. I thought of my workmate, Quiggy, who had won around £600,000 on the Lottery recently. I know how ecstatic he had been then. But, right at that moment there was no happier man on God's earth. My prayers had been answered.

Russell interviewed me and I couldn't have sounded happier. Like Amanda, he also urged caution, reminding me it was only an offer, but I was on a high and dismissed any hint of negativity. As I left *Radio Clyde* many of the staff waved and gave a thumbs-up sign. I could see that they were happy for us, and it was a great feeling.

At the reception desk we intended to book a taxi home. However, *STV* had tracked me down, and wanted to do a live interview. Virtually all my previous interviews with *STV* had been done with Alan Saunby. However, on this occasion it was a female interviewer who I was unacquainted with and who was not totally conversant with details of our campaign.

Due to the state I was in I felt the interview was a disaster. Still, as long as we had a new owner, my performance was incidental. The journey home in the taxi was a blur. I was riding on pure adrenaline.

Isabel was waiting at the door as we arrived home. Excitedly she said,

"Jamie, it's been pandemonium. You've had twenty-odd phone calls in the last two hours. I've got a list of them for you to call back. The media, union officials, workmates, everyone and their granny."

It wouldn't be the first time we had both spent hours answering phone calls on matters relating to the campaign. Isabel was by now a seasoned campaigner. After a call to a joyful Sarwar followed by further calls to a couple of newspapers, an incoming call interrupted the euphoria. It was a journalist from the *Press Association* in London, named Richard.

"Hello, Jamie. Have you heard the news?"

I replied,

"Yes, I am absolutely ecstatic."

He continued,

"But have you heard the latest news?"

"What do you mean the latest news?"

"Kvaerner have rejected the offer. I am really sorry to be the one who told you. I hope it works out OK."

My heart sank and I felt physically sick.

I put down the phone, and went into the living room where Isabel was sitting. She knew immediately something was wrong.

"The deal's fallen through."

She looked despairingly at me. I glanced at Amanda, and she looked away. I could imagine what she was thinking,

"Dad, calm down, calm down. It is only an offer."

The naïve 17-year-old had proved to be more accurate in her appraisal of the situation than her dad. I had let my judgement become clouded due to my obsession to save the yard. My mind started racing again towards all my workmates and their families. Oh my God, two hours ago it would have been happy homes and happy families. They would have been in seventh heaven. What a body blow to now be told that it was back to square one.

I told Isabel that I was going out for a walk and did not want to make or take any more phone calls. I walked about for about an hour and couldn't focus on anything positively. By the time I returned to the house I had made up my mind that the returning of the redundancy letters to London was now futile.

I believed that the workers would have heard that the deal was off and would see no point in bringing their unopened letters in. Furthermore, I was going to call a mass meeting to tell the workforce that we had lost our struggle for the yard and our jobs. Months previously I had promised them that if at any stage the shop stewards felt our campaign was doomed to failure we would tell them. We would not live on false hope or string them along.

I hadn't reckoned on Isabel's response,

"While you were out, Joe Brown phoned."

Joe was the yard outfit convenor and a good friend. Isabel continued,

"Joe was feeling sorry for himself and saying it looked as if it was all over. I told him in no uncertain terms that he was out of order and that you were going to London tomorrow and needed everybody's support more than ever."

I looked at Isabel and told her that Joe was right and that returning the letters to London was useless. I also told her of my intention to admit to the workforce that it was all over. Her response was sharp, stinging and to the point. She snapped at me,

"No way are you throwing the towel in now. If you do that the workforce and the campaign will fall apart at the seams. You're going to London tomorrow and I'll not allow you to give up the fight. The workers need you and the stewards more than ever now. You can't let them down."

A little shocked, I replied,

"Give me one other good reason to keep on going."

Quite emphatically, and with a wry smile she replied,

"My housekeeping money. I have to put food on the table."

I looked at her. That wee woman had sorted both Joe and me out big time.

Of course she was right. I knew it and she knew it. Tomorrow had to be faced. The fight had to go on. My mind had to return to a total focus on what would happen the next day, and whether the workers would hand in their unopened redundancy letters. I wanted to be confident that they would all stay resolute and bring them in. However, I had a nagging doubt because of the bad news that had broken only hours earlier. If I had been on the brink of giving up hope how could I blame them for feeling the same way?

That evening was to end with an unexpected visit to *STV* studios to do a live interview at 11 p.m. Business reporter Alan Saunby phoned about 10 p.m. asking if I would like to respond to the news of the breakdown in talks between Kvaerner and GEC. I knew Alan very well and respected him, but my gut reaction was to say no. It had probably been the most emotional day of the campaign and I was mentally drained. It was Isabel who urged me to go and do the interview.

She said it was an opportunity to let the workers know that the visit to London and the fight was still on. Once again, my 'household spin doctor' was right. I did that interview and lambasted both companies publicly for their crass insensitivity towards the workers and their families. I also said that I saw little decency or integrity within either company. I emphasised that the only place I saw those qualities was when I went through the gates of the yard every morning.

I heard at a later date that the interview broadcast that night had severely dented the public image of both companies. It was clear their negotiations had lacked common sense and common decency, and the public were entitled to know it.

I had a restless night in bed as I knew the next day would be an important and testing one.

WEDNESDAY
7 JULY 1999

Red letter day…

11

I GOT my usual lift to work but I was not my normal chatty self with Donny and John, my fellow passengers. Neither of them mentioned the disappointment of the previous evening's announcement, but I sensed that they were aware of it.

As we arrived at the yard and got out of the car they handed me their redundancy letters unopened merely saying,

"Good luck in London today, Jamie."

As I continued my walk to the gatehouse my heart was racing, my stomach was churning and my mouth was dry. On reaching the gatehouse I asked anxiously,

"Have the night-shift workers and back shift workers returned their redundancy letters?"

Jimmy, the security guard on duty, with a wide grin replied,

"Yes, Jamie, they're all here. Two boxes full of them."

I am sure he saw the colour return to my ashen face. As I stood at the gatehouse many of my day shift workmates were arriving. I was deluged with letters, with lots of back slapping and endless comments wishing us good luck in London.

At that moment a strange mixture of emotion engulfed me – humility and pride. My God, what dignity and resilience they had shown. Once again I had been inspired by their refusal to be negative or broken in spirit. It was a privilege to represent such people. I felt totally rejuvenated by their response. I was raring to go to London. Within an hour the shop stewards had collected all the day shift letters. After they'd been boxed up Davie and I were ready to leave for the airport.

Before leaving the yard, I did numerous media interviews and told them all,

"We're going to London to tell Kvaerner and the government we're fighting to keep our jobs, our families and our self respect."

I also challenged Prime Minister Tony Blair to publicly support our fight for our jobs. One of the interviews I did was for *Radio 5 Live*, heard across the UK. In that news item the reporter stated,

"There are union convenors coming down from Glasgow shipyards today to London. They want Tony Blair to acknowledge their fight to keep their jobs. There are no bland comments from the convenors. They are talking about people's lives and maintaining self-respect. This is passionate stuff."

That news report hit home as later that day in Parliament Blair made a statement in the House of Commons, acknowledging the commitment and passion shown by the shipyard workers on the Clyde in their fight for the right to work.

As we left for the airport a group of our office workers came out to see us off. As we waved goodbye, both Davie and myself geared ourselves up for what would almost certainly be a challenging day.

Prior to boarding our flight I heard from the media the specific terms of reference that related to the bid submitted by GEC for the purchase of Govan the previous day. Had I known these details at the time, I would have known immediately that Kvaerner would never have accepted them as there were many complex strings attached to the offer. One thing remained unchanged. The mind games between both companies were still ongoing.

When we arrived in London, I heard that First Minister Donald Dewar had been quoted that morning as stating that the unions in Govan should not have challenged Tony Blair to make a statement on our campaign. I was asked to respond to the First Minister's comments. My answer was simple,

"We're citizens of the UK. We're down in London to let people know of our struggle. Why should we not have the right to ask for the support of our Prime Minister?"

As I reflected on the statement made by Donald Dewar I formed the opinion that his input on this occasion had again been negative and that we had deserved better. Would the Scottish public not have been proud to see Scottish workers fighting to save their jobs and taking their struggle to the heart of government?

Surely a Labour First Minister should have applauded the action taken by us to keep our industry alive. We hadn't said anything to shame Scotland and I saw no need to apologise for the comments I'd made about Tony Blair.

At the entrance to Kvaerner Headquarters there was a large media presence as Paul Emberley, communications director of Kvaerner, greeted Davie and me. After listening to countless bland statements made by Emberley to the media over the last few months, I was interested to see the true nature of the man. Antti Pankakoski, head of the marine division of Kvaerner, joined him at the entrance.

To me, Pankakoski looked especially ill at ease as the media grilled both of them. Emberley waxed lyrical about how much Kvaerner would regret the certain closure of Govan if a deal could not be struck. I stood there, unimpressed. Their comments were exactly what I had come to expect from corporate business androids. Beneath the glib presentation their contribution, to my mind, was of little substance.

As Emberley escorted us to one of the upper floors I was aware of the sanitised coldness of the whole building and the people within it. Not a smile or acknowledgement from anyone to anyone. We had even noticed the atmosphere at the reception desk when we received our security passes.

It was as if everyone in the building had withdrawn into their own shells. Davie and I both felt smothered.

We also had no doubt what caused that environment; fear. It was etched on many of the faces we saw that day. It almost certainly was a result of the mass cull of jobs that had recently been undertaken at the Head Office. It wasn't only workers in the shipyards on the Clyde whose jobs were at risk. Everyone in the Kvaerner Empire was affected.

It was clear that Almskog's spectre loomed large in that building. I thought back to February when we had met him at the Scottish Office with Lord Macdonald and it reminded me of that same chilly atmosphere.

As we got out of the lift I wondered what kind of reception we would get. It was not clear if Almskog would attend personally and Pankakoski and a H.R. Director initially conducted the meeting. Both Davie and I pressed for Kvaerner to extend the proposed redundancy date to August to enable the talks with GEC to continue. As the meeting went on we felt that possibly we were making inroads there.

Pankakoski asked for a recess, and returned about ten minutes later, accompanied by Almskog. The cordial greeting and warm handshake from Almskog initially took the wind out of my sails. Was this the same man I met in February?

Loudly and boldly he proclaimed,

"Jamie, how nice to see you again. Oh, and I must thank you for your comments about me in the *Lloyd's List* newspaper, and the Norwegian press. I didn't know you held me in such high regard."

Taken aback, I went on the defensive by replying,

"I said things as I saw them."

He didn't pursue me on that and he asked me to outline our proposals. I reaffirmed our view that Kvaerner should extend the first proposed redundancy date from 16 July until mid-August. He mused over this for a moment, and then replied.

"I genuinely compliment both yourself and your trade union colleagues for the dignified and committed campaign you have conducted to save the yard. I have no desire to appear insensitive to the possibility of all the workers losing their jobs. Nevertheless, I have a responsibility to look after the interests of the shareholders. If I genuinely believed that delaying the redundancies would result in a deal, I would do it. However, I am not convinced it is the solution. I would only be delaying the agony for all the workers in Govan. We must get GEC around the table and negotiating seriously."

His last comment to me was,

"I advise both you and your convenors to get the politicians to persuade GEC to put a realistic bid on the table."

We left the meeting, disappointed. However, at that stage I was still convinced a deal could be done. A game of corporate poker was now being played. GEC's trump card was that they believed Kvaerner would be reluctant to pay considerable redundancy payments if they had to shut down Govan. There would also be significant costs in clearing the site to a standard that would be accepted by the Department of Environment.

It was clear GEC felt they had Kvaerner over a barrel and were in a position to dictate terms. On the other hand, Kvaerner were firmly of the view GEC needed the Govan yard to build the second Auxiliary Oiler for the MoD. The contract was now even more behind schedule and GEC would incur heavy penalties if the contract was late. Kvaerner were banking that GEC had to buy Govan to solve their contract dilemma.

The thousand plus workers in Govan were being used as pawns. Something, or somebody, was needed to kickstart meaningful discussions between both companies. If not, it wasn't beyond the realms of possibility that the yard could be shut because of two pig-headed multi-national companies. That would be tragic and totally unacceptable. I was determined that it would not happen.

From Kvaerner HQ it was on to the House of Commons where Govan MP Mohammad Sarwar was waiting for us. We were joined by one of my local union full time officers, Frank Carrigan. I was glad to see Frank, as he was someone who was blunt, direct, and to the point, just my type of person.

Sarwar took us to a committee room where about a dozen Scottish Labour MPs were present, including my own local constituency MP Maria Fyfe. To be fair, she had been very supportive of the campaign, although she must have been sick of the sight of me due to my numerous lobbies of Parliament. It was rumoured that behind the scenes some other MPs were saying,

"Those bastards on the Clyde just won't go away."

Both Davie and I gave the MPs a report of the meeting with Almskog. We reiterated the gravity of the situation and how time was running out. One Labour MP almost took my breath away when he asked me if I did not get rather emotional over the issue of the yard and our jobs. For some strange reason, I can't remember which MP this was although I do know that it wasn't one of the Glasgow members.

After hearing such a callous and insensitive statement I replied,

"Yes, I do get very emotional about the possibility of over a thousand workers losing their jobs and the impact it would have on their families. And the day I do not get emotional about an issue like that I'll be a lesser man for it."

The atmosphere could have been cut with a knife. I sensed the total embarrassment of the MP and his colleagues. He probably wished the ground could have opened up and swallowed him. Despite his lack of tact I believe his words had been ill chosen rather than ill intentioned.

The meeting continued with the other Labour MPs doing their best to counteract those previous comments. It was probably a relief for everyone when Sarwar indicated that

Davie, Frank and I were to go to the Scottish Office at Dover House to meet Secretary of State for Scotland John Reid.

As we made our way there I was now firmly of the view that if a deal was to be done at this late stage, John Reid would almost certainly have to be a main component in delivering it. As we entered the room I was warmly greeted by him, and then caught sight of Gus Macdonald sitting a few feet away. Trite though it may seem I felt reassured by the presence of them both due to the fact that I had the greatest respect for them. They were blunt and open in their assessment of the situation between GEC and Kvaerner.

They both indicated that the situation was grave as they were dealing with two major companies with egos to protect. As I had previously suspected, if serious talks were to be resurrected, heads would have to be banged together.

I could detect both men had real doubts a deal could be done. John Reid stated that in the few days remaining both Gus and himself would leave no stone unturned in an effort to get a deal concluded. They emphasised that they could promise nothing other than total effort. Both of them only asked that I do my best to continue to hold things together in the yard as they worked as brokers with GEC and Kvaerner to get a deal.

We shook hands on it. I could ask no more than they give it a hundred per cent. If that failed, there would be no fall out with them or political recriminations.

Outside the meeting there was a large media presence. Both Sarwar and I gave interviews. The media focused strongly on the fact that there were only days remaining to secure a deal, as if I needed reminding. I was emphatic that one would be done and that I had confidence that the joint efforts of Reid and Macdonald would deliver success.

On the flight home that evening I was physically and mentally drained. Nevertheless, I fully intended to take the message back to the workers in Govan, 'we can, and will save our yard.'

I called a shop steward meeting early the next morning, as they were all obviously eager to get a detailed report of the meetings that took place with Almskog and the politicians. I told them that the final outcome was now in the hands of Reid and Macdonald and that a decision on our future was going right to the wire. I informed them of the plea made by both the politicians for the shop stewards to hold things together in the yard. We had to keep up spirits and morale and decided that it was appropriate to hold a mass meeting that afternoon.

Not surprisingly, the canteen was full to capacity for that one. I began my report to them. There was total silence as I drove home the fact that discussions were continuing between Kvaerner and GEC. I emphasised that John Reid and Lord Macdonald were personally involved in talks with both companies. As always, I tried to assess the mood of the meeting as I gave my report. However, on this occasion I struggled to understand what vibes I was receiving.

Inwardly I had always expected somebody to break ranks and slam our lack of tangible progress. I had promised so much since February, but it was now 8 July and only eight days from a rundown to closure. I wound up the report by urging them not to lose faith. I informed them that the following day I would be attending what would probably be the last Task Force meeting and that there was still everything to play for. As usual, Joe Brown had chaired the meeting and at the end asked if anybody wished to speak.

A plater, Jim Gardiner, who'd been time served in the yard for twenty years, came up and took the microphone. He said,

"There's just over one week to go to save the yard and our jobs. I have no criticism of the campaign. It's been well led and tactically astute. However, we now may lose our struggle."

I flinched as he uttered those words. They hurt.

He continued,

"At the beginning of the campaign you and the rest of the shop stewards hammered home that our fight was to focus totally on saving the yard and our jobs. You were adamant that we shouldn't talk about the enhanced redundancy scheme. The shop stewards view was that to even contemplate talking to the company about the scheme would have sent a negative message out that we didn't have total commitment to our fight. The workforce accepted this in good faith. In the harsh light of day have we now not lost any opportunity to negotiate better redundancy terms if we close?"

I didn't know what answer either he or the workforce expected. Nevertheless my response was clear and concise.

"Yes, we are too late to negotiate an enhanced redundancy scheme. We have burnt all our bridges and there's no way back. With all our eggs in one basket it was success or bust. We are getting a new owner for the yard."

Months previously I had known that if we lost our fight and we had not negotiated an enhanced redundancy package the shop stewards risked a possible backlash. That was the risk we had chosen to take, as we had decided that there would be no side issues to distract us.

I waited to see if there were howls of disapproval as I laid it on the line.

"We set out to let everyone see our fight was for our jobs and our yard. The next few days will determine if our quest had been worthwhile."

There was a profound silence, which indicated that everyone had known from day one that we had a one-track dimension to our campaign. There was no dissension, just a stony silence.

After the mass meeting I watched intently as the workers dispersed and returned to work.

What did I detect? Anxiety. It was etched all over their faces. I re-convened a meeting of the shop stewards to enable us to do a quick appraisal. We generally agreed that the view of the masses was that we have come this far and that we must all stick together and see it through to a conclusion.

Two of my co-convenors, Johnny and Joe remarked that the pressure on me personally was immense. They suggested that they meet me outside the Scottish Office the following morning after the Task Force meeting as they felt that there was a genuine concern among all the stewards I may have been feeling isolated at times. I appreciated their concerns and agreed that they should meet me after the meeting the following day, as I had a gut feeling that whatever transpired, the company of a couple of allies to share a couple of pints with would be a welcome relief.

FRIDAY
9 JULY 1999

On the brink…

12

"I FULLY understand the strains and pressure you and all the workers at Govan have been under. If you feel it's all too much and want to call an end to it, then perhaps it's for the best."

I couldn't believe it. Donald Dewar was throwing in the towel. Our First Minister, the so-called Father of the Nation, was a total defeatist.

A surge of despair hit me after Dewar's comment. But, I could have kicked myself for letting my guard down by saying that if the companies weren't going to do business then they must stop playing games with our lives. What had I said? What did I say that for? I might not have had the chance to retract the statement. If it appeared I was admitting that we had given up the struggle and were accepting closure of the yard we would have been letting the politicians off the hook.

My disappointment at Dewar's input was evident to everyone in the room. I was raging and would probably have let rip and said something I would have regretted.

"You're a bloody disgrace," came to mind.

Fortunately, John Reid interjected,

"Jamie, a few days ago in London both Gus Macdonald and myself promised that we would give one hundred per cent effort to break the stalemate and get a good deal. You accepted that commitment in good faith. Have you changed your mind on that, or does it still stand?"

My mind was in turmoil, but I knew that I had to trust Reid and to get a deal done between GEC and Kvaerner therefore I felt obliged to reaffirm my trust in them.

"I haven't changed my mind. It still stands."

As we wound up the meeting I thanked all the Task Force members for the amount of hard work they had put in over the last few months. They had done a lot of hard slogging groundwork and I knew regardless of the final outcome no criticism could be aimed at them.

In the lift on the way down I knew that the media would be waiting. What would I say? I was totally confused and in my current state of mind was unsure if I would be able to deal with them.

On the ground floor Alan Saunby from *Scottish Television*, the *BBC's* Hayley Miller, Lorraine Herbison from the *Evening Times* and Russell Walker of *Radio Clyde* were waiting, along with some newspaper reporters. I knew Alan, Hayley, Lorraine and Russell well and they immediately saw I wasn't myself.

Obviously, they were keen to find out how the meeting had gone, especially since John Reid and Donald Dewar had been present. They were astonished when I told them that I would prefer to make no comment.

I was feeling shattered, utterly, utterly hyper and looking back with just a few days to go to save the yard, my guess is I wasn't that far away from a nervous breakdown.

The sudden appearance of GMB full time official Jim Moohan resulted in a ferocious exchange of views as he attempted to discourage me from saying anything controversial to the media. He'd seen my reaction to Dewar's comments and I think he realised I was close to breaking point. It was obvious to anyone that I was not in a stable state of mind.

I don't know exactly what was said after I'd left, but having witnessed similar incidents in the past I am as certain as I can be that someone would have dispatched Moohan to get a grip of me. They really thought I was a loose cannon. I still believe his main concern, and the reason he came after me so quickly when the meeting ended, was that he'd seen me struggle to hold my temper in check with Dewar and he was worried about what I was going to say to the media.

I told Moohan that I was ready to blow a gasket and he urged me to show some restraint. He told me that if I said anything critical about the First Minister it would damage the Labour party. It was the usual line from the full time officials. That's the theme that comes to the fore at times like this.

For a moment, we had each other by the coat collars as we went toe to toe and eyeball to eyeball in the atrium of the Scottish office building. I was still hyper. I'd been disgusted by the negativity of Dewar and had been pulled back from the brink by Reid. I had no idea if there would be a deal or not so the last two things I was willing to consider were someone trying to humour me or stop me in my tracks by gagging me.

I always felt the full time officials never stood firmly beside us in our time of crisis, instead preferring to chastise us for what they saw as political incorrectness and unorthodox methods. I felt isolated from them and believed they were just waiting for me to fall flat on my face.

I caught a glimpse of Johnny and Joe restlessly pacing up and down outside in the street and felt relieved they were there. Both knew me better that most and had seen what happened with Moohan through the window. I called them over to the entrance of the building and told them I had left the Task Force meeting utterly bamboozled and as a result of this I was unsure of what to tell the media. After a brief chat, and having regained a degree of composure, we decided to speak for one main reason.

The workforce knew that I was attending a meeting of the Task Force. I was also very aware that it was Friday with another long weekend ahead filled with uncertainty for the workers and their families. There was no way I was going to heighten that uncertainty. I was determined to put on a brave face despite the gravity of the situation.

I hoped I could do that, as I am not particularly good at hiding my emotions. I felt ill at ease during the interviews, which was unusual, as I was normally quite relaxed. Once again it would be a stressful weekend for us all. How I appreciated those couple of hours with Joe and Johnny after the meeting. A few pints with a couple of mates helped me unwind and return to relative normality.

By Monday 12 July we were only days away from knowing our ultimate fate. The convenors called the shop stewards together at 8 a.m., and gave them a report of Friday's Task Force meeting. It was strangely subdued, probably due to the fact that we all realised we had done everything that we could over the last few months and that matters were now out of our hands. We could do little else other than continue to keep everyone in a positive frame of mind over the last few crucial days. We decided to hold a mass meeting on Tuesday morning to give the workforce an update.

Later that morning our MD, Gunnar Skjelbred, summoned the convenors to inform us that he had been instructed to issue two hundred and forty-one employees with notification of formal redundancy for Friday 16 July. Although that announcement was not totally unexpected, it still rocked us. We knew that if those redundancies went ahead on Friday we were on an irreversible road to total closure by October. Word quickly got about the yard, and it was obvious that the mass meeting the following day would test our resolve to the ultimate limit.

On my way home from work that night I reflected on many aspects of our campaign over the previous few months. The shop stewards had constantly appraised the strategy and tactics. We assessed if at any time it was necessary for us to change direction. I felt that if I had to lead the fight again I would alter nothing. At times we had adopted unorthodox, and some people would argue, controversial tactics. However, as I had often said, desperate times called for desperate measures. We had been accused in some circles of being 'politically incorrect'. I often reminded people that we had never set out to be politically correct; we set out to be politically effective.

It was a very restless and sleepless night as I tossed and turned in bed. Thousands of thoughts went through my mind. Constantly I asked myself how I could convince the workers that a deal could still be done even at this late time and in the same breath tell them that two hundred and forty-one of them would get a letter that afternoon making them redundant three days later.

At past mass meetings I had continually expected criticism to come from somewhere within the workforce. Who could blame them? I had promised so much since February, and yet here we were, five months later, within three days of apparent closure and no tangible evidence of our future being secured. Yet, despite the gravity of the situation I was still driven by a profound belief that a deal could and would be done. Well into the early hours of the morning I eventually fell asleep knowing in my mind that it was imperative I successfully transmit that message at the mass meeting.

TUESDAY
13 JULY 1999

From despair to joy…

13

BY NOW I had became well accustomed to my usual reaction to nerves and stress. Since I had got up that morning at 5.45 a.m., my stomach was churning and my mouth was dry. On the way to work I tried feebly to indulge in everyday run of the mill chitchat with my regular travel mates Donny, John and Andy, but failed woefully. I am sure they saw I was a bag of nerves.

I clocked on as usual and went to the office with the intention of having a sandwich and a cup of tea. What a joke, my nerves were jangling and I could almost hear my heart pounding out of my chest. I walked round to the canteen accompanied by a few of the other shop stewards. As we entered through the canteen doors my thoughts were,

"God, give me the inner strength to get me through this meeting, and keep the workers with us."

There was complete silence as Joe opened the meeting and handed the microphone over to me to give the report. I glanced quickly across the mass of workers. There was an intensity etched on their faces that I had not yet experienced. I began.

"I admit that the equation I am about to present to you will defy logic. At 2 p.m. today two hundred and forty-one of you will get a termination of employment letter for the end of this week. But, we will still secure a new owner and our future."

As I had expected, confirmation of the lay-offs and the apparently illogical statement I'd just made led to many workers looking confused, muttering to each other, trying to make sense of it all. The low murmur became louder. I held up my hands to quieten them down and continued.

"Talks are still ongoing between GEC, Kvaerner and the government and let me remind you that last week a deal had appeared to be done only to collapse at the last moment. There is nothing to say our fortunes cannot change for the better in the same period of time. The show isn't over until the fat lady sings. Well she's maybe in the dressing room getting ready. Our job is to stop her coming on stage."

I finished and asked if anybody wanted to raise any points. This was met with a dignified silence. I urged them to keep their belief and to stay strong despite the traumatic events that would unfold that day.

When we got back to the office I asked several of the shop stewards,

"Was that silence a sign of resignation to defeat, or are they still with us?"

They all replied,

"They've come this far. They're still with us."

The remainder of the morning dragged, as we all waited for the dreaded handing out of the letters. At 2 p.m. every employee would find out if they had been selected for the first batch of redundancies. The line supervisors had been given the responsibility for the handing out these letters. It was an unenviable task and speaking to several of them earlier in the day I had detected a distinct nervousness from many of them. I knew the task of handing those redundancy letters to workers who had perhaps been under the supervision of that supervisor for many years would be a soul destroying exercise.

Dinnertime passed and 2 p.m. loomed. As they had been instructed to do, the supervisors collected the letters for the employees under their control from the main administration building at 1.45 p.m.

I watched as groups of them left the building and headed for their respective work areas. Perhaps I imagined it, but at that moment I felt a dark cloud come over Govan shrouding the yard. I went back into my office and sat for a few minutes feeling ill at ease as to how I should respond as the notification exercise commenced. I looked out the office window and saw a group of my workmates from the steel preparation area being given their envelopes.

As they all opened them I could see the supervisor fidget nervously with his protective helmet. I watched intently as the workers scanned the contents of their letters. There were six of them in the group and I could see from their body language that two of them had received the dreaded news that they had been selected for redundancy on Friday. I switched my attention to the supervisor who looked close to tears. He approached one of the men I believed had received a redundancy notification and put his arm around his shoulders.

Helplessness swamped me as I realised what I had witnessed was happening throughout the yard. I had no second thoughts now. I knew I had to get out and about the yard and show face. At the mass meeting that morning I had urged the workers to keep faith and remain strong. I had an obligation to remember my own words.

Everywhere I went I got the same message. Many that had got letters indicating that they were not in the first batch of redundancies felt guilt due to the fact that close friends had received them. Many were serious when they said that they would have been more at ease with themselves had they also got a redundancy notice as they agonised about how to react to close workmates that had been told they were to lose their jobs.

Several supervisors also approached me and told that it was the worst experience of their working lives. Some of them had been supervisors for many years, yet despite having vast experience they had found the task of handing out the letters painful and distressing. I found this gut wrenching.

However, my worst experience of that afternoon was when I was making my way back to the office around 3.30 p.m., when I passed an elderly workmate who I'd known for about twenty years. I had the greatest respect for Danny Halligan as he had many of the human attributes that I had grown to admire in my lifetime in shipbuilding on the Clyde. Endearing qualities like honesty, decency and fair mindedness. He had always been courteous and friendly and he acknowledged me with a nod as I passed by. However, his facial expression painted a picture of despair and I could tell without asking the question that he had been selected for redundancy.

Almost apologetically I asked,

"Hi, Danny, how're you doing?"

Dolefully he replied,

"Oh, it's a bad day Jamie. I got one of the redundancy letters."

My heart sank. What could I say? He saved me from the awkward task of replying.

"Listen Jamie, regardless of how this ends, I want you and the stewards to know that no fault can be attributed to the campaign. You boys have led a first class fight and if I lose my job it won't be because of a lack of effort from you and the stewards."

How sincere and dignified his words seemed at a time of such personal crisis. I replied in an upbeat tone hoping that it would perhaps perk him up and help him sustain hope,

"Thanks for those comments Danny, but remember, the fat lady's not sung yet."

As our discussion ended I didn't dare look at him face to face. My throat almost closed up and I felt my eyes well up. I could have let tears flow then. I would be surprised if, across the yard that afternoon, or in many homes that evening many were not shed.

I arrived home from work at teatime. Isabel had heard on *Radio Clyde* about the workers receiving redundancy notices. She was under enormous stress what with my work situation and the failing health of her parents. She had left her job the previous year to become virtually a full time carer for both of them. They lived nearby and Isabel had to visit them at least three times daily to attend to their numerous personal needs. It was taking a toll on her and many friends and neighbours were commenting on it.

I would periodically feel guilty for compounding her problems. I should have been more visible in my support of her as she never was less than totally supportive of me throughout the campaign. Her mother had recently been admitted to a nursing home as her health continued to worsen and she was in need of twenty-four hour care. Her father could not be left alone in his home so we urged him to come and live with us.

As is the case with many of the older generation, he was very independent and did not want to be an additional burden. I persuaded him that he was more than welcome in our house. Not least of all because I knew that it would give Isabel a degree of peace of mind.

She would, however, frequently wind me up by telling me that her father was bombarding her daily with all the media reports of the events in our campaign. She told friends,

"My God, now there are two of them rabbitting on in my ear about the campaign."

At the dinner table that evening Isabel and the rest of the family noticed my anxiety and as was the normal script tried hard to distract me by discussing run of the mill family business. But, as I sat at the table I just couldn't concentrate. The conversations were literally running by me as I was in another train of thought. We settled down around 7 p.m. to watch television. I gazed at the screen totally oblivious to what was on. Amanda chirped over,

"Dad, are you enjoying the programme?"

"Yes."

"Dad, you're not watching any programme. You're only staring into the screen. You haven't moved your head or batted an eyelid."

I was jolted out of my trance as the telephone rang. I looked at the clock as Isabel answered the phone. It was just after 8 p.m. Isabel handed me the phone and said,

"It's Richard from the *Press Association* in London."

I froze as my mind instantly raced back to the previous week. There was a hush in the living room. The chatting ceased and Amanda turned down the volume on the TV.

It was Richard that had broken the news the previous week that the deal had fallen apart. My heart was pounding as I dreaded another negative message.

"Hi Jamie. Congratulations."

There was a pause for what seemed an eternity when in fact it was probably two or three seconds. He followed on,

"A deal has been done and John Reid Secretary of State for Scotland has just made an official statement."

My head spun and I physically felt a surge of relief and elation throughout my body. Richard continued,

"Jamie, after the major disappointment of last week I'm delighted to be the bearer of glad tidings. Good luck in the future, you deserve it."

Isabel, Fraser and Amanda were itching to get me off the phone so I could tell them the outcome of the call.

"Yes. We have bloody well done it," I shouted as I punched the air in a triumphant salute.

An agreement in principle had been reached between Kvaerner and GEC Marconi after ten hours of talks at the Scottish office in London, led by John Reid and Gus Macdonald.

Although the final details had still to be hammered out, it was clear both sides wanted to complete the deal.

The joy on all our faces was a sight to behold. Was there a happier household anywhere in the world? Perhaps a ridiculous overstatement to outsiders, but a realistic viewpoint from where I was. Isabel was quickly on the phone to tell my eldest daughter Julie the good news. And to tell her I was sitting on the sofa looking like the cat that had got the cream. Even Gizmo our dog got in on the act as he wagged his tail and licked my face.

The following hours were filled with the inevitable calls from the media to get my reaction. How did I feel? Quite simply it was one of the happiest days of my life. I reminded them that more than one thousand families would sleep easy tonight. Their lives were not to be torn apart by the blight of unemployment. And, if as I expected the behind schedule oil vessel at GEC's Barrow yard came up to the Clyde, we would have work to occupy us for months.

Later, I got the phone call that impacted on me the most. It was from Joe Brown, one of my co-convenors and a good friend. He was a stalwart throughout the campaign and had put up with a lot of my demands and often bolshie attitude. Joe was ecstatic.

"Jamie we did it. We bloody well did it. You told the workforce this morning at the mass meeting that a deal could be done. The belief that we maintained throughout our campaign has been rewarded."

I replied,

"I can't wait to get into the yard tomorrow morning to be among the troops."

I also told him that I had encouraged the media to come down to Govan and witness for themselves the happiest place on earth. I ended the call by informing Joe that we would call a mass meeting sometime the following morning.

WEDNESDAY
14 JULY 1999

Enjoying the moment...

14

THE NEXT day I was up with the larks and I was sure the sky looked totally blue, the sun shone and I think I was walking on air. Donnie the car driver and my co-passenger John were extremely chirpy and bubbly as I got into the car. We were certainly not suffering from early morning blues. We arrived at the yard about 7 a.m. and as I got out the car I was amazed to see a posse of media waiting to interview me.

It was frantic stuff and endless shouts and thumbs-up from many of my work mates who were arriving for work constantly distracted me. I drew the attention of the media to my colleagues.

"Look at the demeanour of the workers as they enter the yard. There are no slouched shoulders or glum faces. Look at the spring in their steps."

As I watched them arrive I felt so proud of them all. They had been through so much they deserved that day.

I called the shop stewards together briefly to get the mass meeting organised for later that morning. And by now the shipyard banter was in full flow.

"Jamie where's the bevvy to celebrate? The drinks are all on you."

I replied,

"We don't need alcohol to get high now. Our adrenaline will give us a buzz."

I arranged for a few of the shop stewards to put notices up in the yard calling a mass meeting for 11 a.m.

I was keen to go and see Gunnar as soon as possible to shake his hand and thank him for his unstinting support over the last few months. His face was beaming as I entered the office.

"You will be a happy man today no doubt. I am so glad for all the workers. They deserve a good future. Whether or not I remain here in the long term with the new owners I don't know. The most important thing is that the Govan yard remains open."

Throughout our campaign some people had commented that we had carried a lot of luck. We certainly were fortunate to have had a managing director with such high principles and integrity. Everyone in the yard held him in high esteem and he commanded their total respect. As I left his office I sincerely hoped he would remain in his position with the new owners GEC, however deep down I doubted it. My past experiences with takeovers were that they brought in their own people. Gunnar was a Kvaerner man and I feared he would be replaced.

As I headed to the canteen accompanied by a couple of my fellow shop stewards I could hardly believe that for the first time in months we could deliver good news. As we approached the main door I looked in one of the windows. The canteen was bulging at the seams and I saw a sight that gladdened me. There were rows and rows of smiling faces. At the entrance, Davie Torrance the staff convenor stopped me. He said,

"Jamie, today is a memorable day and we feel it should be celebrated as such. We've brought a lone piper into the yard to pipe you into the meeting."

I was somewhat taken a back, however I was on such a high that I would have been agreeable to any suggestion. Like most proud Scots the skirl of the bagpipes stirs the heart. That music reminded me that this was a good day for Govan, Glasgow and for Scotland.

Our industry and our yard was a part of Scotland's proud industrial heritage. We had fought to keep our industry alive to enable us to contribute to Scotland's economic wealth. But most important of all our fight had been for Scottish jobs.

As I took my first tentative steps into the canteen the roof almost came off the building. Rapturous applause and chorus after chorus greeted me,

"Jamie, Jamie, Jamie."

At that very moment I swear that the hairs on the back of my neck stood on end. It was a display of emotion the likes of which I had never experienced in my life. The atmosphere was energising and for a brief second I was certain that a tidal wave of all my pent up stress, frustration and despair was sweeping by me and out of the door.

As I made my way to the main table I passed many of my acquaintances from the media. Newspapers, TV and radio were all there. Handshakes, thumbs up and even an embrace from one female journalist all reinforced my long held view that the reporters and journalists I had dealt with throughout our campaign were simply workers like us. Human emotions have no boundaries and like the rest of us they were caught up in the euphoria.

A journalist from the *Independent* newspaper later remarked to me that he had never witnessed such raw passion. Similarly a journalist from *The Mirror* told me that so overwhelming was the emotion that he felt it almost physically knocked him over. An avid follower of our campaign Alan Saunby of *Scottish Television* joked that the only ingredient missing to make it the party of all parties was booze. He said it was an exhilarating experience for everyone present. I told him it was simply heaven on earth.

As I reached the table all the crew from the BBC had congregated. They had filmed our campaign over the last few months for the forthcoming documentary, *'Forgotten Britain'*. James Hayes the producer approached me and said,

"What a finish this is to the campaign Jamie. What a finish it is for our documentary. All of us are delighted that you have succeeded against all the odds. You, your fellow shop stewards and all the workers have been inspirational."

I paused for a second and saw a mixture of joy and pride on the faces of the stewards. I reflected for a brief moment on how fortunate I had been to have been surrounded and supported by men of such character and integrity. I knew that during periods of the campaign I had been a moaning faced demanding tyrant. For tolerating that alone they all deserved a commendation.

Joe Brown handed me the microphone. I took it from him and at that moment I had no idea what I would say. I opened up,

"Yesterday we stood on the brink of disaster, our struggle lost. Many had written us off and were preparing our obituary. I asked you all to rise above such negativity and maintain your belief that we would succeed. I want you all now to reflect on this memorable day for our yard and our industry.

"You will all look back on this day with fond memories and pride, as indeed I will. Certainly if I live to the age of a hundred I will never forget the last few months and all that we have been through. No doubt more challenges lie ahead of us, however, having come through a period of such adversity nothing should daunt us. On behalf of the joint shop stewards and myself I want to thank you all for the unity, resilience and determination you have displayed throughout our campaign.

"The majority of you will start your summer holidays on Friday. Go. Enjoy the break with your families. You deserve it. When we return after the holidays under new owners we will continue to work towards obtaining a long term secure future for our yard."

Just as I was winding up, Joe opened a few bottles of champagne. Corks popping and champagne flowing, it was the ideal way to end such a glorious day. I watched many of my workmates as they left the meeting in small groups. Beaming faces exchanging Clyde shipyard banter.

Later that day I received a phone call from John Reid offering his congratulations. I expressed profound appreciation for the major contribution both Gus Macdonald and he had made. They had promised total commitment over the last few days and had given it.

Reid did, however, temper my joy somewhat by implying that I should exercise a degree of caution. We had secured a deal for a new owner for the yard, but there would be other difficulties ahead. I took on board what he said but reckoned it was broad general advice relating to our long-term future.

The day ended with a visit from Gus Macdonald and all the members of the Task Force. I was genuinely happy to see them as it gave me an opportunity to thank them all personally for the work they had done. I fully recognised the early graft done by Gus Macdonald and senior civil servants like John Mason, Andy Bishop and Ben McGuire.

Without their help and the Task Force members our shipyard would almost certainly have closed, of that I have no doubt. And, I also have to make mention of the sixteen Scottish Labour MPs who tabled a motion in the House of Commons praising the campaign and its leadership. I headed home looking forward to a night of normality with my family. That was something I had not experienced for months and it was long overdue.

Later that night in a moment of financial weakness I relented and treated them all to a Chinese takeaway. As my elder daughter Julie reminded me,

"Dad if you can't open your wallet on one of the happiest days of your life, there's no hope for you."

It was domestic blackmail but I gave in gladly.

THURSDAY
15 JULY 1999

A sting in the tail...

15

THE FOLLOWING morning when I woke up I was at last was able to have a pleasant thought. Tomorrow, Friday 16 July was the start of the Glasgow Fair; three weeks holiday. Yippee!

In my head I had it all planned out.

Week one, unwind and relax. Week two, five days in Rhyl, north Wales with the family. I looked forward to a week away with Isabel, my younger daughter Amanda and her friend. And just to put the icing on the cake my terror of a granddaughter, Emma, would be joining us. Boy was I determined to enjoy myself. Isabel badly needed a break too as by now she was doing a daily shuttle service to see her mum who was in a nursing home and her dad who was in hospital and very ill. And week three, relax before returning to the yard we'd all fought so hard to save.

On my way to work I thought through the schedule for that day. Priority number 1 was to address what I regarded as being a formality. That was, confirming with Gunnar that the redundancy notices for the two hundred and forty-one workers had been officially lifted. Little did I know that within a few hours the previous days words of caution echoed by John Reid would come back to haunt me. Furthermore my naïvety in the world of corporate business skulduggery would be cruelly exposed.

Over the past couple of days the story of how the deal was put together began to emerge. After ten hours of talks in London, led by John Reid, Kvaerner had agreed to sell the Govan site to GEC Marconi Electronic Systems for just over £2 million.

Marconi had agreed to transfer work to the yard and Kvaerner would have to foot the bill for any redundancies during the forty-two months after final completion of the contract in September 1999.

At the time, John Reid was asked if any public money had been spent clinching an agreement. He said then,

"We have always made it plain that if someone wanted to take over the yard we would be prepared to give financial assistance in return for their investment. That's something that's already on the record. We have to make sure the workforce and the management are able to compete in a very competitive world."

Kvaerner's top kiddie Kjell Almskog was describing the deal as "balanced" and he was also widely quoted in the media.

"Uncertainty has surrounded the future of the Govan yard ever since we made a strategic decision earlier this year to make a complete exit from our global shipbuilding activities. The past few weeks have been extremely difficult for our workforce.

We still have some way yet to go to make this deal really work–but all the parties are now determined to make that a reality."

Early in the morning I contacted the co-convenors and suggested that we should go and see Gunnar at 10 a.m. I was laid back and relaxed when shortly afterwards several members of the media contacted me about doing interviews that afternoon in the yard.

When we arrived at Gunnar's office he was his usual co-operative self, yet I sensed he was agitated. I knew him well enough by now to realise that something was bothering him. I kept calm as I enquired when the redundancy notices would be lifted.

He fidgeted with paperwork and avoided direct eye contact with me. That's always a worrying sign for me with anyone.

With Gunnar it was very unusual as he was always up front and open with the stewards.

He told us he was still waiting for official confirmation from head office in London, but that he didn't see a problem. He went on to explain that technically under the rules of heads of agreement signed between Kvaerner and GEC, we were all still employed by Kvaerner.

Gunnar also indicated that over the next few months until a formal deal was concluded we would witness an ever increasing number of GEC people coming into Govan to conclude the legal process of due diligence. In layman's terms that would result in GEC going through every part of our yard with a fine-tooth comb.

It was agreed we'd go back to see Gunnar shortly after the dinner-break when hopefully he would have official confirmation regarding the redundancies. As we left the office I felt uneasy rather than alarmed. I convinced myself it was merely a minor delay in concluding the formalities.

Back in the shop stewards office I got a call from *STV*'s news programme *Scotland Today* asking if I would do an interview at home with Isabel on the subject of how the campaign had affected our personal lives. I was apprehensive about doing it. Isabel is quiet and very unassuming, quite the opposite to me according to most people. I was far from sure she'd agree.

I phoned Isabel and after a lot of cajoling she reluctantly consented. I got a taxi home and told the other shop stewards I'd be back in the yard by lunchtime.

At home, Isabel was the proverbial bag of nerves when Shareen Nanjiani from *STV* arrived to do the interview. However, Shareen displayed great tact and diplomacy and soon had Isabel relaxed. In fact Isabel performed like a star trouper much to my amazement, although she did emphasise it would be a once in a lifetime effort. Despite several offers in the future to do similar interviews, it was a vow she was never to break.

I returned to work around 1 p.m. and sat with my co-convenors waiting for Gunnar to send for us. Time passed slowly as we all clock watched, each of us becoming increasingly anxious. The phone rang about two and Joe answered it. I fully expected it to be Christine, Gunnar's Secretary to ask us to come along and see Gunnar. I was wrong. It was *Radio Clyde's* chief reporter Russell Walker. Joe handed me the phone and Russell asked,

"Jamie have you heard anything yet?"

I replied,

"No, we're still waiting for Gunnar to send for us."

Russell went on,

"I'm getting vibes from people in London that the redundancy notices are not being lifted at present."

I felt my face go red with rage. I had never known Russell to get 'vibes' wrong in the past so I knew there was the likelihood that his information was correct.

"What are you going to do now?" he asked.

My answer was blunt and brief.

"Bloody well go to war along the corridor with the company."

I came off the phone realising instantly that Joe, Johnny and Alan had seen from my reaction that all was not well.

"What's wrong? Is there a problem?" Joe enquired.

"There sure is. Those bastards haven't lifted the redundancy notices for the two hundred and forty-one."

Without even allowing any debate on the issue I barked,

"Let's go and find out what the hell is going on."

I glanced at Alan as I stormed to the door. He jerked back and looked surprised at my explosive reaction to the phone call. I had known Alan for many years but I don't think he had ever seen me so angry.

Gunnar's secretary Christine was sitting in his outer office. Normally I would be polite and courteous, however, on this occasion I was livid and the red mist had descended upon me. Decorum was discounted. I nearly took the door off its hinges as we barged into Gunnar's office. He was visibly startled.

Davie Wilson the personnel manger was sitting beside him and he seemed equally taken aback. I had known Davie for many years and dealt with him on a daily basis. But he had seldom seen me display such a confrontational approach.

I knew that I had lost my self-control but somehow seemed powerless to stop myself exploding. I even detected apprehension in the faces of Joe, Johnny and Alan as I let rip.

"What the bloody hell is going on? We've been sitting along there for hours like diddies waiting for an answer about the redundancies. You said you'd send for us after dinner. Well it's now after two and we're still waiting. Meanwhile, we get a phone call from *Radio Clyde* telling us the redundancies aren't lifted. Tell us the bloody truth now."

Gunnar looked at us ashen faced and Davie put his head down and looked at the floor.

"I am sorry Jamie, I apologise. Your information is correct. The redundancy notices have not been lifted. I've known since 11 this morning but couldn't face telling you and the other convenors. It's unforgivable that I didn't face the music earlier and tell you the situation."

I could scarcely believe what I was hearing. Yesterday we thought the yard and all our jobs were secure yet twenty-four hours later two hundred and forty-one jobs are still at risk. It was outrageous. Gunnar urged me to calm down but I couldn't be pacified. Alan and Johnny intervened, also urging me to calm down. I have to admit that only made me worse. I was beyond reasoning with and stormed out the office yelling at Johnny, Joe and Alan to follow me or just sit listening to the company's bullshit.

As I made my way along the corridor and into my office I literally felt the steam coming out of my ears. I vaguely remember brushing past several of the media in the corridor who were obviously expecting a statement from me. I'm glad I didn't do any interviews at that time as I almost certainly would have said something that perhaps later I would have regretted. The convenors entered the office a couple of minutes after me.

As I restlessly paced the room Alan rapped,

"Jamie you were totally out of order in there. Your conduct was disgraceful."

"Too bad. They deserved it. They've treated the workforce and us with contempt."

Alan continued,

"The information they relayed to us wasn't of their making. They were under instructions to do that. They're just like us sometimes, the messengers with bad news."

Joe intervened,

"Alan's right Jamie. There's no good blaming them. Although they should have told us earlier."

Alan and Joe's comments brought me down to earth with a bump. My behaviour was inexcusable. In the past I had always tried to conduct myself in a dignified manner and expected the shop stewards and workforce to behave similarly. I had let everyone and myself down and experienced a horrible feeling of guilt.

Word soon leaked out that the notice for the redundancies had not been lifted. That news immediately engulfed the yard in a climate of uncertainty. I knew that we would have to go to another mass meeting on Friday.

Later that day Govan MP Mohammad Sarwar's secretary Caroline phoned to inform me that Sarwar intended giving all the workers a Glasgow fair Friday surprise before they stopped for the summer holidays. He was arranging for caseloads of beer and lager to be delivered to the yard so that the workers could celebrate their success in getting a new owner. He was unaware that the redundancy notice had not been lifted. It was a kind gesture, however, I had to decline as we could hardly have a celebratory drink while uncertainty surrounded two hundred and forty-one of our workmates.

FRIDAY
16 JULY 1999

Some holiday…

16

IT WAS Glasgow Fair Friday and the euphoria of the previous couple of days was waning. As a conciliatory gesture the yard treasurer of the shop stewards committee had bought a bottle of champagne. He suggested I give it to Gunnar in appreciation for the tolerance and sensitivity he had displayed over the past few months. All the convenors agreed that we should put yesterday's incident behind us, Gunner was as much a victim of circumstances as we were.

We went along to see him early that morning, all of us somewhat apprehensive. Christine had a quizzical look on her face as we entered the office. I supposed she was trying to see if there was going to be a re-occurrence of the previous day's explosive meeting.

"Good morning Christine. Can we see Gunnar please,?" I asked.

"Wait here and I'll tell him that you want to speak to him," she replied as she entered his office.

Within seconds she returned,

"The boss awaits you," she said with a smile on her face.

Gunnar stood up as we entered the office. He immediately opened up,

"Jamie yesterday was a bad day for all of us. Nobody was at ease with what developed regarding the on going redundancy notices."

He asked us to take a seat and continued,

"When I came here last year it was with the intention of making Govan a success. Had I known that I would have to preside over such a messy situation resulting in many people possibly losing their jobs, I would never have accepted the position of Managing Director. Both Davie Wilson and I fully understand the enormous strain and pressure you are under at this time.

Your reaction yesterday was totally out of character and I suppose it was inevitable that at some period you would blow up. Both Davie and I want you to know that we harbour no grudges or animosity. It's water under the bridge."

I offered my apologies for the previous day's outburst and handed him the champagne. I said,

"This is a token of appreciation from the Govan workforce."

We all laughed when he replied,

"Thank you, although yesterday Jamie you would probably have hit me over the head with it."

I was glad we were back on an even keel with Gunnar again. I had grown to greatly respect him and nothing would change that. He went on to explain that GEC in conjunction with Kvaerner had indicated that the redundancy notices for the two hundred and forty-one employees would remain in place until GEC had undertaken a review of their future labour requirements. That review would be completed by the time the workers returned from their three-week summer holiday break early in August.

Gunnar informed us that he would be in constant discussion with management representatives from GEC and assured us that he would put a strong case for the retention of all the workers in the yard. The convenors did not doubt his word on that personal commitment and we thanked him for his support. I asked him if I could keep in regular contact with him over the holiday period although I would be away for part of the Glasgow Fair. He was perfectly happy with that and asked that we relay to the workers his personal pledge that he would do everything in his power to secure all their jobs.

As I headed to the canteen for the mass meeting I knew that there would be no triumphal scenes like a couple of days previously. I was never the less utterly determined that we would not let our spirits drop and that we would remain positive minded towards securing everybody's job. At the meeting I could sense an aura of confusion and disappointment.

The workers had assumed as I had that by securing a new owner all our jobs had also been safeguarded. I explained to the workforce GEC's intention to conduct a labour requirement review during the holiday period. I assured them that I would be spending the first week of my holidays presenting as strong a case as possible for the lifting of the redundancy notices and the retention of all the jobs.

The convenors were urging everyone to remain optimistic in the hope that we could achieve our aim. After the meeting ended I did numerous media interviews. I emphasised that having secured a new owner we would now channel our efforts into having the redundancies lifted. Having put so much into our campaign over the last few months we had no intention of faltering now.

In the first weekend of the holidays I met Govan MSP Gordon Jackson in Byres Road in Glasgow. He expressed his concern that *The Herald* newspaper had printed a quote attributed to a Govan worker. When the worker had been asked about Gordon Jackson's contribution to the campaign in his role as local MSP, the worker had responded by saying that Govan would be just as well off in having Michael Jackson as MSP for all the use his namesake had been.

I told Jackson that he had a lot to learn about brutal shipyard humour. It could be cutting and merciless at times. I conceded that my workmate's statement had been somewhat overcritical but reminded him that he would be best advised to adopt a higher profile in his involvement with the yard. Shipyard workers are not renowned for airs and graces and tend to shoot from the hip. They would criticise or praise politicians without fear or favour. That chance encounter must have impacted on Jackson as from that period he was more visible and accessible throughout the campaign. I always felt that his legal background and lack of knowledge about the industrial manufacturing arena had put him at a disadvantage.

So much for my plan to relax during the first week of my holiday. During that period I kept in contact with Gunnar and some senior managers in Govan discussing the implications of the two hundred and forty-one HR1's. I had a lot to learn.

I had assumed:

New Owner + Work = Zero Job Losses.

But, this wasn't the case. The equation really was::

New Owner + Work = Some Job Losses.

I'd been naïve to think otherwise. I just didn't think that would ever happen. We'd been so unified throughout the campaign I hadn't even thought GEC would be considering damage limitation as they sought to maximise their investment in us.

But, surprisingly as the week wore on, a picture was evolving that the number of redundancies was gradually decreasing. As I went on holiday with my family in the second week I was increasingly upbeat that there would be no compulsory redundancies.

I had two feelings as I took the family to north Wales. First, I knew I had to give them a good time because after all I'd put them through they deserved it. The weather was glorious, just what Isabel, myself, my daughter Amanda, her pal Emma and my grand-daughter Emma needed. We stayed in a little guest house on the front and I for one was able to relax as much as I had for many, many months.

But, second, I couldn't forget about what was happening back in Govan. Although I was getting more confident GEC would minimise the lay-offs I was still worried about the future of the yard. I was concerned about the result of the review and the more I thought about it the more I convinced myself that there would have to be compulsory redundancies. Maybe I felt less confident because I was away from the place.

I kept in contact with Gunnar while I was away. He felt all the jobs could be saved but I wondered if he was saying that to keep me happy or did he really believe it. I was certain Gunnar was being deliberately kept out of the loop of corporate decisions and had been turned into a bit part player.

After we got back home from Rhyl I was anxious for a current update on the redundancy position so I contacted the yard on Monday 2 August, one week before the workforce were due back.

The general view appeared to be that there would be some losses, although probably a relatively small number. The sources I was getting the information from were reliable, so I attached a fair degree of credibility to it. Over the last few days of the holidays I phoned the other convenors to give them an update and also to prepare them for what to expect when we returned to work on 9 August.

MONDAY
9 AUGUST 1999

Meeting the new owners…

17

IT'S BACK to the grindstone. The first day at work after a long break usually brings with it a short period of post holiday blues. It was clear, however, that the issue of the redundancies superseded everything else that morning. Although I had told everyone to enjoy their break and try to unwind, on reflection that must have been very difficult for the two hundred and forty-one who still had the cloud of uncertainty hanging over them and their families.

An early phone call from Christine informed me that Gunnar wanted to see me immediately. I made my way to his office realising that such an urgent summons could provide a definitive position regarding the redundancies. He told me that some of the Directors of GEC were coming into the yard later that morning and had requested a meeting with the convenors. I prodded Gunnar for an insight into what might happen at the meeting. Gunnar looked uncomfortable and indicated that it was best left to GEC to outline their plans.

The meeting was fixed for 11 a.m. and I contacted my co-convenors and told them to be present. As we headed for the boardroom to meet our new owners for the first time I felt like a schoolboy going to meet the headmaster and heads of departments. Well, that was my initial thought. It was quickly replaced by a compelling urge to make sure that our 'New Masters' would not overawe us. First impressions can be misleading, but those first impressions can also be very important. We had to leave our mark at that initial meeting and at the same time create the right atmosphere.

I was very apprehensive. I was still worried about the climate of brinkmanship that ran through GEC. They'd taken us over but did they see a long term future for us or were they going to finish the work we had and do a runner?

But, I also realised I had to go with an open mind. Be single-minded not stubborn. I had listened to hundreds of people since the campaign had begun but at the end of the day my best advice was my own. I hoped this wasn't arrogance, but rather a realisation that you had to go with your gut feeling. I had confidence in my own decisions. The whole campaign had rotated around the mass meetings where you'd had to keep the workforce with you.

In the boardroom Gunnar made the formal introductions and introduced us to Chief Executive, Ron Leggater, Bob Rigby the Managing Director and a senior representative from Human Resources, Peter Wilkinson.

Leggater was well made and heavy, reminding me very much of the schoolboy character Billy Bunter. He did, however, come across as down to earth and approachable. Surprisingly, he lacked the presence of 'The Iceman' Almskog.

Rigby was a total contrast. In his late 50s he was clearly an introvert. He never relaxed and always seemed to want to be in control and his opening remarks had 'boffin' stamped all over them.

Peter Wilkinson was much younger, in his thirties.

After concluding the formalities it was down to business. Leggater welcomed us to the meeting reaffirming that GEC and Kvaerner had signed heads of agreement for the sale of the Govan yard. He indicated that although he was confident that a final agreement could be reached he could not give a specific date. He indicated that there were still many technicalities to be sorted out between both companies. But he was still confident they could all be resolved.

He complimented the trade unions and workforce at Govan on the very positive campaign that had been conducted. He also confirmed that the contract for the building of the second Auxiliary Oiler for the Ministry of Defence would be transferred from GEC Barrow to Govan immediately. He informed us that during the current transitional period Gunnar would remain in charge as Managing Director and it would be business as usual. He concluded by indicating that the GEC labour requirement review was almost completed and would be announced within a couple of days.

The input from Marine Managing Director Bob Rigby was less reassuring and made us all rather uncomfortable. He tried to be cordial but came across as aloof. And I couldn't help but compare him to Gunnar. Chalk and cheese would be the most apt phrase to explain how different they were.

Rigby hit a sour note almost immediately with us when he made a veiled implication that our high profile campaign with the media was not the way he liked the unions to behave. I am sure that he detected from the look on my face that perhaps we would be agreeing to disagree on that issue. Legatter then invited us to comment on any of the issues that had been raised.

I had been hyping myself up and as usual the adrenaline was flowing and my heart was thumping. Inwardly I said to myself,

"I must state our case, clarify the hopes and aspirations of the workers and put forward the merits of our yard."

I assured them that we welcomed the arrival of GEC as new owners of the yard. I stated,

"You'll like the Govan yard and the Govan workforce. You'll find the workers loyal, committed and progressive in their thinking. If faith is shown in them and they are treated with dignity and respect they'll repay that faith tenfold.

"We have excellent industrial relations at Govan. In fact, it's one of our main strengths. I would, however, stress that you should never confuse our willingness to co-operate and compromise as a sign of weakness. Should anybody shit on us from a great height you will find us firm in our resolve to fight any injustices. May I also assure you that despite the fact that there are already prophets of doom forecasting that GEC's stay at Govan will be short-term, the workers and the trade unions here are totally committed to becoming a star player within GEC and not a bit part player on the fringes."

I watched the reaction from Legatter and Rigby as I laid it firmly on the line. Rigby remained impassive. However, the response from Legatter was more pertinent.

"Jamie your reputation precedes you. I heard that you're someone who speaks his mind and is direct and I share that approach. I believe we'll get on fine on the basis of that."

The meeting wound up with the assurance that the company would make a formal announcement relating to the redundancies within days.

But, I realised there would be a problem with Rigby because I'd be dealing with him on a more regular basis than Legatter. I was convinced he wasn't a plain speaker and I knew he'd hated the high profile media campaign we'd waged. His approach was obviously 'we talk, you listen.'

Conversely, I didn't envisage the same problems with Legatter. I felt he was a man we could negotiate with. As an aside, I must say the Human Resources manager was astonished at the frankness of the dialogue that took place at that meeting.

When we returned to the union office the convenors called a shop stewards meeting. We agreed that immediately the formal announcement regarding the redundancies was made we would hold a mass meeting of the workforce.

I urged the shop stewards to get about the yard to calm the workers nerves and to assure everyone that the position would be clear within a few days.

WEDNESDAY
11 AUGUST 1999

A prayer for Eddie...

18

GUNNAR SENT for the convenors and informed us that the labour review had been completed. The result was that there would be a reduction in the number of redundancies from two hundred and forty-one to ninety-seven.

I suppose in my heart I knew that the review would not result in all the jobs being saved. I had, however, expected that the number would be no higher than fifty. Gunnar indicated that all two hundred and forty-one employees would be formally informed if they had been removed from the redundancy list or if they were still to lose their jobs. We left the meeting somewhat deflated and downcast.

Back in our office, we reviewed our current situation and came to the conclusion that although from the outset of the campaign we had urged workers not to volunteer for redundancy in order to maintain unity, it would be necessary to reverse that policy and ask any employee wishing to volunteer to do so now.

I did feel somewhat hypocritical that after trying so hard to dissuade workers for months not to volunteer I would now almost be encouraging it. Nevertheless it would be important to let those wishing to leave to do so thus reducing the number of compulsory pay-offs.

I suspected that in the sixty-plus age group we would get a reasonable response. There were quite a few who had spent most, if not all, of their working lives in shipbuilding. It is a tough and physically demanding industry and often took its toll on worker's health. The industry was rife with health conditions such as occupational asthma, bronchial disorders and arthritis to name but a few

Word soon got about the yard that with the inevitability of some compulsory redundancies volunteers from the areas affected would be accepted. For the remainder of that day I kept in constant touch with the personnel office to ascertain the level of response there had been. By the end of the day around fifty employees had volunteered. As expected many of them were aged sixty or over.

I had the greatest respect for many of my older workmates because they could have broken ranks months previously and volunteered. It was to their credit that they supported the shop stewards plea not to volunteer during the campaign for the sake of keeping a united front.

I had always believed that if there had been a run of workers volunteering for redundancy at the height of our campaign the floodgates might have opened and our struggle would have been lost.

We arranged a mass meting for Thursday morning to inform the workforce of the final position. Again I knew it would be a stressful night for the remaining ninety-seven still on the compulsory list. No doubt they would be hoping that their jobs could be saved by another workmate volunteering. I fully expected that the mass meeting would be a tense and emotional affair.

At home that evening I received a phone call that would cast a dark cloud over everyone in the yard. John Shearer, a manager on the back shift, was in a distressed state. He told me that Eddie Urie, a plater, had committed suicide at home that morning.

Eddie was in his early thirties and had served his apprenticeship in the yard alongside his brother Michael who was a welder. Being a welder myself I knew Mick much better than Eddie. I had always found Eddie very quiet, unassuming and very easy to like. He got on well with his workmates on the back shift where he had worked for several years. I was numb with shock.

Immediately I asked myself, why? He was a young man with his life in front of him. What a tragedy. John went on,

"Jamie, did you know that Eddie was on the original redundancy list? He was removed from it yesterday and was not one of the ninety-seven remaining redundancies."

I was discussing the loss of Eddie with Isabel when the phone rang again. It was a reporter from *The Daily Record* asking for information about the tragedy. He immediately homed in on the fact that Eddie had been targeted for redundancy. I constantly dealt with the media and as a general rule was co-operative and open with them. However, on this occasion instinctively I put my guard up.

This death was personal and sensitive. I found myself being evasive as I was very conscious about the feelings of Eddie's family. Nevertheless I knew that with the numerous sources available to the media they would soon acquire all the information they needed. My worse fears that Eddie's suicide would be widely reported were proved well founded when major articles appeared on the radio and in newspapers the following day.

The next morning prior to the mass meeting I discussed the situation with the other shop stewards. It was quite apparent that Eddie's death and the circumstances surrounding it had affected everybody profoundly. We unanimously agreed that after I had given the report on the redundancy situation we would recommend that all the workers go home for the remainder of the day.

I found giving a precise and pragmatic report was difficult as my mind kept flashing back to the news of Eddie's death. Focus! Focus! Bloody well focus I kept telling myself as I related the details of the labour review that would now result in the number of redundancies being reduced from two hundred and forty-one to ninety-seven.

I informed them that fifty volunteers had applied and been accepted for redundancy. The number of compulsory redundancies was now down to forty-seven. My report was met with a strange eerie silence. I felt confused and guilty as I wound up. I was confused, as I tried to do an instant analysis as to whether our campaign had been a success and guilty because somehow everything seemed irrelevant in light of Eddie's death.

I also found myself incapable of expressing my true feelings towards the forty-seven workers who would be made redundant the following day. There was no point in patronising them as I knew they would be too distressed and hurting inside. There was an uneasiness creeping into the meeting. I could sense that all the workers who had retained their jobs were relieved on a personal basis, however, that was counteracted by feelings of guilt that although they had survived others had not. We finished with a minute's silence for Eddie and the recommendation for us all to go home. In a way it seemed like relief.

Friday 13 August, or 'Black Friday' as we remember it, was another emotional day. Many of us said goodbye to workmates who we had known for many years and it was a painful experience. However there was no acrimony from those that had been forced into redundancy.

They all echoed the view that every effort had been made to save all the jobs. Nevertheless I still felt guilty that we had all gone into our struggle together only for some not to survive.

Later that morning I did interviews with the media. Talking later to them informally about the final outcome I mentioned the fact that perhaps the campaign had not been the major triumph it had been perceived to have been. I reiterated the fact that some workers had lost their jobs and that such an outcome had been a bitter blow. Alan Saunby of *STV* and Hayley Miller from *BBC* expressed surprise at my downbeat appraisal of the situation. Alan told me,

"Some jobs were lost but many were saved and the yard is still here. How can that possibly be regarded as failure?"

Perhaps a balanced viewpoint was that we aimed for the stars but didn't quite get there.

At noon that day I was tidying up some paperwork before finishing for the weekend. I looked out the office window across to the area at the steel stockyard. I caught sight of two large lorries arriving at the stockyard entrance. It was a delivery of steel for the Auxiliary Oiler that we would now be building. In biblical terms those lorries were the equivalent of manna from heaven, our salvation. It reminded me that despite the disappointment I felt earlier that morning there was a new dawn, our yard was still here, and we were still building ships at Govan.

The following Monday I went to see Eddie's family along with a couple of my fellow shop stewards. Needless to say it was a very emotional experience for us all and not surprisingly Eddie's family were distraught. The fact that Eddie's brother Mick currently worked in the yard and that I knew Eddie's mother Cathy when she had previously worked there in the canteen made me feel more at ease than if they had been complete strangers.

We all sat around talking about Eddie being on the original redundancy list and how it had affected him. Certainly we all knew he was agitated about the situation but then again, most of us were. A couple of managers had tried to buck up his spirits on several occasions but he seemed to be struggling in coming to terms with the possibility of losing his job.

In hindsight one lesson I learned about the redundancy experience is that we all react differently to the pressures it presents us with. Some cope with it better than others, some put on a braver face than others. Some can talk openly about it, while others retreat into their shells. I suppose that is what makes us human. For me, the hardest part in coming to terms with the loss of Eddie was the fact that his name came off the amended redundancy list.

He would not have been one of the final ninety-seven. His job was safe. The fact he didn't live to find that out always leaves me, and I dare say many of my workmates, posing the question "what if?" One thing I do know is I seldom reflect back on any period in the campaign without Eddie crossing my mind. After everything was done and dusted Eddie's mum sent me a couple of gifts, including a new watch. I still wear it and every time I look at it I think of Eddie. I feel a very willing obligation, indeed a duty, to keep it on my wrist.

It was now late August and we were all trying to get back to a degree of normality. Yet little did we realise that what we had been through in the last six months would only be a chapter in the story of us securing our long-term future. We were oblivious to the fact that we were all about to embark on a journey, on an 'emotional roller coaster' that would last another two and a half years.

August witnessed a constant flow of people from GEC into our yard. They went through us like a fine toothcomb. Slowly we began to realise that our Govan site no longer had a separate identity. We were part of GEC Marine that now consisted of Govan, Scotstoun (formally Yarrows) and GEC Barrow (formally Vickers).

This position would be further confused by the fact that GEC Marine were expected to be taken over by British Aerospace in the very near future. For the present time it was abundantly clear that at Govan we were 'new kids on the block.' We were joining a new family but we would not be welcomed with open arms.

Barrow's background was steeped in Ministry of Defence naval work, principally the building of submarines. It was much bigger than Govan both geographically and in manpower with in excess of five thousand workers. Scotstoun was also exclusively involved in naval work specialising in the building of frigates for the UK and other overseas countries. It had a workforce of more than two thousand.

Govan with a workforce of about eight hundred plus our pool of contract employees was principally a commercial yard building a wide range of ships. These ranged from supply vessels to gas and chemical carriers. Occasionally there would be rare sorties into MoD work such as the helicopter carrier HMS *Ocean*.

I realised from that early stage that bringing together the three very different cultures would be a gigantic task. Industrial mindsets do not change overnight; they evolve over years if not decades. Previous to the takeover the trade unions in Govan were well acquainted with the unions in Scotstoun and Barrow. We met regularly on a national basis with other shipyard convenors from all the other UK shipyards. Generally speaking we all got on well with each other. However, it would be different now. We were now joined at the hip whether we liked it or not.

It would be fair to say that given the choice the three yards would have preferred to retain their individuality. In the coming months, however, we would find out that the company planned a radical new marine business structure that would change the shapes of the yards forever.

SEPTEMBER
1999

Brinkmanship and bereavement...

19

TAKE-OVER TALKS were still ongoing between GEC and Kvaerner. Any illusion that the companies were adopting a more amenable attitude than previously towards one another were dashed when it began to leak out that there were still some serious issues to be resolved. Major differences existed in relation to who would be liable for future redundancy costs if Govan did close soon after the oiler was built.

More concerning was the issue of contaminated land on part of the Govan site. The cost of cleaning up the area was rumoured to be in the region of several million pounds. Which company would be liable should such an exercise ever have to be undertaken was to become a complex and difficult problem to overcome.

Both companies continued to play a game of 'industrial posturing' similar to the tactics they had adopted prior to signing the heads of agreement in July. However, as time went by it became apparent that Kvaerner were the more intransigent throughout the negotiations. Although the workers were just glad to get back into building the new oiler contract I was getting twitchy that a final deal had not been concluded.

All the union reps in the yard also knew that we would have to continue to drive hard in our efforts to secure the roll-on roll-off ferry contract from the Ministry of Defence. We were fully aware that if we failed in securing work to follow on from the oiler the prophets of doom that had predicted our closure could well be proved correct. It was abundantly clear that we would have to continue our political, media and public campaign to secure more work.

I was still keeping in regular contact with Gunnar although there were increasing vibes that he was living on borrowed time in his role as Managing Director. Speculation was rife that the chances of Gunnar remaining in Govan when GEC finally took over were very slim. Nevertheless I did have to rely on him to keep me abreast of any ongoing developments

Unfortunately, his Kvaerner bosses were telling him little and GEC were telling him even less. Quite simply he was to manage the Govan site and oversee the current shipbuilding programme. He would not be a decision maker in the big picture.

Despite these restrictions he kept his dignity and integrity and remained active about the yard keeping in touch with the workforce. He constantly reminded me,

"No matter what happens externally in the yard let's all work together in a policy of business as usual."

I had no problems supporting him on that philosophy as it had taken us through a perilous few months. Hopefully it would take us through the difficult times that lay ahead.

In mid-September I wrote to every MSP at the Scottish parliament asking for their support in our efforts to secure the Ro-Ro ferry contract from the MoD. Despite the fact that the decision on this contract would be made at Westminster I knew that the Scottish Executive could lobby on our behalf. I was pleasantly surprised when twenty-two MSPs agreed to come into the yard to allow us to put our case for securing the order.

Our strategy of cross party involvement continued as we had always maintained that all political parties should support a campaign for securing Scottish manufacturing jobs. I approached Gunnar for permission to bring in the delegation of MSPs on 20 September and I was astounded and taken aback when he refused.

Gunnar had always been very supportive of any previous requests for assistance and I quizzed him about the reason for his decision. He was uneasy and edgy and I sensed that the decision not to let the MSPs into the yard was not his. I suspected he had been pressurised into this course of action. I challenged him on this suggesting that a person or persons in the yard had encouraged him to take that stance.

In the hectic and traumatic previous months spent trying to secure a new owner the unions had been given support and encouragement from all levels of employees in the yard. Manual workers, technical staff, administration staff, line and senior management had all fought to save the yard.

At director level Gunnar was appreciative and understanding and so were a few of his co-directors. However, I always knew that there was not universal support at this level for the campaign.

At director level there was a minority school of thought that the unions had gained too much influence during the period of trying to secure an owner for the yard. There was resentment to the fact that the boiler suit division (manual work shop stewards) had led the workforce through a nightmare period. I expressed grave disappointment to Gunnar on his decision and strongly urged him to reconsider.

I also emphasised that he should remember that the delegation represented our government and that it would be insulting and disrespectful not to show them courtesy and hospitality. I also indicated that should permission not be given for the visit the meeting between the MSPs and the Govan union convenors would still go ahead. If necessary we would hold the meeting and a press conference in a local community hall.

Inevitably the MSPs and the media would question why they were not allowed into the yard. I told Gunnar he would have to answer that question.

Finally I reminded him of the excellent relationship he had with the trade unions and the workers within the yard. I urged him not to tarnish that. I concluded by informing him that I would come back the following day for his final decision.

Later that day the grapevine told me that a director, Paul Friedberg, had been quoted as saying at a recent meeting,

"The unions in the yard have outlived their usefulness now that a new owner seems to have been secured. It is time to batten them down, put them in their place and not allow them to bring politicians or the media into the yard."

It now looked like my suspicions had been vindicated. I felt disgusted that such comments had been made from a senior representative of the company considering the fact that Friedberg himself was still in employment in Govan due to the efforts of the trade unions in their campaign to secure the yard's future.

Friedberg, I always felt, was a fly in the ointment. In Glasgow parlance, he 'fancied his barra'–he had a high opinion of himself. He was in my opinion very anti-union and resented Gunnar's good relationship with the convenors and workers.

I remember at one of the launches Lord Macdonald brought his wife Tina. She and I had a good old natter for ten or fifteen minutes. Friedberg was looking over as much as to say what is Lord Macdonald's wife doing talking to him? In fact, Friedberg came over later and asked me what we'd been talking about for so long. I told him to ask Lady Macdonald if he was so interested. Just as the guests were leaving, Lady Macdonald came over and said she'd enjoyed our wee gab.

Friedberg's done okay for himself. He's now President of Goltens Worldwide Services. This company, which was established in New York and Oslo in the 1940s, provides specialised repair, maintenance and reconditioning services for worldwide shipping, offshore marine installations, industrial plants and power stations. He's one of the bosses in a company that employs almost a thousand people across fifteen sites.

Prior to the signing of the heads of agreement the directors at Govan had been conspicuous by their absence. They kept a low profile and, with the exception of Gunnar, there was a distinct lack of leadership. But when GEC bought the yard they all breathed a collective sigh of relief and tried to convey the image of being totally purposeful and in control.

My perception of what was going on politically between the various camps was this. Kvaerner were still there along with GEC and, waiting in the wings, was BAE. So, there was a frantic jostling for position by our directors trying to sell themselves to the new bosses. I believe there was a certain amount of backstabbing going on.

Early the following morning I went to see Gunnar. Our conversation was brief.

"Jamie, I have given consideration to your views yesterday. I've never found the judgement of you and your co-convenors less than sound in the past. On the basis of that I will continue to support you. You have permission to bring the MSPs into the yard. Go ahead and make the appropriate arrangements."

I shook his hand and thanked him. He had restored my faith in him by rejecting a petty negative viewpoint voiced by a co-director.

Could Gunnar, a good man, have ever survived under GEC? It's possible, but unlikely. All other directors at Govan would have had to endorse him and stand by him and there's no way they would have done that. They smelled blood. There was also the fact that Gunnar created the impression he was too cosy with the unions, and that damaged him.

But, I always thought Gunnar knew exactly what he was doing and he did it to satisfy his own conscience. Effectively, and honourably, Gunnar Skjelbred, fell on his sword. He's now back as MD of another yard in Philadelphia but I truly believe

Govan could have gone on from strength to strength under Gunnar.

On the home front all was not well. Isabel's dad was in still in hospital and his condition was giving cause for great concern. Furthermore with her mother now in a nursing home Isabel was totally stressed out due to the daily shuttling between both her parents. I tried to accompany her on the evening visits often expecting her to flare up at some time about the amount of time I was still spending on our ongoing campaign.

Amazingly it was quite the opposite. She showed great resilience in continuing to support my efforts in the yard. I have always regarded her fortitude during this period as remarkable. It is a strange coincidence that Isabel's favourite song is 'Wind Beneath My Wings' by Bette Midler. I have never told her this personally but she was undoubtedly the wind beneath mine.

Back in the yard the convenors received an invitation to meet a delegation of Labour MPs at the Party Conference in Bournemouth at the end of September. This would be the first occasion when we would have a joint delegation of convenors from both Govan and Scotstoun shipyards. We would now be pushing together for the Ro-Ro ferry contract to come to the Clyde. We were now in reality one Clyde shipyard on two sites.

Wednesday 20 September witnessed the arrival of the MSPs to the yard. As the convenors greeted them at the reception door I thought, 'What a motley crew.' But, to their credit, Labour, SNP, Lib Dem and Conservative, were all in to support our campaign.

The proceedings were brightened by the appearance of Scottish Socialist leader and MSP Tommy Sheridan and Independent MSP Denis Canavan. The fact that Sheridan hobbled in with a distinct limp due to a football injury incurred the previous day remains etched in my mind.

Likewise Canavan was MSP for Falkirk West, a constituency a considerable distance from Glasgow. Certainly I did not expect him to come and I fully respected both him and Tommy for making the effort.

We had a good session with the politicians in the boardroom as we pushed the case for our yard and for the need to acquire the Ro-Ro contract. We hammered home that the possibility of this order going abroad was totally outrageous and emphasised that it must stay in the UK.

That meeting also remains memorable as it witnessed the remarkable sight of Tommy Sheridan and Annabelle Goldie, now the leader of the Scottish Conservatives, singing off the same hymn sheet. Poles apart in their political beliefs our fight for Scottish jobs had brought them together. I found myself reflecting on how politicians would get so much more credibility and respect from the public if they jointly addressed social issues instead of being blinkered by political dogma.

The MSPs joined the convenors on a walkabout around the yard to let them to have an informal chat with the workers in a relaxed environment. It also helped the convenors to remind the MSPs that we were still building ships at Govan.

Back in the boardroom afterwards I was chatting to some of the politicians when my mobile phone rang. I felt the colour drain from my face as it was my daughter Julie to tell me to get to the hospital as fast as possible. The doctor had told Isabel that her dad was slipping fast and would soon pass away. Instantly the importance of the meeting seemed irrelevant compared to my getting to the hospital on time to see Johnny. Sadly, despite the fact that a work colleague drove me immediately to Stobhill hospital Johnny passed away ten minutes before I got there.

This reminded me of when I lost my mother. I'd been with her all night and felt I should stay. But, she insisted I went to work. When she passed away and I wasn't there I felt so guilty at first but then I thought, no, my relationship with my mother was much stronger than the fact I hadn't physically been at her bedside when she died. And, I realised I felt the same about Johnny's death. He'd supported the campaign right from the start and had insisted that I went on the May Day rally when he took ill. I respected him for how he was. I would have liked to have been there at the end for him, but although I felt guilty at the time, I realised I was doing something Johnny was proud of.

On my way back home it began to rain heavily and became overcast. What had started as a feel-good day had ended with great sorrow. It was a stark reminder of the painful ups and downs of life we must all endure. Isabel was distraught and inconsolable. She and her dad had been very close.

She may have been a middle aged woman but to Johnny she was just still a 'daddy's girl.' I got a week off work as arrangements were made for the funeral. Isabel had been a rock for me and I hoped I could be of similar support to her.

I knew I had neglected my family. Isabel had totally backed me throughout all the moans, the gripes and the depressions. I tried my best to be there for her now although I don't think I was ever the mainstay she could and should have had. That said, the campaign to save Govan could have been the death of our marriage. In fact, it made our bond all the stronger.

Returning to work a week later I had hardly got my feet in the door when it was time to go down to Bournemouth for the Labour party conference. In recent months I had become acquainted with a considerable number of MPs therefore the ice had been broken. Nevertheless although many of them were sincerely supportive, I felt others were either going along with the flow or were reluctant followers. Doubtless some were still conscious of the incident in February when we had named the thirteen Scottish Labour MPs who had not responded to our letter asking for their assistance.

BACK FROM THE BRINK

I was given the opportunity at the meeting with a delegation of MPs to provide an update on the current position on the Clyde. I drove home the importance of securing the Ro-Ro ferry contract. I reiterated the position that if a UK Labour government allowed that MoD contract to go abroad it would be a total disgrace.

I provided evidence that in recent years no European country had allowed any similar kind of contract to leave their domestic shores. We only expected that the UK government would show a similar commitment to our home shipbuilding industry. I could see that my forceful and uncompromising stance on that issue caused a degree of consternation among some of the MPs. They were aware that under the terms of reference structured by the MoD for this contract the work could indeed go to another European country.

I reminded them that there would be uproar and a political backlash against Labour if that happened. This would result in significant job losses in the UK not only in shipbuilding but also in numerous marine supply companies.

Unexpectedly, First Minister Donald Dewar arrived and proceeded to give his perspective of the situation relating to the Ro-Ro contract. Conjecture rather than definitive statements dominated his input. The overall theme suggested was that a decision would not be made till the end of January 2000 at the earliest. More importantly he hinted that GEC would have to 'sharpen their pencils' in the tendering stakes for the Ro-Ro's.

Again I felt Dewar was going through the motions to support Govan. He was certainly never a driving force. He seemed to respond when he was forced to. Remember him using the back entrance at the STUC conference? I always thought Donald Dewar was a conscript and not a volunteer.

The comments about sharpening pencils worried me, as it was not the first time similar comments had been made in relation to GEC's bid. Reliable and knowledgeable sources were sounding alarm bells that GEC's input on Govan's bid had sent our yard's price rocketing up from the one originally submitted by Kvaerner.

Kvaerner's tender would have been lower than GEC's as they were from the commercial shipbuilding market and were aware of the ferocity of competition in that arena. GEC came from a market almost exclusively dominated by defence work. It was clearly evident that the significant overheads carried by them in their operations would be transferred onto Govan's bid thus escalating the price submitted. I was getting seriously concerned that GEC would price us out. That would be disastrous.

At the end of the meeting I expressed my concerns with local MP Mohammad Sarwar who was now taking a much higher profile in our campaign to secure the Ro-Ro's. However, like many of his political colleagues he could be extremely sensitive to criticism. In an article in the *Evening Times* I had commented that Sarwar did not get ten out of ten for performance in our campaign. He was somewhat miffed by that. Indeed I had to remind him that a score of ten was excellent and that five was a pass mark. My comments must have had a further motivational effect on him as his work rate and efforts in the future well warranted appreciation and praise.

OCTOBER – DECEMBER
1999

New beginnings…

20

DURING OCTOBER I had a couple of further meetings with GEC Managing Director, Bob Rigby. I witnessed little at those meetings to reassure me let alone inspire me. I continued to find him a very difficult man to feel at ease with.

Outwardly he was polite enough but his dialogue was constantly abstract and theoretical. He displayed all the characteristics of a boffin. Maybe I much preferred and understood earthy dialogue from those in the real world. I was reassured in the knowledge that I was not alone in my view of Bob Rigby; it was widespread across the company.

He was distant and certainly not a people person. I remember once stopping him outside Gunnar's office and asking him a couple of questions about how the purchase of the yard was going. His answer was unintelligible. I didn't understand one word he said – it was corporate gobbledygook that left me baffled. If this was what the ongoing dialogue was going to be like then we had a major problem.

At a private meeting in mid-October he again raised with me the high profile that the trade unions in Govan, particularly me, were having in the media.

"Are you aware that GEC are monitoring every comment you make to the newspapers, television and radio?"

I responded by stating that I would have been very surprised if the company had not been observing.

I added,

"I'll be even more surprised if my comments are interpreted as being in any way negative towards either our campaign or the company. I have a responsibility to not only look after the interests of the workers in the yard but to reflect their views to the public, politicians and the media."

I pressed Rigby further as to whether the company had any grievance with any particular comments I had made, however, he reassured me that up until the present time my remarks had indeed been positive and objective. I left that meeting further bemused by our conversation and fully realised that informal chats between us would probably be the exception rather than the rule.

A few days later the convenors along with various local and national union officers visited the Scottish Parliament in Edinburgh. The union delegation had been invited to hear Govan MSP Gordon Jackson raise the debate on the Ro-Ro ferry contract and also to meet a delegation of MSPs. We arrived in Edinburgh a couple of hours before the debate began and gave several media interviews. Outside Parliament a significant number of MSPs stopped to speak to us and wished us well for the future.

I was chatting to Johnny and Joe my co-convenors at Govan when the SNP's Nicola Sturgeon, a staunch ally of our campaign, tapped me on the shoulder. Nicola was her usual chirpy self and as always was offering to help in any way she could. She assured me that our campaign would continue to get total support from her and all the SNP members.

Indeed she indicated that in the Parliament there was genuine and committed support from all the parties. She attributed that to the fact that the unions in Govan had been courteous to every party throughout the campaign. As she left to go into the Parliament building, a union official approached me and with a degree of sarcasm attempted to chastise me for 'fraternising with the enemy.'

I was livid and he was left in no doubt that as far as the workers and the trade unions in Govan were concerned Nicola

Sturgeon commanded the highest respect. I reminded him that the workers on the back shift in Govan had invited Nicola in to the yard to present her with a bouquet of flowers on the day that heads of agreement had been signed in July. I emphasised that the workers would be the judges of who they should be indebted to and needed no outside advice on that issue. I also indicated to him that the gesture made to Nicola did not have any political undertones and was merely a personal thank you from the workers. In a final shot across the bow I asked him to keep his opinions to himself and not to dictate to me who I should or should not speak to. He didn't like my reply but he got the message.

During the debate there was broad support from all the parties for our campaign. No sniping, back biting or scoring political points which I found refreshing. The fact that we had shown courtesy to all the parties in September when they visited the yard ensured that we received genuine support. After the debate Gordon Jackson took me aside and informed me that the First Minister wanted to speak to me about the on-going difficulties regarding the contaminated land on the Govan site.

As I've said, this issue was complex and if it wasn't resolved it could jeopardise the actual takeover of the yard. It was apparent that there was considerable political activity taking place on how to solve this problem. When Dewar arrived he eased my fears somewhat by indicating he was confident that a solution to issue would be resolved satisfactorily in the near future. It transpired at a later period that a deal involving Clyde Port Authority taking over the land and leasing it back to GEC would be the acceptable solution to all parties.

By November the vibes indicated that the takeover by BAE was possibly only weeks away. I prayed it would be. The thought of it dragging into 2000 was depressing and would continue the uncertainty. It now looked like the buy-out of Govan would result in us never really being owned by GEC, but going directly to BAE.

On 23 November, we handed over the last ship to be built under the Kvaerner Govan banner. It was an icebreaker for a Norwegian ship owner. It was a relatively low-key affair and if the truth be told I believe that everyone just wanted to put life under Kvaerner behind them and look to the future.

The end of the month saw the first formal meeting between representatives of GEC and the trade unions from Govan, Scotstoun and Barrow. The principal item on the agenda was the integration of the three yards into one marine shipbuilding group. With different wages and conditions, vastly different working practices and overall different cultures existing in the three yards there was little doubt that these issues would present major challenges to us all.

I could only look at this from a Govan perspective. But, clearly Scotstoun and Barrow had their image of Govan. Barrow's track record was submarines and prior to the Auxiliary Oilers they hadn't built a surface vessel for what I reckoned had to be thirty years. It was also generally felt Barrow was also isolated geographically and for this reason was, on the Clyde, jokingly known as Jurassic Park.

Govan had a commercial background but had seen much turbulence and change during the Kvaerner years. Their commercial customers were hard taskmasters. New working practices and adapting to new technology had been thorny issues in the past at Govan. It had been a painful experience but it had made us leaner, meaner and sharper even though we'd lost about eight hundred jobs in a decade. The one positive thing Kvaerner left us with was that every employee in all areas of the company felt that they were multi-skilled, from craft tradesmen to office workers, from purchasing to procurement. It actually worked because people were flexible and adaptable.

The yard at Scotstoun was deeply entrenched in naval work, a non commercial shipbuilding background. It had long standing dealings with the MoD. But the Ministry was now ditching the blank cheque philosophy and moving towards what it called smart procurement. It was all about getting value for the taxpayers' money.

In my view, Scotstoun was going to have to deal with a much tougher customer which would inevitably expose them to the uncomfortable experiences Govan had gone through in the last ten years. What would be high on the agenda of GEC and when they were taken over, BAE, would be rationalisation, flexibility and multi-skilling. These changes would be difficult and would not be well received in some quarters at Scotstoun.

I fear, and think, I've been proved right. Govan has often been seen as the villain of the piece with our concepts appearing to be forced upon the other yards in the group. The business plan decreed that the yards changed their structure and to oppose that would have been futile. Govan's experiences with Kvaerner resulted in our workforce becoming more pragmatic, based principally on those hard lessons and our fight for survival.

Not surprisingly, the perspective at Scotstoun was different. Up until then they'd more or less been masters of their own destiny. Govan was now seen as the 'cuckoo in the nest' and it had created the base upon which GEC/BAE would decide the cross-fertilisation of the workforce. Some elements of Scotstoun's workforce were antagonistic and fearful of the consequences of Govan being brought into the fold. There has been a transfer of labour, but it was a difficult and at times awkward experience which took a number of years to bed in.

Mike Salmon, the Marine Company's operations director, in conjunction with Tony Williams, operations director for Govan and Scotstoun, asked me about the concept of two sites effectively operating as one integrated yard with one working culture. He asked how long I thought it would take for this to be accepted. I told him in my opinion he was looking at a decade.

This surprised him but I told him in shipyards cultures don't develop over a week, a month or a year. As an apprentice, I had witnessed the differences at yards like Fairfields (now Govan), Yarrows and Scott Lithgow in Greenock and I knew how difficult it would be to effect change.

Salmon thought I was being overly-pessimistic but I warned him it would be three years before he saw workers starting to even understand the concept of two sites, one yard. Over eight years later significant progress has been made but my prediction of ten years has turned out to be a good first guess.

Needless to say December would not be December without thinking of Christmas. In the yard we had our usual party in the first week of the month for local disabled children. Many of the parents and support workers told us they had followed our campaign with interest and congratulated us on our success. This was not surprising. Many had attachments to the yard through the charitable work done by the workers. Their comments reminded me the role the yard played outside our gates in the community. The yard was Govan and Govan was the yard.

On Monday 10 December, the nerves were jangling on two fronts. Firstly my elder daughter Julie was about to make me a grandfather for the second time. Her baby was due at any moment. Secondly, stories were doing the rounds that the official takeover could be only days away. Would I settle for such a joyful double? I most certainly would.

In the early hours of 12 December, part one became a reality with the birth of my second granddaughter Robyn who was to be a record breaker in her own right. Weighing in at eleven pounds and eleven ounces Robyn was the heaviest baby born at the Queen Mother Maternity Hospital in 1999. Everyone therefore understood when I temporarily nicknamed her

'Sumo.' Bleary eyed it was off to work as normal later that morning hoping, just hoping, that it could be the joyful day I craved.

During the course of the day rumours abounded that BAE were on the verge of concluding the takeover of GEC. This would almost certainly result in the conclusion of Govan being formally taken over by BAE. We waited and waited but by the end of the shift there still had been no official conformation. I temporarily dismissed my disappointment and looked forward to what was certain to be an eventful evening for me.

A visit to see Julie and the latest addition to our clan followed by the annual pre-Christmas night out with a few close workmates would be the basis of a very enjoyable evening. Isabel and my younger daughter Amanda had spent a significant part of the day at the hospital and I arranged to be there at 7.30 p.m.

As I made my way along Dumbarton Road towards the hospital my mobile phone rang.

"Hello Jamie. This is Henry McLeish from the Scottish Executive. Let me be the first to inform you that the formal agreement for the purchase of Govan has been completed. I would like to congratulate you and all the workers at Govan for your remarkable campaign. You and the workforce have commanded great respect from everyone for the positivity shown through very difficult times. Good luck for the future and please pass on my best wishes to everyone in the yard."

I thanked him for the political support we had received from the Scottish parliament in finalising the deal. A new granddaughter! The deal concluded! A night out with the boys! This was a Good day with a capital G. I didn't walk the remaining distance to the hospital, I bounced. It was just as well it was pitch dark in the street otherwise people passing by would have seen the original Cheshire cat that had got the cream.

My co-author, Russell Walker, who's watched this story since the beginning, has since told me that all was not well in the Scottish Office that night right until the end. He and a couple of other reporters had been there with McLeish waiting for the official word that everything was okay.

A spanner was thrown into the works right at the death. I'll never know who by, but according to Russell, Paul Emberley, Kvaerner's PR man who I didn't like, was on the telephone at 7 o'clock trying to smooth out last minute problems with the contract. At 7 o'clock that night! What else could have gone wrong?

A new granddaughter and a new owner added up to not a bad day's work. The following day some of my workmates said that they had never seen me so exuberant. What they really meant was that I had hogged the show all night. As the Christmas holiday break loomed large, like everybody else I looked forward to a break away from the grindstone.

However, it was abundantly clear that early in 2000 we would have to actively step up a gear in the political lobbying for the Ro-Ro contract. Sarwar our local MP had arranged a meeting for mid-January with the Defence Procurement Minister Baroness Symons to enable us to present the case for the Clyde securing the order. This contract was becoming a political hot potato. There was still a hue and cry that the order could be built abroad.

Behind the scenes much of the blame for the structuring of the tender for the Ro-Ro's that could allow it to go outside the UK was being laid at the door of previous Defence Secretary George Robertson. I thought these comments were credible. With a little foresight the contract could have been structured in such a way that outside predators could not have been allowed to tender for it. It could be argued that such an attitude is protectionist. Possibly so, but what was indisputable was that in other shipbuilding countries in Europe work of a similar nature would never be allowed to go to a foreign competitor.

Yet again the UK had been fair and generous to a fault and was playing totally by the rules. That's all very commendable providing everyone else in Europe was doing the same. However, some of our European competitors were receiving hidden subsidies from their regional or national governments which enabled them to cut their costs and therefore their prices.

The European Commission periodically instigated investigations into allegations of malpractice. However, it was inevitably wishy-washy and was never pursued with vigour. Indeed in recent years UK shipbuilding companies and the trade unions had formed strong suspicions of unfair practices abroad. Repeated delegations to meet UK MEPs on this issue always proved to be fruitless. Personally speaking I had never been over impressed by the majority of UK MEPs. They seemed to me to be a relatively impotent crew.

JANUARY–MARCH
2000

Yet more change…

21

EARLY JANUARY witnessed the first formal meeting with the company on the issue of harmonising wages and conditions across Govan, Scotstoun and Barrow. Even getting past first base on wages would not be easy as all three sites had different rates of pay, Govan having the highest and Barrow the lowest. The company intimated that they hoped to harmonise everything in the period of the proposed two year wage deal. As I knew well, this would be fraught with many difficulties.

On 14 January we got a visit from the Secretary of State for Scotland, John Reid. He received a very warm welcome from all the workers when he went on an informal walkabout in the yard. He was at ease in such surroundings as he was an MP from a constituency in the west of Scotland industrial heartland. He spoke our language.

The major role he had played along with Gus Macdonald in the securing of a new owner for the yard was also universally acknowledged. I accompanied him on the tour with Bob Rigby and Gunnar. There was a considerable media presence in the yard that day with the main item on the agenda not surprisingly being the Ro-Ro ferry contract. In media interviews Reid emphasised that the competition for this was fierce, however, he emphasised that BAE Systems would be afforded every opportunity to secure the contract.

He went on to say that the actual building of the ferries constituted only a proportion of the total overall contract. The main proportion was for a twenty year servicing agreement and the operating of the ferries for commercial use when they were not in active service with the navy. BAE Systems bid was linked to a consortium under the banner of Sealion. It was beginning to emerge that our most serious competitors were a French consortium, Maersk a well-established European ferry operator and a Scottish based company called Andrew Weir Shipping.

I found myself more interested, however, in the comments that Rigby made to the media on the subject of our bid. I was somewhat surprised that he agreed to do interviews as I had always felt he was extremely apprehensive about the media in general. I listened intently to the comments that he was making.

"BAE Systems have submitted a bid that we believe will match any of our competitors."

I was buoyant. Although I might never have become his most ardent fan I never got the impression that he was one for making rash statements or for flying a kite. Following those comments I convinced myself that Rigby would never have made such a bold prediction without real justification.

Two years previously I attended a shipbuilding seminar in Glasgow organised by the Scottish Engineering Association. A director of Andrew Weir's was present and I was gob-smacked by the venomous attack he mounted on UK shipbuilding. He talked about how we'd lost the ship-owner/ship-builder relationship, the industry had a bad profile, there was no investment in yards, there was government apathy and a concerted campaign to kill off the industry.

In the experience of this director, and he'll be thankful I can't remember his name, the last twenty years had seen yards become antiquated in structure and facilities, not customer friendly, inefficient and with bad industrial relations. In his opinion the UK shipbuilding industry was getting what it deserved. He didn't actually say it, but the message I took from his comments were that we deserved to get nothing. He concluded by saying his company had the right to take work away from Britain to Korea where they understood how to treat customers.

I remember leaving that seminar hoping that I would never have to cross swords with a Scottish company that I thought had an entrenched anti-UK attitude towards our industry. The fact that they now emerged as serious competitors in the competition to secure the Ro-Ro ferry contract sent a shiver down my spine. If they were successful I had no doubts the boats would not be built in Scotland.

On 18 January, the convenors from Govan and Scotstoun travelled to the Ministry of Defence offices in London to meet Defence Procurement Minister Baroness Symons to present our case for the contract coming to the Clyde.

She was friendly, charming and very knowledgeable. However, nobody in the trade union delegation was naïve enough to think that she would have had, or would be having in the near future, other delegations from our competitors. In fact we already knew that at least one other UK yard, Cammell Laird in Birkenhead was also making strong representation at Westminster.

Whereas the unions on the Clyde made open declarations of our determination to secure the contract we were equally aware that BAE systems had an efficient and powerful political lobbying process of their own. We also appreciated the fact that business decorum and sensitivity would often restrict the comments that the company could make publicly.

Nevertheless I personally believe that the company was overly secretive. This was much more noticeable under GEC whereas BAE systems appeared to be slightly more open and transparent with the trade unions.

In late January a high-powered delegation from the MoD visited the yard to monitor progress on the Auxiliary Oiler. I was astonished later that day when I was asked to go to the director's boardroom to meet them. There is a general view that most Ministry of Defence visits are stuffy affairs principally because the mandarins are not renowned for informality or congeniality. As I made my way to meet them I wondered what might unfold.

I knew that delegations like this seldom met union convenors during these visits. There was a broad perception that the MoD was a faceless monster that had never actually been humanised. When there was a visit from dignitaries, politicians or a potential new ship owner customer there would always be a buzz about the yard. A visit from the Ministry, however, created a completely different climate.

I was greeted at the door of the boardroom by the head of the MoD delegation. They all heaped lavish praise on the yard's progress and performance on the Auxiliary Oiler which amazed and delighted me. I was so pleasantly taken aback that they must have noticed it. The delegation leader remarked,

"I see you're surprised at us complimenting the workers for their excellent performance on the oiler."

I found myself nervously laughing and responding,

"Well to be honest I am a bit surprised. Not about our performance on the oiler. I promised everyone we wouldn't let anybody down on that front. At Govan we value our customers and pride ourselves on the ships we build. The MoD is no different. You are a customer."

In hindsight my comments might have sounded sugary and patronising, however, they were not meant to be and more importantly I am certain they knew that.

Unfortunately for a split second my mouth ran away from me as I continued,

"Without intending to be rude the general working population in shipbuilding tends to regard MoD personnel as faceless people from the black lagoon. You're also rarely associated with making compliments."

Instantly I wondered whether or not I'd put my foot in it with my blunt comments even if they were principally made in jest. But, almost spontaneously they all burst out laughing.

One said,

"We are aware of how we are perceived. The only difference is few people say it to our face."

The remainder of the meeting was very cordial, however, it wasn't lost on me that getting positive reports from them could only bolster Govan's reputation.

February revealed BAE Systems conducting a comprehensive review of best practices in operation across Govan, Scotstoun and Barrow. I was confident that despite us being a new arrival on the scene and the smallest of the yards in the marine group we would come out well in the review.

This was not a biased self-appraisal. Life in the ultra competitive commercial shipbuilding market under Kvaerner had made us a flexible, adaptable and progressive workforce. I was a strong advocate of one of Govan's greatest attributes, our 'can do, will do, must do' philosophy. No doubt we could learn some things from Scotstoun and Barrow, however, I genuinely believed that there was much that they could learn from us.

In those early days, Barrow was 'big brother', Scotstoun was 'wee brother' and Govan was 'the wean.' As such Barrow was most likely to get its own way. At Govan we thought all the reviews and surveys would be weighted in favour of the north of England site and then Scotstoun simply because the reviews were not independent since they were conducted in-house. I was being told by some in management at Govan that there was a serious risk many of our strongest points were to be overturned in favour of how they did things at Barrow and Scotstoun.

How did I respond? I knew the workforce at Govan would be open-minded. They knew the methods worked. I had to tell them our best course of action was to continue doing what we do well and hope enough eyes were open in high places to see things were being done well.

Barrow is still the main player in our arena. In fact, in 2007 BAE Systems landed its first export order for submarines in twenty years. Spanish shipbuilding firm Navantia placed a multi-million pound order for parts for four diesel-electric subs. Under the deal, BAE had to make eight pressure domes at its base in Cumbria. BAE saw off competition from Germany, France, Russia and the US to win the order. So, in some ways, but not in all, times are better at Barrow, as they are at the three yards. But, more of that later.

Back in 2000, I believe Govan's practices and more flexible attitude were beginning to make small inroads. But there were many people who were still unwilling to change. Barrow saw itself as dictating things from top management levels to the shop floor. There was an inbuilt business and industrial arrogance in thinking that a smaller yard like Govan had little to teach them. We had to continually prove ourselves because we knew we were never going to get the benefit of the doubt.

On the Ro-Ro contract front, Donald Dewar's prediction about a decision being made by the end of January had proved inaccurate. However, he could hardly be faulted as the contract continued to become a moving target. The vibes were that a decision was not now expected until some time in March.

Over the next few weeks we switched our attention away from the Ro-Ro issue to negotiate our annual wages and conditions with the company in conjunction with Barrow and Scotstoun trade unions.

We managed to reach a reasonable settlement and also signed a ground breaking labour mobility agreement that allowed the transferring of workers from the Clyde to Barrow and vice versa on a temporary basis. It was hoped that this new innovation would assist in partly solving the continual peaks and troughs in work that often blighted our industry. It meant we'd be using contract workers less, but hopefully it would help safeguard staff at the three facilities.

9 February was a red-letter day for Govan under our new owners BAE Systems. It heralded the launch of the Auxiliary Oiler RFA *Wave Ruler* amid much pomp and fanfare. Royal Marine pipe bands, hundreds of local school children and approximately four thousand members of the public witnessed the launching of the ship by the wife of Geoff Hoon the UK Defence Secretary. It was fitting that even this early in the year the sun chose to shine for such a memorable occasion in our yard.

As usual there was a considerable media presence and when interviewed I exuded confidence that this was the dawn of a new era for the yard. My comments were somewhat tempered by those made by Simon Kirby, acting Managing Director, who was at that period standing in for Rigby. Whereas I portrayed a picture of extreme optimism, Kirby expressed concern regarding a short-term gap in work that was looming at both Govan and Scotstoun. Although I couldn't disagree that his comments were accurate they did to a degree take the shine off a day of celebration.

In early March the twitchiness on the Ro-Ro's contract resurrected itself again. Hints were being dropped from the political domain that BAE Systems were playing hardball with the government in their bid for the contract. There were now strong indications that our bid would not be good enough to secure the contract. These vibes were causing great concern throughout the workforce at Govan.

There were constant mutterings in the yard that Kvaerner's original tender price had been increased due to the considerable overheads inherited from the GEC dynasty. The general view was that BAE Systems were trying to win a semi-commercial contract using MoD contract costing systems. I found myself reflecting on Rigby's words in January when he had stated to the media,

"We are confident that BAE Systems have submitted a bid that will match any of our competitors."

Those words now appeared to have a hollow ring to them.

Despite our increasing concerns, the convenors decided that it remained imperative that we continue to make representations to the company emphasising that our bid must be competitive. At the same time we had to maintain a high profile in the public, political and media arenas on the need for the Clyde to secure the Ro-Ro contract.

Around this time, the convenors took a phone call from Gunnar which informed us that he would be leaving the yard by the end of the month. This announcement although extremely disappointing was not unexpected. My fears that Gunnar would be replaced had unfortunately proved to be accurate.

Gunnar had earned respect from us all. He had treated the workers with compassion and understanding during a very difficult period. On a personal basis he had gained my total respect principally because he had treated every employee the same regardless of their position in the company. He was definitely the least pretentious director I had ever encountered.

The high esteem in which we held him in was such that the shop stewards decided to arrange a presentation evening for him the week he left. We gave him a model of a fishing vessel engraved with the words 'To Gunnar, the adopted Govan-ite, from the workers of Govan shipyard.' Some would say that our union forefathers would have turned in their graves at the thought of workers giving a presentation to a Managing Director. Our view was that he contributed significantly to our campaign and fully merited our appreciation.

Surprise, surprise! In mid-March the goal posts moved once again on the Ro-Ro's with the announcement that the MoD had re-opened the tendering process for the contract. There was mounting speculation in the media that this had been done to afford BAE Systems a final opportunity to secure the order. The Ministry of Defence strongly denied these allegations emphasising that their prime concern was to ensure that they delivered value for taxpayer's money.

The following week the convenors from Govan and Scotstoun were invited to Edinburgh to meet First Minister Donald Dewar and Enterprise Minister Henry McLeish. Both emphasised that the re-tendering process gave BAE Systems and their consortium Sealion every opportunity to secure the Ro-Ro's. Once again, however, the First Minister's demeanour during the meeting did little to reassure me.

I continued to form the impression that he was always several levels below being an optimist. A number of my union colleagues maintained that I was, and still am, overcritical of Donald Dewar. Perhaps they were right although I remained unconvinced.

Sarwar phoned me a few days later and suggested that the trade unions should consider collecting signatures for a petition to send to Defence Secretary Geoff Hoon emphasising the Clyde's case for the ferries. He indicated that several MPs such as Douglas Alexander (Paisley South), Des Browne (Kilmarnock), Ian Davidson (Pollok) and Sandra Osborne (Ayr) as well as others had offered to organise petition signing in their constituencies. Both of us agreed that the shop stewards from Govan with assistance from Sarwar and several of his local party workers would travel to a variety of locations over the following few Saturdays. During this period we collected signatures throughout Glasgow covering areas such as Govan, Pollok, Shawlands, Partick and Maryhill to name but a few.

As our petitioning gained momentum we received numerous invitations from MPs representing constituencies outside the Glasgow area. They invited us to visit busy locations in their areas to enable us to enlist the support of the public across the whole of Scotland. Obviously we were restricted in the number of constituencies we could visit over a period of several Saturdays. However, we did manage to get to Coatbridge,

Livingston and Edinburgh. It was hard work but it was very rewarding and helped to bolster our spirits.

We received fantastic support everywhere we went. It was abundantly clear that the average person related closely to our struggle to maintain our jobs and supported us whole-heartedly. The most persistent comment made to us by the public during the petitioning was,

"It is good to see people actually fighting for their jobs instead of just rolling over and accepting it."

It was during that period that I finally realised how vital the media had been in reporting our campaign. The extensive coverage had made most people aware of our struggle. In one of our first petitioning exercises in Partick, a reporter from *BBC TV* arrived to interview a couple of members of the public that had signed the petition. As expected the people spoken to echoed their total support for maintaining jobs on the Clyde.

In the interview that followed, I seized upon the opportunity to remind the public of the philosophy for the future as stated by the then Chancellor Gordon Brown.

"Those who can work will work."

I confirmed that the workers on the Clyde totally supported his sentiments. I took the opportunity to remind the Chancellor,

"That we were in work, wanting to work yet ironically if we lost a government MoD contract we would be put out of work."

During the interview I was also asked how the government would regard the fact that we had made our fight for jobs a political issue. My answer to that question was blunt and to the point,

"Having people in work is a political issue and any government that does not subscribe to that view isn't worth tuppence regardless of what political party is in power."

Many people commented that during this interview I got in a subtle dig at the government. I will always maintain that the intention was to focus the politician's minds on the importance of people continuing to be in employment.

A few days later Patricia Ferguson my local MSP for Maryhill phoned and asked if I could join her and some of her party workers at the local shopping centre the following Saturday to collect petitions for the campaign. She indicated that an old ally of our campaign, Maryhill MP Maria Fyfe, would also be there. Sarwar had made prior arrangements for us to petition in Pollok on the same day, however, it was agreed that it was appropriate for me to gain support in my local area and that he would petition at Pollok with the remainder of the shop stewards.

That Saturday morning as I made the short five-minute walk to my local shopping centre I felt strangely nervous at the thought of petitioning on what was virtually my own doorstep. This would be a more personal experience for me as this was where I was born and bred and home territory.

Any doubts I had about the reception I would receive were dispelled almost immediately. Neighbours, friends and local shoppers all offered their full support and best wishes. It was overwhelming. I didn't realise the vast number of people I was acquainted with in the area until that day.

Maria and Patricia seemed amazed by the number of people I knew until I reminded them that I had lived there for my whole life. During the course of the morning I met various people I'd not seen for several years including a couple of ex-members of a local youth club I used to run during the 1970s and '80s. My initial thought was how old they made me feel, as they were now wives and mothers.

We spent a few minutes reminiscing and leg pulling about old times at the club. I also got engaged in more of the same when a former team mate from my football playing days appeared on the scene. He quipped,

"You're still the same old Jamie. You're never backwards at coming forwards in speaking your mind. I wasn't surprised to see you leading from the front."

Near the end of the morning session a man thrust a ten pound note into my hand and said,

"Jamie, go and get you and your helpers a cup of tea. You're doing a great job."

He disappeared in a flash and to this day I never found out who he was. What I do know, however, was that his gesture reminded me that there are people who have a genuine concern for others involved in a struggle.

Throughout our campaign I found out that many share those values.

APRIL–JUNE
2000

Ashamed to be British...

22

THE BAE directors announced their future business plan for Govan and Scotstoun shipyards or BAE Marine Clyde as we would now be known. The proposals they put forward were radical and when implemented would drastically alter the current shape and roles both yards would play on the Clyde.

You can go back to my naïveté in July 1999 when the Heads of Agreement were announced or even to December of that year when they were concluded, and I was still of the belief that the two yards would continue to be part of the Empire and they'd have their own identities. Nothing much would change. We'd be building ships, Scotstoun would be building ships.

But, it became clear the company had a much different plan to that. Cross fertilisation was coming in and the company was determined that Govan would keep their expertise in steel fabrication, because that was our strong point and that Scotstoun would be principally confined to the export work they were getting and also outfitting.

In hindsight that was only part of the plan because one of the things I've realised is that they have a master plan with a time-scale in which the various components will come in piecemeal. You have to remember Scotstoun was very big, Govan was smaller and to have done something totally radical in one move probably wouldn't have worked.

But, the strategy paved the way for later events where Govan has ended up in charge of steelwork which would mean a lot of steelworkers would have to transfer over from Scotstoun and they would then concentrate on outfitting. But, if you looked further down the line it became clear what BAE Systems were saying was that this was just part of the overall plan. If we'd read between the lines we'd have seen the message clear and simple, both yards were to be changed forever.

People don't like change; it makes them nervous and apprehensive. If the workers at Scotstoun had known how much of an impact those changes were going to have then I think they'd have been a lot more hostile towards them. The two yards were losing their individuality and their traditional roles.

The biggest impact the changes had on a day to basis was that it forced people to sign up for the cross fertilisation concept. It resigned you to the fact that there would be a great upheaval to the workforces, with a relatively small number, no more than a hundred, moving from Govan to Scotstoun, but several hundred transferring in the other direction. That was later to pose a big challenge to me and my shop steward in terms of leading the workforce at Govan.

Despite the certainty of difficulties arising, at Govan we realised that it was essential we committed ourselves to supporting the company's vision for the future. The following week the convenors attended the National Union Shipbuilding seminar in Manchester. Alan Johnston a junior minister at the Department of Trade and Industry was guest speaker. With his knowledge of many issues concerning the shipbuilding industry we anticipated a detailed insight into how the government perceived the future of the industry in the UK.

What we did not expect, however, was that he would 'let the cat out of the bag' in stating that there was the likelihood that the Ro-Ro ferry contract would probably be going to Germany.

Initially those remarks left me dumbstruck, quickly followed by the view that what we were now hearing was an organised leak. During his address I had also detected uneasiness among some of the national union officers leading me to believe that perhaps they knew more than they were revealing, that they'd been pre-warned.

As the meeting ended and we headed to collect our belongings I remarked to my co-convenors Joe, Johnny and Davie,

"I smell a rat. There were bad vibes at that meeting."

Those words had hardly left my mouth when a full time official raced up to me waving *The Guardian* newspaper,

"Have you seen this article? It's claiming the Ro-Ro contract is going to Germany. There's another piece suggesting the German bid is fifty per cent lower than Govan's. It also suggests Govan may not have the capability to build Ro-Ro ferries."

I almost exploded with rage. The comments from Johnston followed by *The Guardian* article were too much of a bloody coincidence from where I was standing. Driving home from Manchester was a long arduous journey as we all sat fuming at the contents of the article. The trip was punctuated with calls to my mobile from the media in Scotland who had latched on to the story.

I was convinced that it was almost certainly a leak from a MoD source with the intention of testing what the reaction would be from the unions, media and public should the Ro-Ro contract go abroad. I arrived home around 7 p.m. and received a phone call from *BBC Scotland* asking if I would do an interview early the next day on the issue of the contract.

As I arrived at the studios I was determined to react strongly to the previous day's events. I was asked to comment on speculation that the article in *The Guardian* was indeed a leak from the Ministry of Defence. I agreed with that view adding that if that was the way government bodies treated their own home based industries it was a national disgrace. I told the interviewer,

"If there's any truth to the view that this is a leak from the MoD, then I'm ashamed to be British."

That final comment became front-page news that day. It caused uproar in political circles and it was implied in some quarters that I had been unpatriotic. But, I regarded what I said as being quite the opposite. A government was elected to inspire, motivate and extol the virtue of its people. I was not prepared to sit back and let some faceless bureaucrat undermine our yard or our industry.

My revelation that junior minister Alan Johnston had indicated the Ro-Ro contract was going to Germany also caused a rumpus at Westminster. I received phone calls from the media telling me that some national union officers who were present at the seminar in Manchester were trying to suggest that I had misinterpreted Johnston's statement.

Those comments were ludicrous and I felt obliged to ask my co-convenors if they were certain that the contents of the minister's speech were as I had reported. They were a hundred per cent sure that I was correct. What followed was a whispering campaign in certain union circles that we should not have gone public on the minister's speech.

That may have been the fine moral high ground from where some of the union hierarchy stood, however, considering that the minister's comments could have affected the livelihood of twelve hundred workers on the Clyde I felt we had every right to reveal the contents of the meeting and in doing so attempt to find out the truth.

The following day Lesley Riddoch from *BBC Scotland* asked me to appear on her mid-day programme to defend the Clyde's corner in relation to the ferry contract. I was informed that a shipbuilding expert from *Lloyd's List* newspaper in London would also be on a phone link to the programme supporting the merits of the comments in *The Guardian*. I was ready for him and hoped he had encased himself in a suit of armour.

In the studio Lesley grilled me about the statements made that the German bid for the ferries was about fifty per cent lower than Govan's. She also asked my views about claims made that Govan did not have the capability to build Ro-Ro's. I totally refuted the speculation that the German bid was half ours. I said that anybody with a genuine knowledge of the industry would have dismissed those comments out of hand.

I supported my argument by reminding everyone that under Kvaerner we had close links with many of their other European yards including the one in Germany. All Kvaerner's European sites constantly undertook exercises to compare costs across all their facilities. The fact that labour costs in Germany were higher than in the UK and that major material costs from suppliers across Europe would be at best only marginally different cast serious doubts about the validity of the claims that any shipyard in Germany could submit a bid fifty per cent lower than a UK yard.

Furthermore there was no evidence to support the view that German shipyards were more productive than their UK counterparts. Indeed the only area where I would concede that perhaps the German performance would be superior was in the process planning of the ship.

I also referred to the fact that in previous exercises undertaken by Kvaerner in comparing prices for shipbuilding contracts across Europe, the differential was more likely to be five per cent rather than fifty. It was my assertion that if there was a substantial difference in the price put forward by a German yard as compared to a company in the UK there was most certainly a hidden factor.

Many people in UK shipbuilding are of the opinion that some European governments are more innovative in assisting their shipyards. There was a firm belief that aid given by regional or federal government was in the form of 'grants'. In recent years trying to get UK government at Westminster to investigate our suspicions were constantly met with a lukewarm response.

Or alternatively, the bureaucrats at Whitehall would always respond to us with the old chestnut, 'prove it, and provide evidence.' It was our view it was their role to safeguard UK jobs by investigating thoroughly our suspicions. I believed then and still believe that there is too much of a culture of going through the motions in looking after our interests in Europe. We should have been major players in the European arena but we were not.

In responding on the second issue raised with regards to Govan's capability to build the Ro-Ro ferries that surely was the ultimate insult, on the basis that one of Govan's strongest assets was our versatility. We had proved that consistently in building a wide array of ships in recent years. I emphasised we could built Ro-Ro's standing on our heads.

Three years previously we had built the *Sea Launch Commander* for a Boeing Consortium. It was one of the most technologically advanced ships in the world and had been featured on *BBC's Tomorrow's World* programme. And it had received rave reviews for its performance at sea. If there were any criticisms of it, they certainly would not be on the grounds of lack of capability or skill.

Lesley then invited the *Lloyd's List* guest from London to respond to my defence of the Clyde.

"You have heard Jamie refute the allegedly fifty per cent lower costs in Germany for the Ro-Ro's and rubbish suggestions that Govan couldn't build the ferries. Would you like to respond Richard?"

"I didn't say Govan couldn't build Ro-Ro ferries. I suggested that Germany had more experience in building them. Actually, I agree with Jamie that the differential of fifty per cent in relation to the alleged bid put forward by a German yard is absurd"."

Lesley interjected,

"Rather a watered down version of earlier comments attributed to you Richard, are they not?"

I had put to bed some of the nonsense that had been circulating in relation to the fantasy price submitted by a German yard. Despite that I was still very concerned that the leak in *The Guardian*, almost certainly from political circles, indicated that securing the Ro-Ro contract was going to be an uphill struggle.

Back on the domestic front Isabel's mum's health was continuing to be a cause for great concern. She was suffering from a combination of conditions including the superbug, MRSA. It was also becoming apparent that her mind was beginning to wander almost certainly due to the onset of senile dementia. As many people will know from their own personal experience it can be a painful and emotionally distressing period for any family to go through. Isabel had only recently come to terms with the loss of her dad less than seven months previously and I dreaded the thought of her having to cope with the possibility of losing both her parents within such a short period of time.

Unfortunately in mid-April her mother's condition deteriorated rapidly and she passed away on the eighteenth. Once again, Isabel was inconsolable and her spirit was almost broken. However, as is often the case in times of adversity the family pulled together with everyone reminding Isabel that no daughter could have done more for her parents. I have often reflected on the period between 1998 and 2000 and the pressures and stress put on Isabel both in caring for her parents and supporting me actively in the campaign, whilst at the same time looking after the home and family.

Those experiences opened my eyes to the blessing that I had received in having such a remarkable wife. I had learned the true meaning of having the 'ultimate soul mate.'

It was May Day rally time in Glasgow again and to my great surprise I had been asked once again to be a guest speaker. On the day the weather was glorious and there was a massive crowd at Glasgow Green to meet the procession.

Minutes before I was due at the rostrum I decided on my theme. Where is our manufacturing base disappearing to, and do we care?

I put a staunch case for the necessity to maintain a strong diversified manufacturing base.

I opened up with.

"Never mind if it is a shipyard, textile factory, oil refinery or ceramic factory, we need to maintain the capability to produce manufactured goods."

I stressed that the 'dot-com', financial and service industries would not sustain our economy. We had to have a diversified economy and attempt to balance all our employment activities and opportunities.

I was not anti the others, merely pro manufacturing. I was neither politically minded nor active, however, I did remind the audience,

"...the Thatcher years had created a dismissive and contemptuous attitude towards manufacturing. That had damaged our economy and made many of us brow beaten and defeatists towards the defence of many of our manufacturing industries. I had expected such an attitude and policies from the Tories, however, I did not expect a continuation in the same vein from a Labour Government."

I was pleasantly surprised that when I left the platform several female workers from a textile factory in Lanarkshire approached me. They thanked me for having the decency to relate to the audience the difficulties their own industry was currently experiencing stating that my comments of support had been more than they had encountered from many in the political arena.

As I stood outside the marquee after speaking I was very surprised to be approached by Malcolm Clark an old ally from the Task Force that had assisted in us getting a new owner the previous year. Malcolm had held Senior Executive posts worldwide in the engineering industry and somehow the surroundings of a May Day rally seemed a strange arena for such a high profile businessman.

I believe he saw surprise in my face as he quipped,

"Hi Jamie, are you surprised to see me here?"

"A bit, yes," I replied.

"I heard your speech in the marquee and I had to chuckle to myself."

I was curious to find out why he'd been so amused.

"I heard you say that you were not politically minded. That may well be the case but my God since we first met you've managed to turn many of your views into political issues."

He paused and then added,

"Incidentally did you realise you took the biggest gamble of your life when from the beginning of your campaign you got heavily involved with the media? Were you aware how fickle they could be? And how at any time they could have turned on you and destroyed the campaign? Having said that you conducted yourself very well and the media seemed to switch on positively to the campaign. You did well."

I replied,

"Desperate times require desperate measures. We had to get a high media profile from the outset of our campaign otherwise the politicians would most probably have been dismissive of us. I was fortunate in that I developed a very good relationship with the media. Perhaps I was just a lucky bugger."

I was happy to have met Malcolm that day as it was always interesting to hear other people's perspective of things. It always provides food for thought.

Throughout May we were heavily involved in our on-going national petitioning across Scotland. Sarwar was continuing to get a fair degree of support from Scottish Labour MPs who were organising petitions in their own constituencies. Surprisingly many of our most ardent supporters among the MPs represented constituencies outside Glasgow.

That was in contrast to some of the Glasgow MPs who remained lukewarm in their support for the petitioning. Sarwar had hired a campaign bus during May and suggested that we should target Coatbridge, Livingston and Edinburgh all on one Saturday. The shop stewards agreed and with the aid of Sarwar and some of his local constituency workers we set out to make hay while the sun shone.

I have nothing but praise for those local party workers who gave up their free time on numerous Saturdays to assist us in the petitioning. I was well aware that they could have been spending their weekends relaxing. My two daughters, Julie and Amanda who periodically had assisted in our petitioning, also insisted on accompanying me on our trek to Lanarkshire and the east with a couple of their friends coming along.

We arrived at Coatbridge shopping centre mid-morning and were met by local MP Tom Clarke (Coatbridge & Chryston) and Govan MSP Gordon Jackson. I had a lot of respect for Clarke as he was perceived as being 'Old Labour' and he had been extremely supportive throughout our campaign. His constituency was a true industrial heartland that had lost many core manufacturing industries in recent years like steel making and mining.

I believe he admired the determined stance that we had taken in defence of our industry and jobs. He reinforced the view that in Westminster prior to us getting a heads of agreement for a buyer for Govan in July 1999, the vibes a few days previous had indicated that the Govan yard was 'going under.' It was also being rumoured that in some political circles the advice being given was that it was advisable to distance oneself from the campaign or risk being associated with failure.

There is no doubt that despite the fact that our campaign had enlisted genuine and committed political allies, we had also acquired some fair-weather friends. Needless to say in Coatbridge we got a very warm welcome from locals. A countless number of them told us of their anger and frustration at having witnessed numerous manufacturing industries going to the wall. They commended us for 'having the guts to put up a spirited fight.'

We travelled through to Livingston and arrived at the shopping complex just after mid-day. Livingston in recent years had become a major base in Scotland for sunrise industries, electronics rather than heavy manufacturing. I wondered if they would be knowledgeable of our campaign and more importantly would they identify with us and support our fight for jobs in Glasgow. Once again my fears were dispelled within minutes. The power of the media had once again broken the ice for us.

It was West Lothian, but the local population still supported Scottish jobs for Scottish workers. Livingston Labour MSP Bristow Muldoon and several local councillors greeted us. The local MP Robin Cook was unable to be there due to overseas commitments in his role as Foreign Secretary. It was an enormous shopping centre so we split up into small groups to maximise our impact.

The support for the petition signing was solid. However, I did experience a slightly different climate to that of the one in Coatbridge. A significant number of people questioned why a Labour MP and party workers were accompanying our union campaign delegation. I explained that Sarwar was the Govan MP and that I would have expected any community MP regardless of his or her political party to actively support a fight for jobs in their respective constituency.

I emphasised that our campaign had always attracted political cross party support and that our appeal was to working people, from working people. We were asking the people of Scotland to support our fight for jobs not the politicians. I realised that many of the people we asked to back our campaign may not have been Labour voters and perhaps could have been put off by the presence of a Labour MP. However, in fairness not one person declined to sign when I repeated that it was ordinary workers that wanted their support.

We stayed there for just under two hours before travelling on to Edinburgh. However, the Livingston visit always reminds me of one of the funniest events that happened during the campaign. It occurred while my younger daughter Amanda and her friend Emma were getting petitions signed at the car park entrance.

They had approached a couple of middle-aged women and on hearing the petition was to support shipbuilding at Govan they willingly signed. Just as Amanda and Emma prepared to walk away one of the women enquired,

"Do any of you personally know Jamie the union convenor who's always on the TV and in the newspapers?"

Amanda replied,

"Yes, we know Jamie."

"How well do you know him?" the woman continued.

"Very well. I live with him," Amanda replied.

"What! You live with him? Did you hear that Mary?" she said to her friend.

She went on,

"I read Jamie's diaries in the *Evening Times* and it said he was happily married to Isabel."

"He is," Amanda chuckled. "Jamie is my dad. I was just winding you up."

The banter continued when Amanda told us the story before boarding the bus for Edinburgh. Again there was an outburst of laughter from everybody. One of the shop stewards added,

"Jamie, it looks as if you may have established yourself as a male pin up for the middle aged blue rinse brigade."

A bit of humour could always lighten the spirits during a tiring day.

It was now last stop Edinburgh city centre, namely Princes Street. Although I had been quite laid back about us getting solid support in Coatbridge and Livingston, Edinburgh was an unknown area that I had a degree of reservation about. Everyone knows about the rivalry between Glasgow and Edinburgh. Gritty Glasgow as opposed to elegant Edinburgh many would say. This was not Argyle Street in Glasgow this was Princes Street in Edinburgh.

We quickly erected the union banner and set up the tables for the petition signing. I decided to put any apprehension behind me and take the bull by the horns. I approached a group of men and women at a bus stop near by. Before I got the opportunity to utter one single word one of the men of the group instantly remarked,

"Jamie Webster, Union Convenor at Govan Shipyard. The yard is not shutting and the Germans are not getting the Ro-Ro ferries."

I was amazed as he rhymed off that statement. The whole group burst out laughing as I stood there struggling to find a response.

One of the women in the group must have felt almost sorry for me as she said,

"Of course we'll sign your petition. It's good to see workers fighting for their jobs. There have been too many jobs lost without a fight all over Scotland."

I chatted for a few minutes with them until they boarded the bus waving and giving us the thumbs up as they moved off.

Any apprehension that Edinburgh would be less supportive than any other part of Scotland was instantly gone. If we needed further evidence of that it came when I spoke through the loud hailer asking for the people of Edinburgh to support our campaign for jobs on the Clyde.

I watched in amazement as many people on the other side of Princes Street crossed the road and came over to sign the petition. That day we collected over three thousand signatures in under two hours in Edinburgh. When we finally departed for home I realised that the only difference between people from Edinburgh and Glasgow was the accent. I realised we all wanted jobs for people in Scotland regardless of the location.

On Sunday 11 May, the *BBC* broadcast Fergal Keane's documentary *"Forgotten Britain"*. A *BBC* crew had arrived at Govan in February 1999 with the intention of showing the changing face of British heavy manufacturing industries and how that had affected the communities that were reliant on them. By total coincidence they arrived just as our fight for survival had began. The producer James Hayes and Fergal asked if they could follow us throughout our campaign and be permitted to film fly-on-the-wall style. Deciding on allowing such an in-depth look into our everyday activities throughout the campaign needed serious consideration.

I eventually satisfied myself that we should let the public nationwide see behind the scenes, warts and all. It would be a story about ordinary people fighting for what they believed in, namely the right to work. Regardless of whether we would ultimately be successful or not I thought that people would understand and appreciate the merits of our struggle. We would be required to give the *BBC* access to film in areas never seen before on television.

Included would be our shop stewards meetings where we constantly reviewed and appraised our campaign strategy and tactics. They would also be allowed access to our mass meetings where they would capture a wide range of human feelings being expressed. They would have frequent informal chats with the workforce at different periods during the campaign. I felt we had nothing to hide and certainly nothing to be ashamed of.

Firstly, however, I had to get agreement from the shop stewards committee, the workforce and Gunnar the Managing Director. I was far from convinced they would give approval. I initially raised it with the stewards and although there was a degree of apprehension within a small minority of them it was overwhelmingly accepted.

Weeks previously the workforce had committed themselves in supporting the shop stewards in the fight to secure our jobs. We were now asking them to allow the *BBC* to record their experiences. I was delighted when they gave it their unanimous support. The last remaining part of the jigsaw was Gunnar and I knew that he could be caught between the views of the workers and the sensitivity that Kvaerner might have towards the documentary. However, as was generally the case with Gunnar he trusted our judgement on the matter and gave his permission.

The film crew were in the yard on numerous occasions between February 1999 and January 2000 when the yard was finally and officially bought over by our new owners BAE Systems. When they had finished filming they all emphasised how privileged they had felt in being allowed to film our campaign. James and Fergal said it had been an emotional experience for them all as they had shared out highs and lows. They also said that perhaps they would come back and film us a few years down the line to see how it had all panned out. Being in a buoyant mood at that time I said,

"Perhaps you should come back and see the ultimate fruits of our endeavour. You'll see a prosperous, thriving shipbuilding industry on the Clyde that many had prepared the obituary for. We'll be here for many decades to come."

When the documentary was shown it received considerable acclaim from the media TV critics. 'Gritty stuff', was how one newspaper TV programme critic described it. For weeks after the documentary I received lots of letters from members of the public all across the UK. From as far north as Inverness down to Dorset in the south of England, they all said how much they had enjoyed the documentary and wished us every success in the future. I made a point of replying to them all over the course of the next few weeks.

One letter touched me deeply. It was from a very elderly lady in Perthshire whose late husband had held a senior position in the Foreign Office in London in the 1950s. He had been given the honour of launching a ship from the Govan yard, then called Fairfields, during that period.

She told how her husband had often spoken to his children and grandchildren about what he had always regarded as being one of the most memorable days of his life. At that launch he had been given the small wooden mallet that triggers the launch of a ship as a memento by the company. She told me that a couple of years later her husband was sent to be a senior British UN representative in New York. He chaired many meetings, and always used this prized keepsake to open them. It was a much valued possession even when he retired and returned to Scotland.

It had pride of place in a cabinet in the dining room, and she told how he would regale people about the day he launched a ship from Govan on the Clyde. Sadly, he had died in the mid-nineties, but the mallet remained in the cabinet. She had watched our campaign and the documentary, and it brought back all the old memories. She sent her best wishes for our campaign, assuring us that her late husband would have also been an avid supporter of it. I am only sorry I don't still have the letter.

It was fitting that soon after the documentary was shown I was invited down to London to hand copies of the programme into the residencies of Tony Blair and Gordon Brown at 10 and 11 Downing Street. I trust they watched it. They certainly should have because it would have reminded them of the fact that there was a real world with real people out there with hopes and aspirations. Surely it was their responsibility to help people fulfil those aspirations.

Fergal Keane also used some of the material from the documentary in his book 'A Stranger's Eye', which accompanied the programme. He was able to go into much more depth about the crisis we had faced and re-reading the book several years later, I am still amazed at Fergal's insight into problems he only experienced over a short period of time, albeit at close quarters.

In early June there was still no decision on the ferry contract. There were no words to describe the frustration we were all feeling in the yard. I attended a national BAE Systems union seminar held in Farnborough where the Corporate Chief Executive John Weston conducted a question and answer session during which he also gave a broad summary of the company's performance. It was the first time the unions from BAE Systems Marine had attended such a seminar and we were all interested in the views that he would express on the recent purchase of the three shipyards. I listened intently as he raised the issue of the Ro-Ro's.

He said he expected a decision within weeks and remained optimistic. Much to my surprise he went out of his way to indicate that he had received very positive and favourable reports of the performance by the Govan workforce on the Auxiliary Oiler and of the commitment shown. I was chuffed at the fact that he had taken time to mention Govan in his report, as apart from the fact that we were the most recent acquisition to the BAE Empire we also represented less than one per cent of the company's total workforce.

After the seminar Marine Chief Executive Ron Leggater took me aside and emphasised that Govan had sent out very positive messages to the main board of their willingness and determination to succeed. He assured me that the board would match that commitment by redoubling their efforts to secure work. As we travelled home that night I was upbeat and optimistic due to the positive comments made by both Weston and Legatter and I was convinced that those comments would auger well for our future.

During that same period various sections of the media were continually running articles speculating that the reason why the ferry contract was continually being re-opened for tender was to allow BAE to get another bite at the cherry. They further speculated that this was due to the fact there was considerable concern in the political arena that should the contract go to Germany there would be a backlash against the government. The position at that time was further confused when the decision by the MoD to re-open tendering resulted in the European Commission demanding to know why the re-tendering process had occurred.

In the yard we were concerned that if the European Commission deemed that there was any evidence of impropriety it could lead to a long protracted investigation being carried out that would result in a lengthy delay in the awarding of the contract. If that situation arose it would have been potentially disastrous, as we needed to secure new work now. I was relieved when the vibes I got reassured me that the MoD were confident that they had not breached European competition laws. My relief was complete when two weeks later it was announced that the investigation by the European Committee had been completed resulting in no further action being taken.

Although we were apparently still in the hunt for the Ro-Ro's I was continually haunted by the name Andrew Weir Ltd., the Scottish based shipping company. As I've mentioned previously my experience with the Senior Executive of that company in 1998 had left me hoping I would never have to cross swords with them. Sod's law was now indicating that my worst fears were coming to pass and that they were becoming our principal competitor for the contract. Having experienced the extreme anti-UK shipbuilding views expressed by an executive of Weir's, I did not fancy the chances of that contract landing in the UK let alone the Clyde.

Near the end of June I discussed with Sarwar the issue of taking the petition to Defence Secretary Geoff Hoon in London. By now we had gathered approximately eighty thousand signatures over a period of about ten weeks. It was jointly agreed that we would wind up the following Saturday in the Shawlands district of Glasgow before making arrangements to go to London with the petition in the first week of July. Shawlands is generally regarded as one of the more affluent areas in Glasgow. However, toffs or not, they gave us great support in the last leg of our petitioning.

When I reflect back on the people who signed I often wonder if they followed the events that ensued over the coming months. I believe many of them would have. I sincerely hope that some of them will stop me in the street some day and I will be able to personally thank them for the small but symbolic part that they played in our campaign.

JULY–DECEMBER
2000

Taking our fight to the Ministry of Defence...

23

WE WERE all geared up to arrange for the petitions to be handed to Defence Secretary Geoff Hoon in London. Sarwar had arranged for the numerous boxes containing the signatures to be taken down to his London based office, situated only five minutes walk from Whitehall.

A couple of days before we went down the media asked me how difficult it had been to collect eighty thousand signatures. Not difficult at all I said and reminded them that we had received fantastic support everywhere the petition had been presented. I was totally sincere when I told them that had we been given more time or resources we could have got eight hundred thousand signatures. I certainly did not doubt that and I do not believe the media did either. I had personally witnessed the support and good will our campaign had received across Scotland.

On 5 July co-convenor Davie Torrance and I went down to London to deliver the petitions to Hoon. It was only when we arrived that we were told they were now to be handed in to the Prime Minister's residence at Number 10 Downing Street. We were joined at Sarwar's office by a delegation of Scottish Labour MPs who were to assist both Davie and me in carrying the boxes along to Downing Street.

It did not go unnoticed by the media or me that while many of the MPs present had been staunch allies, there was a minority that were merely there for the photo shoot at Number 10. It reminded me of when we'd been petitioning in Glasgow. Des Browne MP for Kilmarnock had organised one in his area.

Tom Clarke had invited us to his constituency in Lanarkshire. How many Glasgow MPs did that?

The involvement of people like David Marshall and Jimmy Wray, (to say he'd been conspicuous by his absence would be complimentary), was pathetic. The areas they represent, Shettleston and Baillieston (Wray left Parliament in April 2005) are heartland Glasgow, the essence of working class, the soul of who we are, our life blood.

But, there was no great enthusiasm from any of them. What was to stop them showing more support on the ground? Nothing. I'm not saying they didn't support us at Westminster but locally their profile was almost non-existent.

We handed in the petitions at Number 10 and following that I did live interviews for *BBC* and *STV.* During them I couldn't help but reflect on the fact that I had been given the opportunity to present our case to the nation whilst standing outside the Prime Ministers residence. I was happy our industry and our yard had been given a platform to tell everybody,

"We want to work and we intend to succeed in our campaign."

As the yard went on holiday in mid-July there was speculation that an announcement on the Ro-Ro's could be made during that period. Some cynics were suggesting that if the news was bad for Govan then that would be the most opportune time for the government to announce it. It did not happen.

We returned to work in early August with no announcement having been made. Our concern about the delay was exacerbated by the fact that Parliament was now in recess until early October. The silence was deafening and it was a very worrying time. Furthermore there was no point in making representations to the company as they always maintained that they were as much in the dark as we were, although I was never totally convinced of that.

In early September, nearly eighteen months after our campaign started, the convenors were invited to attend the STUC conference as visitors. Our strategy was again high on the agenda. Unfortunately none of the convenors were allowed to speak at the conference since we were not official delegates. I have never been the greatest fan of such conferences. There is a pretence that debate is encouraged when in reality it is often stifled due to the expectation that everybody toes the official line.

I witnessed an example of this when during the conference a vote took place on the abolition of Clause 28 which opposed the teaching of anything to do with homosexuality to children in schools.

This proposed legislation had been a source of much controversy in Scotland with the STUC proclaiming that all trade unionists supported the abolition of the bill. My experience in the grass roots was that this was far from being the truth as many shop floor workers I had spoken to opposed abolition of Clause 28.

Furthermore during the debate I overheard three delegates sitting in front of me indicating that they were against supporting the abolition of the clause. However, they had all agreed that to publicly vote against the motion would have been unwise and futile. One of them personally stated,

"We'd be outcasts and sent to Coventry."

I find it sad that although the conference was supposed to be a platform for open debate it would appear that the rule of thumb was to doff the cap and go with the flow.

It also came to our attention at the conference that a minority of delegates belonging to the, 'New Labour' division had been fiercely critical of my style of leadership throughout the campaign. Abrasive, confrontational and politically incorrect were only a few of the comments made about me. They stated that there had been no need to project our campaign into the media and that my approach in the political arena had been both unnecessary and over the top.

Their view was that we should have left it all to the national union officers to deal with the government in a softly-softly approach. They maintained that such tactics would have assured a secure future for the yard and saved our jobs. That may well have been their view, however, it was certainly not one shared by workers in Govan, the public or the media.

It has always been my belief that had we not maintained a high and positive profile in the media Govan shipyard would have shut. I have always had an affinity with Labour. However, neither Labour nor any political party deserves blind loyalty. They must be accountable and receptive to justifiable criticism. To have lesser expectations would further belittle the image of politics.

The 'New Labour Luvvies' I encountered were often weak-minded individuals, sometimes, I thought, incapable of standing up for what they personally believed in. They gave the impression that any trade unionist critical of the Labour party was ill informed or a traitor. They were tied to political dogma. Their creed is blind obedience, they are total conformists.

I don't believe it is right to toe the party line because it is the party line. If Labour does something wrong it needs to be questioned and brought to book. It doesn't mean that by criticising them the other political parties get the upper hand.

If you criticise it's because you feel something's incorrect, inaccurate or cannot be justified. I have always believed in giving praise where it's due and criticism where appropriate without fear or favour. Needless to say at the conference not one of the snipers ever spoke to me personally to express their misguided views on our campaign. I wonder why? I would have relished the opportunity to openly debate the issue.

I was reassured that I was not becoming paranoid when two solicitors I knew approached me as we left the conference.

They remarked that they had also overheard criticism of the Govan campaign and my leadership and expressed astonishment to hear such comments from people who they maintain should have known better. They both echoed the view that they believed the campaign was excellent and reflected well on the role that trade unions carry out in defence of workers jobs. I was heartened to hear the views of outsiders looking in they tended to be more objective in their appraisals.

By mid-September there was speculation that Govan could benefit from the closure of Ailsa Troon shipyard that had gone into liquidation. It was rumoured that an uncompleted contract for ten landing crafts for the Ministry of Defence could be transferred to BAE Systems in Govan.

We sympathised with the workers at Ailsa regarding the proposed closure of their yard. Despite the fact that numerous representations had been made by both the trade unions and the government to the owners neither party had managed to get the company to reverse their decision of closure. Although we acknowledged it would not be the best of circumstances in which to secure work it was a case of much rather the work remained on the Clyde than going elsewhere.

Around the same time the *Business AM* newspaper ran an article indicating that the Ro-Ro contract was indeed going to Germany. When I contacted the newspaper they insisted that their information was MoD linked. The government immediately refuted the contents contained of the article and maintained that no final decision had been taken. With every passing day I was getting more concerned. The piece in *Business AM* worried me, as there was seldom smoke without fire.

In early October I was told that BAE Marine Chief Executive Ron Legatter was taking up a new role in the BAE corporate body. Speculation was rife that Rigby the current Managing Director would be standing down due to personal family circumstances and was being replaced by Simon Kirby who had undertaken that role on a temporary basis for several months. We had been dealing with Kirby more often in recent months and he seemed reasonably approachable and down-to-earth.

A few days later we were informed that Legatter was visiting Govan to meet the senior management and I was somewhat surprised when he sent for me prior to meeting them. He greeted me warmly and indicated that he would like an informal chat about how things were shaping up in Govan. He said,

"Do you remember our first meeting in Govan fourteen months ago at the time of the interim takeover and the contents of that meeting? What was it you said? That BAE would like Govan, the workers and the culture. You also said the workers would give a good performance on the Auxiliary Oiler. Well I want you to know that you were right on all counts.

"We do like Govan and the workers have done extremely well on the oiler contract. Do you remember what else you said?"

I knew exactly what else I had said as the conversation was still vivid in my memory.

However, before I had the opportunity to recount it he continued,

"You said that if treated fairly and shown respect by the company the workers would repay the faith shown in them ten fold. You also emphasised that we were not to confuse the responsible and reasonable attitude adopted by the Govan workforce as a sign of softness. Indeed the words I remember were that if we ever shit on you from a great height and abused the workforce then we would find a workforce firm in its resolve in facing up to any injustices. I hope we've treated the workforce fairly and with respect because I want it known that whether we secure the Ro-Ro's or not BAE Systems intends to make maximum effort to secure other work that will ensure a future for the Govan yard."

I was relieved to hear those comments as it finally dispelled the fear that BAE would use Govan to build the Auxiliary Oiler and then close the yard. I also appreciated the fact that Legatter had taken the time to speak to me personally prior to him taking up his new role.

Thoughts of our future were put on hold on 11 October. Scotland's First Minister Donald Dewar died aged sixty-three, after suffering a massive brain haemorrhage. He'd fallen on the steps outside his official Edinburgh residence the day before. His health had been in question since April when he'd undergone heart surgery in Glasgow, but the First Minister had been back at work for a month and had in fact gone on the offensive about Labour's chances of winning the next General Election.

But, he'd looked visibly tired during a bruising First Minister's Question Time with the SNP's leader John Swinney on the 5 October and now six days later, the country was in mourning for the man dubbed 'The Father of the Nation.'

I've never been shy about my opinion of Mr Dewar. He was always, I found, lukewarm at best about our campaign and even although many people have told me I got my assessment of him wrong, I just can't reverse that view. However, my thoughts and those of the Govan convenors were with his family. Isabel was still finding it hard to come to terms with the death of her mother in April so I could understand how Mr Dewar's nearest and dearest must be feeling.

On Monday 16 October BAE informed us that a decision on the Ro-Ro's was expected on Wednesday. We were advised that the convenors from Scotstoun and Govan along with full time union officials would travel down to the House of Commons to hear the announcement by Defence Secretary Geoff Hoon. A few hours later I was told by the company that I was in fact to stay in Govan to participate in a joint statement that would be made by BAE Systems and the Govan trade unions.

This decision caused discontent within the Scotstoun convenors and some full time officials as they thought I should be made go to London along with them. I firmly believed I had a duty to be in Govan to hear the news, good or bad.

I discussed this difficulty with my co-convenors to establish if they had any difficulty with me staying at Govan while they went to Parliament. I reminded them that we had worked as a team throughout the campaign and that it had always been necessary to delegate jobs to individuals. I emphasised that our only real concern should be in the delivering of the right result for our yard. They fully supported that viewpoint and I subsequently informed the Scotstoun convenors and the full time officials that my priority would be to stay in Govan and wait for the announcement from Parliament.

The Govan convenors also agreed that immediately after Hoon's statement, regardless of the outcome, Managing Director Simon Kirby and I should address a mass meeting of the workforce. Kirby was in Govan because the Ro-Ro's had always been our contract. We felt that it was vital there was a union presence at that mass meeting in case there were pertinent questions that needed to be answered.

On Wednesday, Johnny Johnson, Joe Brown and Davie Torrance my co-convenors set off for London early in the morning. Hoon's speech was expected around lunchtime and a press conference had been provisionally arranged for 3 p.m. in the Govan boardroom. It was agreed that Kirby and I would address the workforce prior to that press conference. Just before mid-day I was informed that Secretary of State for Scotland John Reid would be coming to the yard later in the afternoon to meet the company and the unions.

Shortly afterwards the announcement came, 'Andrew Weir Shipping have been awarded the Ro-Ro contract' with the added revelation that a major part of the contract would be built in Germany. My heart sank at the news. My initial thought was, "what a disaster, all our efforts lobbying and petitioning had been in vain".

But, there was more to come from Hoon. He continued.

"A contract for four logistic ships for the MoD has also been placed. Swan Hunter on Tyneside will be the prime contractor to build two of the ships with the other two to be built at BAE Govan subject to a contractual agreement being reached between Swan Hunter and BAE Systems."

In my heart of hearts I was bitterly disappointed at losing the Ro-Ro contract as it was to be the mainstay in securing our long-term future. Despite the disappointment, my pragmatic nature told me that all was not lost. The building of two logistic ships was at worst a significant consolation prize. Instinctively my mind turned to the workforce and the media and how they would react to the announcement of losing the ferries and instead be awarded two logistic ships.

I bucked myself up, determined I was not going to wallow in self-pity and conscious that maintaining a positive outlook and high morale was vital in the yard. I accepted that it had to be a case of putting on a face to the workers and the media. Prior to the mass meeting I discussed with Simon Kirby the importance of keeping the workforce upbeat and the necessity that we jointly put the disappointment of the Ro-Ro's behind us. He agreed totally with my sentiments adding that there was a distinct possibility that Govan could be awarded the contract to build the ten landing crafts that were now up for grabs due to the closure of Ailsa Troon. There was still everything to play for.

Before addressing the mass meeting along with some of the shop stewards I spoke to John Reid about the implications of losing out on the ferry contract. He indicated that he fully understood our disappointment but stated that he had total confidence in Govan's ability to come through the ongoing difficult period. It seemed unfair to aim any criticism at the government or Reid personally. He had been a staunch supporter throughout our campaign and we would always be indebted to him for the commitment he gave to our struggle.

By the time I attended the mass meeting with Kirby word had got around the yard about our failure to secure the Ro-Ro's. Initially there was an air of dejection at the meeting as they were all aware how much effort had gone into our attempts to win that order. Nevertheless I urged them to remember that fifteen months ago we had faced almost certain closure. Losing the ferry contract had been a bitter blow but we now had the opportunity to build two other large ships for the MoD.

I concluded by also reminding them that we had faced and overcome greater difficulties than those currently presented to us. We would build the logistic ships. We would get the landing craft contract and we would attempt to secure other commercial contracts to plug the looming short-term gap in work. I could gradually see the gloom lifting and by the end of the meeting was convinced that our greatest attributes of commitment and resilience would see us through the current difficulties.

Later at the press conference I emphasised that there was no use crying over spilt milk. I accepted that although the logistic ships were not as lucrative a contract as the ferries they did still present us with a platform for building a long-term future. When questioned by the media I also admitted that many of the finer details in relation to the logistic ship contract had still to be fine tuned, not least of all when work could begin on the contract, an aspect that would now be of great importance.

I expected the following day to be dominated by acquiring more specific details of the logistic ship contract. Instead I got a phone call summoning the Govan convenors to a meeting of the Confederation of Shipbuilding and Engineering Workers. It was not long before I was getting the vibes that once again I was not flavour of the month.

The meeting was being called to discuss the situation in relation to the announcement of the logistic ship contract. However, it was becoming apparent that the meeting would also be used as a platform to criticise my decision to remain in Govan at the time of the official announcement in London. I also suspected that there would be further criticism of the positive tone I adopted with the media following the statement by Hoon.

In discussing this matter with my Govan co-convenors they told me that some of the full time officials and the Scotstoun convenors were livid at my comments to the media and would be calling me to task.

They were claiming that I had presented an over optimistic picture of the future and were indicating that many questions still had to be asked about the logistics contract. I fully realised that perhaps in time it would be proved that my confidence had been misplaced, however, it was my view that on some occasions they had tended to be too negative in their outlook. More importantly it was my personal responsibility to speak on behalf of the Govan shop stewards and workforce and I was quite prepared to stand up and accept full responsibility if I got it wrong.

Although it was initially intended that all the Govan convenors would attend the Confed meeting, prior commitments ruled out Johnny and Davie from attending which left only Joe and me. I immediately sensed tension in the air and it was clearly evident that my fears that it had all been pre-arranged and orchestrated would be proved correct. I listened intently as initially one of the Scotstoun convenors, George Kerr, followed by a couple of full time officials proceeded to make savage attacks on my reaction to Wednesday's announcement.

Kerr and I are chalk and cheese. He is very political, unlike me, and a conformist. I'd had other antagonistic meetings with him, particularly around the time the heads of agreement were signed. He simply doesn't like my style.

The meeting was not a pleasant experience and I had no intention of letting them dictate to me the whys and wherefores of the campaign in respect of the future of Govan. They said that I shouldn't have stayed in Glasgow and certainly should not have stated that the announcement was good news for Govan.

I responded angrily. Not so much to the criticism that they made of my comments to the media. I could accept that they were entitled to their opinion even if I strongly disagreed with it. What rankled with me was the way that the meeting had been orchestrated in an attempt to hammer me into line. I told them I felt hurt, disappointed and dejected at losing the Ro-Ro order after all the efforts we'd put in but we had been given work on two other boats so I had to get morale back up among the workforce.

I reminded them I was the union convenor at Govan and that it was me who was accountable to the workforce, not any of them.

As I left that meeting I was disillusioned and raging. Once again some full time officials had seemed more intent in petty fault finding in aspects of our campaign as opposed to actively assisting us in guiding the workforce through difficult times. I was fed up of having difficulties thrown in front of us about minor issues like who did or did not go to London when we had a major issue like how to save shipbuilding on the Clyde to worry about. Everything else was superficial. By gaining the order for the two logistic ships we had secured a significant contract that would have a beneficial impact on the Clyde and my main aim was to have the workforce kept on.

Joe joined me for a couple of pints after the meeting. He was a much more calm and measured person than I was. He was also universally regarded as fair-minded and honest. In the pub I asked,

"Joe was I in any way out of order at that meeting? I know you'll tell me the truth."

He replied,

"That meeting was a total sham and set-up. But, they miscalculated what your reaction to them would be. If they thought you would be dictated to or bullied they were badly mistaken. You more than held your own."

Throughout the campaign I had learned many things, not least of all that you had to stand and fight your corner when you felt you were in the right. I believe that meeting was a prime example of that.

The following week as we returned to a degree of normality in the yard I received a pleasant surprise in the mail. It was a personal letter from Lord Macdonald sending his best wishes for the future to everyone in the yard. It was a nice gesture and proved that he had followed developments in our campaign even though he had moved to pastures new in his role as Transport Minister.

As stated previously, it was always my view that his assistance at the start of our campaign was crucial in mobilizing political support. Indeed without the input of Macdonald and senior Scottish civil servants like John Mason and Ben McGuire in those early days I am convinced our yard would have closed.

With many details in relation to the logistic ship contract still vague Sarwar arranged a meeting with Geoff Hoon and Defence Procurement Minister Baroness Symons and requested that the convenors from Govan and Scotstoun attend. At that meeting we asked Hoon when he believed work would start on the logistic ships or ALSLs, as they would now be called. He indicated that to the best of his knowledge steel would be cut on the contract at Govan by July 2001. I detected a hint of frustration in his tone as he further indicated that the

Ministry of Defence could not be expected to continue to be the sole customer of UK yards.

Hoon I always found to be shallow and cantankerous towards us. I never warmed to him at all and nor did he to us. Hoon was hostile and consistently negative. He told us that in his experience over the last twenty years, yards in Britain had become antiquated in their structure and facilities, not customer friendly, inefficient, with bad industrial relations. I believe it was his opinion the UK shipbuilding industry was getting what it deserved. Nothing. Hoon bluntly stated that UK shipyards would have to extend their horizons into the export market, as future MoD contracts would not sustain all the UK yards. He was equally blunt about BAE Systems and their failure to secure the Ro-Ro ferry contract stating that, "BAE Systems bid had simply not been competitive enough."

He emphasised that Govan now had the opportunity to build the two logistic ships and he expressed the view that this contract gave Govan the opportunity to secure a future. As he wound up the meeting his final words echoed in my ears,

"Just get back up to the Clyde and get on with building those ships."

He also indicated that we'd never have got those orders unless we had serious political allies. I've always taken this to mean John Reid, although I've never had any confirmation of it.

Little did I realise that such a simplistic final statement would become the source for much continuing controversy.

As we moved into November Geoff Hoon's statement that Govan would start cutting steel on the ALSL contract by July 2001 was being seriously questioned in many quarters. The indications were that Swan Hunter was not programmed to commence work until January 2002. This sent alarm bells ringing on the Clyde.

As prime contractor and lead yard Swan Hunter would normally be expected to begin work approximately six months before BAE. If that was the case Govan could not start steel work on the ALSL contract until July 2002 instead of July 2001 as Hoon had suggested.

The consequences of such a delay were grave as it could result in a gap in work on the Clyde of approximately one year. It was abundantly clear that we either had to get the commencement of work on the ALSL contract brought forward or we would have to urgently secure some stopgap commercial contracts. It would be fair to say that during this period I reflected on the comments made by some of my union colleagues that I had been over confident on the ALSL contract being the solution to all our difficulties. It was becoming apparent that the observations they had made at that time now had a degree of legitimacy.

Late November saw the company providing more specific details of their future business plan for the Govan and Scotstoun. Kirby reiterated that Govan would become the centre of excellence for steelwork preparation and fabrication. Scotstoun would concentrate on ship outfitting and future export contracts for overseas navies. A couple of lines stated by Kirby at that meeting stuck in my mind more than the rest of his lengthy and detailed presentation. I remember them well,

"The shape and structure of Govan and Scotstoun will alter radically over the next two years to the extent that both yards will be unrecognisable compared to how they are at present. There will be many changes implemented that may well prove to be unpopular and on occasions painful. However, to secure a strong base for the Clyde well into the next decade they will be necessary."

He did not elaborate and for whatever reason, the Govan and Scotstoun convenors didn't pursue him on the issue. However, as I left that meeting I was in no doubt that those few words uttered by Kirby contained all the ingredients for the future of the Clyde. Events in the next year would prove me to be completely correct.

One fact was clear from Kirby's statement. There was going to be a massive upheaval of labour from Scotstoun to Govan on a permanent basis and to a lesser degree from Govan to Scotstoun. This crossover would not be well received in either yard as the majority of workers not surprisingly were accustomed to their own work culture at their home base.

It was clearly evident that for the employees being permanently transferred in either direction it would be a complete shock. The convenors reported details of the company's business plan to the shop stewards and then the workforce. Although the prospect of a long-term future received solid approval, as expected the proposed transfer of a fair proportion of Govan's outfitting, manufacturing and technical base to Scotstoun was initially met with disappointment. However, as was generally the case in Govan, pragmatism finally ruled the day with us all realising that we could not change the blueprint for the future set out by the company.

As it turned out, under a hundred workers moved north of the river to Scotstoun, but since the Millennium, up to a thousand have come across to Govan. There's no comparison, and it paved the way for the next set of changes which would identify the Clyde as one yard on two sites.

There was always a strategy by BAE to drip feed you the master plan. They'd never produce a total blueprint because it was too much too soon for the workforces to accept. Either they were a very uncertain management or they were using the 'softly softly' approach and I was always of the view it was the latter.

By early December we had received some good news with the securing of the contract to build the ten landing crafts that had initially been under construction at the now defunct Ailsa Troon shipyard. The icing on the cake was when we won a further contract to build an anchor handler ship for Stirling Shipping. They were a Scottish based company which Govan had built ships for in recent years and developed a good relationship with. Stirling also had the claim to fame that they had never previously succumbed to having any of their fleet built anywhere outside the UK. How refreshing it was to find that there actually was at least one surviving UK shipping company that had maintained a sense of loyalty to our home based shipbuilding industry.

How our industry could have done with another half-dozen UK shipping companies with a similar approach. I reflected on how Stirling were a million light years away from the other Scottish based shipowners Andrew Weir. Although the landing craft and anchor handler contracts did not constitute a massive amount of work, they nevertheless were extremely beneficial to us due to the fact that work could start on them almost immediately. These contracts provided a vital cushion that would assist us through a low workload period due to the now certain delay in commencing work on the ALSL contract.

JANUARY–DECEMBER
2001

The future unfolds...

24

BY THE time January 2001 arrived, the real vision for our long-term future for the Clyde was gradually emerging.

A gigantic multi billion MoD contract for the new batch of up to twelve Type 45 destroyers was up for grabs. This contract was regarded as the 'golden egg'.

Months previously BAE System's Chief Executive John Weston had openly hinted that the securing of this contract was absolutely vital to BAE's vision for a long-term future for the company's marine division and that failure to secure at least the lion's share could have signalled the death knell for BAE Systems in the marine sector.

Nobody on the Clyde had to be reminded that in the BAE System's worldwide empire Marine was a small fish in a very big pond. The division only constituted seven per cent of the company's total workforce with the remainder being employed in their massive worldwide Aerospace division. Although Weston had always appeared relatively keen on having a foothold in naval defence work, there was a genuine fear that if BAE were not successful in securing the Type 45 contract, his commitment and interest could wane or indeed vanish overnight.

Everybody at all levels of the Marine Division knew that securing the contract was imperative for the survival of all three yards in the group; Govan, Scotstoun and Barrow. As things stood at that time BAE were heavily involved in an imposed 'partnership' with the VT Group, known before 2002 as Vosper Thornycroft, in Portsmouth. The Ministry of Defence rules on competitiveness decreed that in the designing and building of the first three of the Type 45s there must be involvement by both companies.

You didn't need to be a financial wizard to realise that under that structure there could be serious questions of profitability being achievable for either company and it appeared obvious that something would have to give. Ultimately it did.

Shortly afterwards BAE announced that they had submitted an unsolicited bid to the MoD that included proposals for BAE to build the total Type 45 contract. It was also proposed that they were prepared to build two further Auxiliary Oilers for the Ministry on the basis of a build now, pay later agreement. These were radical and controversial proposals that received massive media coverage in the UK broadsheet business sections. It was argued that such proposals flew directly in the face of the MoD's procurement policy in ensuring competitiveness remained within the UK for naval contracts.

BAE refuted that by maintaining that the proposals they had put forward satisfied the prime criteria set out by the Department; that they delivered value for the taxpayer. The essence of the argument put forward by BAE was that in a rolling programme of building all the Type 45s, significant cost savings could be made after the expense of the initial learning curve on the first ships had been absorbed. There was a simple business rational to their proposals, but would the MoD be convinced?

Not unexpectedly the proposals put forward by BAE were met with vehement opposition from VT who accused BAE of aiming for a monopoly of all UK naval defence contracts. This was shaping up to be a titanic struggle. Perhaps rather selfishly, but inevitably, the convenors at both Govan and Scotstoun fully supported the company's unsolicited bid to build all the Type 45s and a further two Auxiliary Oilers. If we secured it all there would be serious consequences for VT's survival, but we had to be parochial and bat for the Clyde.

As expected our trade union colleagues in VT's vigorously opposed our company's proposals and embarked on a campaign of political lobbying in relation to the Type 45 contract. On the Clyde we responded by mounting our own lobbying campaign at Westminster as it was now obvious that the contract was not going to be handed to anyone on a plate. We realised that we had to match or indeed surpass the strong and potent political lobbying base in the south of England that would support the case for VT Group.

It was essential on the Clyde that we ensured Scottish MPs were totally on board with us and that they would match the political lobbying of their counterparts in the south of England. With this in mind I wrote to every Scottish MP emphasising the importance of our unsolicited bid reminding them that winning this order would sustain shipbuilding on the Clyde for the next decade and beyond. No doubt there were re-emerging mutterings at Westminster to the theme of, "will those bastards on the Clyde never go away?"

However, we got solid support from many of them. Certainly on the home front at Govan Sarwar was working like a Trojan and could not be faulted for effort and application. Having said that, by now he was getting to know me well, as on occasions he'd suffered a Webster tongue lashing. I had big expectations of him and in fairness he did have a lot to put up with when I was on my high horse.

Throughout this period we also kept in constant contact with the Scottish MSPs in Holyrood. Although defence was a Westminster responsibility we realised that effective lobbying would activate the Scottish Executive into becoming involved in highlighting our case with the appropriate government ministers in Westminster.

By March the MPs in Westminster had arranged for a trade union delegation to meet the recently appointed Secretary of State for Scotland, Helen Liddell. It was the first time I had met her personally and I couldn't help but think that she would have a hard act to follow, with the departure of John Reid to the Northern Ireland Office.

The difficulty with Liddell was that she came in relatively cold on the state of play in relation to our campaign as opposed to Reid having been totally up to date with all the events. But, she promised her full support, and agreed to arrange a further meeting for us with Geoff Hoon in relation to our unsolicited bid for the Type 45 contract and the two proposed Auxiliary Oilers.

We were also determined that when that meeting with Hoon took place we would raise with him his statement in the House of Commons in October 2000 that work could commence in Govan on the ALSL contract in July 2001. It was a statement that had proved to be well off the mark.

We also realised that pressure would need to be put on the MoD and Swan Hunter to get started on work on the ALSL contract as soon as possible, although the most optimistic starting date was now appearing to be early 2002. Every week or month that the commencement of work was delayed was resulting in a widening gap in the workload in the Clyde which we realised if not resolved could lead to job losses.

With Scotstoun nearing completion on the last of the Type 23 destroyers and the contract for Brunei also being at a very advanced stage our sister yard was in a precarious position.

In Govan we were marginally better off with work still under way on the oiler, anchor handler and landing crafts. It was abundantly clear at this stage how important the securing of two further oilers contained within the unsolicited bid would be if we were to succeed in plugging the temporary shortfall in work

In April we heard the rumour that the MoD had commissioned an American company, Rand, to carry out an appraisal of the UK shipbuilding naval construction capacity. Rand would also be expected to put forward proposals that would put in place best practices for future defence contract procurement. Indications were that the findings of the review would be of paramount importance to us in relation to the awarding of the Type 45 contract. Speculation was rife that the review by Rand would come down firmly in favour of the BAE proposal for the building of the Type 45s.

In the meantime VT was upping the ante and making loud noises in the media castigating BAE Systems for attempting to achieve a monopoly in UK naval shipbuilding. Their managing director expressed grave doubts as to whether his company could match the industrial muscle of BAE Systems. Aware that BAE Systems Marine had eighty-seven per cent of the UK warship building capacity with ownership of Govan, Scotstoun and Barrow, we banked on the fact that as BAE had such a lion's share of the total UK shipbuilding capacity it would ensure they would be capable in meeting any future British naval requirements.

Unlike some of our other UK competitors we had the facilities, resources and skilled labour to meet any of the MoD demands in the future building programme.

Prior to our meeting with Hoon on 11 May, we heard that the convenors from VT had already met him to express their concerns about the Type 45 contract and the possibility of BAE Systems winning the total contract. We could hardly fault them for fighting their corner for their yard. However, what did concern us on the Clyde was the fact that the Shipbuilding Negotiating Committee comprised totally of national union officers had also attended that meeting and supported VT's case.

Our view on the Clyde was that in being at that meeting the SNC compromised the appearance of impartiality which ought to have been maintained towards the case put forward by VT in Portsmouth. Hoon, naturally, would take the SNC view as being representative of union policy across the UK.

We were up in arms at them, as it was an unwritten law that the SNC did not get involved in supporting one region against another. VT should have been represented by local regional full time officials as that would have been normal protocol. Although various national officers tried to justify their actions, in our view they had prejudiced us prior to meeting the Defence Secretary. We made it abundantly clear with the national officers that we would be strongly supporting our company's bid for the full contract, emphasising that the workers on the Clyde would expect no less of us.

When we went to London for the talks with Hoon, we were first met by local MPs Mohammad Sarwar (Govan), John Robertson (Anniesland), Ian Davidson (Pollok), and George Galloway (Kelvin), who was by now giving us his backing publicly. They appeared quite chirpy prior to the meeting and we wondered if they had been dropped any hints.

A last minute surprise emerged with the unexpected appearance of Helen Liddell, who apparently had made a dash from business in Scotland to attend the meeting. We appreciated the effort she had made and past experience had always led me to believe that the closer MPs or ministers were to you in times such as this the more likely a good result would occur. Generally the time to worry was when all the MPs and ministers were busy, unavailable or otherwise engaged. I frequently heard that one of the first rules of survival at Westminster was to ensure that you did not get involved with bad news or lost causes.

As the meeting commenced, Hoon was quickly off the mark in stating that the perpetual lobbying for MoD work by most UK yards was becoming somewhat tedious. Again he was blunt in pointing out that any illusion that existed that the Ministry could or would continually bail out UK shipyards by awarding defence contracts was misguided. He emphasised that MoD work alone would not sustain the current UK shipyards in full employment and insisted that much more effort would have to be made in the commercial market to secure new contracts.

He reiterated that he would not be looking the length and breadth of the country continually dividing up the UK naval defence contracts in an effort to keep everybody happy.

He reminded us that his prime responsibility was to the taxpayer and ensuring that the Ministry got best value on their behalf from the suppliers. As I had previously feared, Hoon also got a subtle dig in at us by indicating that, to his knowledge, the national union officers were opposed in principle to the terms of BAE Systems' unsolicited bid.

He indicated that the officers supported a policy of distributing the naval contracts throughout the UK and I got the impression that he took a degree of pleasure in challenging us as to whether we supported that policy.

However, if he had thought that we would give a wishy-washy answer that would appease our national officials he was in for a rude awakening. Convenors from both Govan and Scotstoun unreservedly gave one hundred per cent support to BAE Systems bid. We put a case forcibly and competently that BAE had submitted a bid that progressively cut the costs on a rolling programme of building all the Type 45s. We emphasised that we had by far the best capability and facilities in the UK to undertake any MoD contract.

We also presented a case that the BAE offer to build two Auxiliary Oilers on the basis of a 'build now pay later' agreement represented good commercial value and further justified our argument by indicating that to the best of our knowledge there was an urgent requirement for the oilers.

This was due to new international shipping regulations that demanded such ships be double hulled. The vessels currently carrying out similar roles for the Royal Navy were part of an ageing fleet and some of them would not be permitted entry into many international waters due to their single hull status.

We believed that this argument supported strongly the case for the building of two new Auxiliary Oilers under our company's proposals.

Normally I would have expected that Hoon would have grilled us on our comments. However, much to our surprise on this occasion he was relatively subdued. He raised the issue of the Rand review, indicating that an interim report was expected some time in July. The review would include recommendations on future MoD procurement policy and we expected that the Rand review would express a viewpoint on the awarding of the Type 45 contract.

We could not allow the meeting to finish without raising the issue of the ALSL contract and the fact that his statement in Parliament in October 2000 had indicated that steel would be cut on this contract in Govan by July 2001. We reminded him it was now May and that recent signs were that a commencement date was now July 2002, a year late.

We told him that the inaccuracy of that statement had now resulted in serious consequences for the Clyde. Hoon was decidedly uneasy, emphasising that the principal responsibility on when the contract could start lay with Swan Hunter in consultation with BAE. He further indicated that his current understanding was that some work on the ALSL could start in October or November 2001, subject to a contract being finalised between Swan Hunter and BAE. He assured us that the MoD and defence procurement agency were making great efforts to assist work being able to begin as soon as possible.

Helen Liddell sat impassively throughout the meeting, listening but not speaking. As the meeting progressed I detected that there was an air of confidence from everyone present that the Rand review would support our case for securing the Type 45 contract.

Nevertheless we had equal concern in respect of getting the oiler proposals accepted within the unsolicited bid. When we pursued Hoon on this issue it drew a lukewarm response from him probably because it could have been political dynamite if BAE were to secure the Type 45 contract and the oilers. There would undoubtedly have been an outcry across all the other shipbuilding regions in the country thus fuelling accusations that BAE Systems were systematically heading towards a monopoly of the UK defence industry.

Although Hoon did not dismiss out of hand our proposals on the two oilers he did dampen our expectations somewhat by implying that there could well be budgetary constraints that could prevent acceptance of our company's proposals. I left that meeting high in expectation that we would secure the Type 45 contract but gravely concerned that the oiler proposals would be rejected thus leaving the Clyde with a considerable gap in our order book.

In June, a new political figure arrived on the scene with the appearance of Scottish Enterprise Minister Wendy Alexander. Throughout the campaign, (apart from his lack of response to our plea-for-help-letter), we had been heavily involved with her brother Douglas, MP for Paisley. We hoped that she would match his commitment. However, I felt we were venturing into unknown territory not knowing how supportive she would be.

My first impression of her was that she was smart and blunt mixed with a sprinkling of the 'nippy-sweetie'. I saw her as being very similar to one of her fellow Holyrood colleagues the SNP's Nicola Sturgeon although I doubt if she would appreciate that comparison. However, neither of them should have got upset at my comments as the above-mentioned ingredients are a good recipe for a competent MSP. As an added side note I do not believe that either of them would suffer fools gladly.

At the meeting with the minister we discussed the position in relation to our bid for the Type 45 contract and our grave concern about the impending gap in work if we were to secure the frigates without the two oilers. This meeting had been arranged as an informal chat and update, however, I suspected that the Minister knew more than she was letting on. She informed us that she had been in constant contact with her colleagues at Westminster, especially Helen Liddell and Brian Wilson who was a Minister at the Department of Trade and Industry. She gave assurances that the Scottish Executive would continue to make representation to Westminster on our behalf.

As I left the meeting I got the impression that there would be considerably more political developments surfacing soon. The following morning in work, I told the rest of the shop stewards.

"Sarwar will contact us soon. Following on from that we'll be invited to meet MPs culminating with a meeting with a government minister."

One of the shop stewards remarked,

"Is that a statement of fact, or a prediction?"

"Let's just say it is a calculated guess, based on past experience." I replied.

The following day there were raised eyebrows followed by chuckles of laughter when Sarwar phoned to tell me that the convenors were to come to Westminster to give an update to Scottish MPs. That was part one of the prediction correct. Would I get part two right?

There was an excellent turn out of MPs at the meeting on 27 June at Westminster. We were pleased that there was such solid political support not only from Labour MPs, but also from several SNP and Lib Dems. Laboriously I once again gave them all an update on the need to secure the entire unsolicited bid for the Type 45 destroyers and the two oilers.

Although we could not complain about the level of support we were receiving from the Scottish MPs I sensed a strange uneasiness among some of the Labour members. It was a feeling similar to the one I had got at the meeting with Wendy Alexander in that they knew more than they were telling us.

At the end of the meeting part two of my prediction came true as Sarwar informed us that another meeting had been arranged at the DTI with Brian Wilson. Poor Sarwar had recently injured his foot and was hobbling about in obvious pain and discomfort as he escorted us to the meeting with Wilson. To his credit Sarwar had been excelling in the increasing role as Mr Fixit when it came to arranging such meetings.

The discussions with Brian Wilson were strange. Limited in definitives, but heavy on hints, was how I evaluated it. However, Wilson's body language told me that all was not well. He was edgy as he raised the issue of what the consequences would be if we did not secure the oilers to plug the imminent gap in work. Although he was pleasant enough throughout the meeting we all got the impression that he could not wind it up quickly enough. The convenors all left that meeting perturbed and firmly of the opinion that a decision on the unsolicited bid was imminent.

Here we were, 10 July 2001 and almost a year to the day since we were saved from certain closure we were awaiting another vital decision. It was early morning, but already the hares were running. The convenors from both Govan and Scotstoun were summoned to the boardroom at Govan and informed that Hoon in Parliament would make an announcement in relation to the Type 45 contract.

It was expected about 3 p.m. with the company intending to call mass meetings in both yards as soon as possible afterwards. The Scotstoun convenors returned to their base whilst at Govan we sat clock-watching as the hours ticked by.

We held our breath as Hoon's statement was read.

"BAE Systems have been awarded the contract to build the first six Type 45 destroyers, along with the possibility of securing the further six."

Yes! Yes! Yes! I thought. Go on! Go on! The two oilers? Sadly it was not to be as the MoD stated that they did not feel that there was a current requirement for them.

The news on the oilers was not totally unexpected, as recent vibes had been indicating such a result. We had just digested the implications of the statement when, bang, disaster struck. The company issued a further statement.

"Due to BAE Systems failing to secure an agreement with the MoD for the building of two Auxiliary Oilers, there is a significant gap in work on the Clyde between now and commencement of work on the Type 45 contract in early 2003. This situation has been exacerbated by the delay in commencing work on the ALSL contract. The company therefore regrets the necessity to issue an HR1 redundancy notice for one thousand job losses between September and December 2001."

We reeled at this announcement and there was cause for further dismay when the company announced their build strategy for the Type 45 contract. Govan would do all steel preparation and fabrication work with Scotstoun concentrating on block unit construction and outfitting.

Then the bombshell! Barrow would launch and complete the Type 45s with only the first of class being launched on the Clyde at Scotstoun.

This news was initially met with disbelief, followed by anger and resentment. The Clyde felt betrayed. We had done all the footslogging and lobbying in London. We had mounted the political and media campaign to assist the company in securing the order.

Furthermore Scotstoun were the experts at the construction of this type of ship and it was difficult to figure out the logic behind the company's build strategy. On the Clyde there was a sense of total betrayal by the company as we had expected all the steelwork to be done at Govan and the launching and outfitting at Scotstoun. The unions at both yards felt as if we had been used and abused by the company.

What a bittersweet day it had turned out to be.

Having won a multi-million pound contract that would secure the Clyde's long-term future what should have been a day for joyful celebration was marred by that horrific sting in the tail resulting from the announcement of a thousand redundancies. It was as if you had won the lottery only to be told soon after that you shared it with a million other people.

The media were keen to get the reaction of the unions. What could you say, other than that we were devastated at the announcement of the job losses. We did, however, remind reporters that despite our disappointment and grave concern at the proposed job cuts, we had to acknowledge that the announcement of us winning the first six Type 45 destroyers would bring years of stability to the Clyde.

I emphasised that the unions regarded the number of job losses as being grossly excessive and that we would be discussing this issue with the company. The combined number of employees at Govan and Scotstoun was approximately three thousand and there was no way that the company could justify such savage cuts.

Personally I was seriously disappointed at the number of redundancies but realistically I knew BAE were restructuring for the Type 45s and we had a gap in work. And, perhaps selfishly, I took the Govan view that although any job losses concerned me I felt we were lean and mean and the impact on Govan would be proportionately small with the bulk of any cuts coming at Scotstoun.

The following day Wendy Alexander called us to a meeting at the Scottish Executive Office in Glasgow. She announced that a Task Force was being set up immediately to look at all issues relating the future of shipbuilding on the Clyde. The announcement of government Task Forces is often met in many quarters by cynicism and disdain. Rightly or wrongly they were often thought of as 'talking shops' or 'smoke screens' to get the politicians off the hook. Generally speaking, their main role was to provide support and facilities to get those affected by redundancy into new jobs.

However, there was a widely held perception that the jobs marketed by the relevant agencies were usually menial, low paid and unskilled. Certainly it had often been said to me that when skilled workers lost their job in manufacturing industries, they did not want to be patronised by being offered jobs in call centres, hamburger stalls or in the service industries.

Workers who have often come from highly skilled and relatively well-paid jobs wanted to be placed in similar work to that which they had left. Unfortunately, reality often dictated that there were no jobs available in their previous field of work.

At the Task Force meeting the convenors emphasised that shipbuilding had an ageing workforce with recent studies revealing an average age of forty-seven, a figure well above other industries. We also explained that a very high proportion of our labour force had spent a considerable part, if not all, of their working lives in the industry. We knew it would be a daunting challenge to get the workers to adopt a positive approach to the apparent need for re-training for an occupation outside the shipbuilding industry.

Unlike many others attending the meeting I had experience of working with a previous government Task Force. The setting up of one in March 1999 under Lord Gus Macdonald had given me an insight in how they operated. That Task Force, however, was significantly different from the one now being proposed by Enterprise Minister Wendy Alexander.

Back in 1999 the Task Force was comprised of only a handful of people with an uncomplicated task, which was to find a new owner for the Govan shipyard and Kvaerner Energy in

Clydebank. The proposals now being put forward by Wendy Alexander would cover a wide range of issues. Although the trade unions supported them all, we emphasised that our principal aim was to reduce the numbers of redundancies.

At this stage of the meeting we felt it was essential to put our marker down with the company and demand that they explore all avenues with us, to reduce the number of job losses. BAE responded by indicating that they would now accept applications for voluntary redundancy. We urged them to make serious efforts to re-train employees from areas affected into sectors where there was a skill shortage. Redeployment and relocation to other BAE Systems UK-wide was another concept that we expected the company to support.

After broad discussion the final structure of the Task Force was agreed. It would consist of representatives from various government agencies such as Scottish Enterprise, the Department of Trade and Industry and the Employment Service. Other representation would be from Glasgow City Council, the Scottish Office, BAE Directors and the trade unions.

Wendy Alexander would head the Task Force with Brian Wilson, George Foulkes MP (Carrick, Cumnock and Doon Valley and, since June 2005, Baron Foulkes of Cumnock) and two MSPs, Gordon Jackson (Glasgow Govan) and Pauline McNeil (Glasgow Kelvin) completing the political involvement. With the first compulsory redundancies scheduled for mid-October there was much to be done.

At the first official meeting on 14 August I detected that the company delegation were rather uneasy in this environment. It was hardly surprising, as they were constantly under the cosh from Alexander and the unions. I immediately put Managing Director Simon Kirby on the spot about the continuing delays in starting work on the ALSL contract knowing that if we had confirmation of work commencing we could pressurise the company into reducing the number of redundancies.

Alexander questioned the company about the proposed investment programme for the Clyde with the convenors adding that presentations on investment were one thing, seeing new machinery, bricks and mortar was another. The company reported that the voluntary redundancy exercise had resulted in ninety-seven applications across both yards. They also confirmed that they would be presenting proposals for various re-training packages to the convenors over the next few weeks.

The following week the main board held a seminar at a Glasgow hotel for senior managers and Clyde union convenors. It was to be a state of the nation style update and a rallying call to us all to meet the present difficulties and challenges with purpose and a sense of leadership. Director after director spoke about different aspects of the company's future and the way forward.

At a similar seminar in March there had been a considerable input from the audience and an air of optimism reigned. This one was different. Now there was a climate of mixed emotions ranging from anxiety to anger, suspicion top disillusionment. This was not a captive audience. There were few questions and a distinct lack of rapport between the directors and the audience. In fairness the directors could hardly be faulted for attempting to motivate those people who were expected to lead the workforces.

Had the directors detected that this meeting was dying on its feet, or were they oblivious to what was going on around them? Had they not sussed that, under the proposed redundancies, a fair percentage of those present would not survive?

I suppose they were in a no-win situation. Damned if they did not hold a seminar to rally the troops, and damned if they were seen to be not leading from the front.

At the mid-day break there was a sombre atmosphere. No buzz, no spark, just an overwhelming feeling that most of those present would have just preferred to be back in Govan or Scotstoun.

I wondered if the directors had any idea of the impact that the redundancy announcement was having across everyone on the Clyde. The uncertainty had unleashed a cauldron of mixed human emotions that would test even the most resilient of us.

Simon Kirby was keen to stress that the directors fully appreciated it would be a difficult period for all of us over the next few months. When he invited questions or points of view from the audience, I rose.

"Simon, you've just indicated that the directors fully understood that this would be a difficult period for us all. You may regard my next comment as over dramatic. Indeed, you may even regard it as negative. If so, it's not meant to be. I want you and your colleagues on the board to fully understand what lies ahead of us. It will not be a difficult time. It will be a nightmare experience that will affect us all. It will be painful, depressing and stressful for all of us on the front line.

"May I also warn you that even after the job losses are completed those of us who remain in the company will not be an all-singing, all-dancing band of happy troupers. We will be traumatised, shell shocked and exhausted. Believe me, the way forward after the redundancies will be as great a challenge to us all as the present difficulties are. I sincerely hope you all realise that, and display leadership that will show compassion and tact throughout this difficult period. Incidentally, in case you are concerned by my comments, let me assure you that I have great personal optimism for the future of the Clyde. I merely want to make sure you do not underestimate the profound sensitivity that needs to exist in our current situation."

Kirby seemed somewhat taken aback and I saw from the expressions on the faces of some of the directors that my comments had not won universal approval. Had I been too blunt and too near the bone? Perhaps, but I felt it had to be said. At least they would be in no doubt in the months ahead as to what the workers would have to endure.

Back in the yard the company's decision to accept applications for voluntary redundancy was continuing to receive a poor response from the workers in Govan and Scotstoun. The convenors in both yards were unconvinced that BAE had been putting maximum effort into reducing the numbers. We made our views known in no uncertain terms that we expected results on re-training programmes and redeployment to other BAE sites.

The Scotstoun convenors indicated that, as there was little tangible evidence that the company was seriously attempting to reduce the number of job losses, there was a risk of industrial action from their workforce.

At Govan, although we shared the frustration felt by the Scotstoun unions and workers, we did not support the strategy of taking industrial action, as we did not believe it would improve the current situation. The view in Scotstoun was that their frustration at lack of progress had to be given a profile in the political, media and public arena. At Govan we had come through a long difficult campaign without losing a single day's production whilst at the same time keeping our profile high in the media.

The unions at Govan could see no gain in altering tactics now and indeed we felt that there was always a risk that in taking industrial action you might damage your situation. If the media were in any way to be critical of such action public support could be quickly lost.

But, it was no surprise that following a mass meeting in Scotstoun on 5 September the workforce decided on a one day stoppage combined with an overtime ban. Over at Govan word of the walk out spread quickly. A small minority of Govan workers and some of the Scotstoun crew currently on transfer made representations to me and my co-stewards that we should support Scotstoun.

A small percentage of the workforce in Govan indicated that they were concerned that we would be regarded as 'bottle merchants' for not showing unity with Scotstoun. I reminded those who raised such issues that it was the Govan shop stewards responsibility to lead the workforce and advise them on what course of action we should follow and that the shop stewards would be accountable to the workforce for all the actions and decisions that were made. We fully accepted that we were accountable to the workforce for all the actions and decisions that we made.

As the day wore on, it became abundantly clear that the vast majority of workers had supported our judgement on that issue. As expected the media had a field day, posing the question continuously that the unions in Govan and Scotstoun had fallen out with each other about Govan's decision to work normally. I refuted this, emphasising that it was the prerogative of Scotstoun to do what they felt was appropriate, and the same held true at Govan.

Despite what people perceived the situation to be, the unions in Govan and Scotstoun agreed on most issues, but not all. We were not clones. There was a degree of animosity within some sections of the Scotstoun yard at our decision to work normally. We regretted that such a view existed, nevertheless we remained convinced that we had to stand by our conviction that a walkout would not improve the situation.

Two days later a planned meeting between the Clyde convenors, full time union officers and the company was cancelled at the last minute, with the company indicating that the talks would not go ahead until Scotstoun had removed the overtime ban and returned to normal working. It was a standoff position that could not be sustained and may have given the company the opportunity to cease further talks concerning reducing the redundancies. A couple of days later the overtime ban was lifted and normal communications with the company resumed.

On the ALSL front I felt compelled to write to Wendy Alexander to re-emphasise that the delay on commencing work on the contract was creating a grave situation regarding the gap in work. I informed her that failure to get that order signed, sealed and delivered soon would significantly hinder our attempts to get the number of redundancies reduced. I was banking on the fact that she would make strong representations in all the right places on our behalf.

The next Task Force meeting on 14 September at last produced signs of progress in relation to reducing the number of job losses. A combination of voluntary redundancy applications linked to re-training and redeployment to other sites had reduced the figure from one thousand to seven hundred. Undoubtedly it was reasonable progress. However, we indicated to the company and the Task Force that there were still opportunities to reduce the number yet further.

At the meeting Danny Carrigan, national officer for AEEU, confirmed the trade union official policy of being opposed to compulsory redundancies. Danny was of the view that the problem could be resolved without any compulsory redundancies. In principle I supported his views but in reality even at my highest peak of optimism I could not agree with his evaluation that there would be no compulsory losses.

In the current climate I told myself that a fifty per cent reduction in job losses to five hundred would be no mean feat. That was not a defeatist attitude merely a realistic appraisal of the situation. In the meantime in Govan and Scotstoun we would bite and scratch for every job.

There was always this fundamental difference between the full time officials like Danny Carrigan and me in terms of our tactical approach. How you say things, when you say them and most importantly what message you put out. Carrigan had made a statement that there would be no compulsory redundancies, but how did he know that for sure and how could this be achieved? I, on the other hand, was devastated when the redundancies were announced but took the view that the challenge was now to save as many jobs as possible.

I couldn't accept the fact that officials like Carrigan were not facing up to the reality that there would be some redundancies because of the gap in work we faced. And Danny wasn't having to talk to the workforce on a daily basis, constantly being put on the spot about how the unions would stop there being any compulsory lay-offs.

I never told them that because I simply didn't believe it. What I did tell them, because I did believe it, was that we could cut those losses. I told them we would move mountains to mitigate the numbers losing their jobs through new start programmes, re-training and redeployment in BAE's vast empire. There would also be voluntary redundancies and we would push harder for the ALSL project. More than anything though, I felt because of everything we'd been through since we fought the closure of our yard, I had to be totally honest with them.

Giving Danny Carrigan the benefit of the doubt, perhaps his comments were made in the laudable, but somewhat naïve, belief that if he hadn't come out fighting the company would have thought they were getting too easy a ride and the unions were showing signs of weakness.

But, a company like BAE Systems will not give in to intimidation and I thought a more subtle strategy was called for. And, of course, it's okay for national officers to adopt the bullish approach, but when ultimately that doesn't work it's never the responsibility of the national officers to explain to the workforce. That painful duty always falls to the local convenors.

Any statement I made to the workers had to be on the basis of what I'd told them before. There would be redundancies but that didn't mean we wouldn't fight to save as many jobs as possible. The question you have to ask the yard is do you want to be told there will be no compulsory redundancies when it's obvious there's a gap in our order book or do you want to be told there will be lay-offs but we'll do our best to minimise them.

The total eventually fell to around four hundred and fifty with about ninety at Govan, one hundred and fifty at Scotstoun and just over two hundred at Barrow, and I, along with the other convenors, had to tell the workforce. But, we took no flak because we never said we could save all the jobs. We'd been consistent throughout. How Danny Carrigan comes to terms with the gulf between reality and his rhetoric I'll never know.

Around the same period there were whispers that BAE were in advanced talks with an unnamed ship owner to possibly build supply vessels for the North Sea. This work was in the commercial field, not MoD naval work. There would no doubt be fierce competition for such a contract. Nevertheless there were indications that this contract could be attainable. We realised that success in securing this would be a godsend. Without flying a kite I genuinely believed that if we could conclude the signing for the ALSLs in conjunction with us securing the Platform Supply Vessel (PSV) contract, the impending gap in work would be drastically reduced. This would enable us to argue strongly for a massive reduction in the number of proposed redundancies.

Achieving both of these aims would be our target over the following few weeks. If the company intended to instigate compulsory redundancies from the expected date of 9 October it was vital that we got positive answers soon.

Shortly afterwards an interesting development arose when the company decided to send the Auxiliary Oiler No. 1 up to the Clyde from Barrow, for completion. The indications were that a considerable amount of Clyde labour would be required to complete this contract. Despite the fact that the company were not definitive in the timescale for this work, we believed that it would extend into early 2002.

With the two Auxiliary Oilers now under the final stages of construction on the Clyde, one at Govan and the other at Inchgreen Dock in Greenock, we were of the opinion that the company would be compelled to review their redundancy programme timescale.

Over the next few weeks we pressed the company to carry out such a review, as we were totally convinced it was seriously flawed. The company remained mute maintaining that the proposed redundancies would be completed by the end of December 2001.

9 October was D-day in relation to the redundancies. In Govan and Scotstoun there was a high level of tension, due to the fact that all the workers were aware that legally the company had met all their obligations in respect of the ninety day consultation period. We were now certain that the oiler transferred from Barrow and now based at Inchgreen still had a considerable amount of work to get done on it before it would be completed.

At our weekly consultation meeting between the company and the convenors we put our cards on the table to the Clyde Operations Director emphasising that the company was on the verge of losing all credibility with the workforce if they did not review the current workload. We urged them to postpone the proposed compulsory redundancies until after the New Year. We were concerned that BAE was reluctant to face up to the fact that they may have got their redundancy numbers wrong.

The convenors were not interested in trying to score points or adopt an 'I told you so' approach merely so that BAE would do a realistic appraisal of the current situation. At this meeting the Operations Director looked increasingly uneasy. We were firmly of the view that he probably agreed with our analysis but that he was under instructions from his superiors to maintain the stance that Auxiliary Oiler No. 1 would be completed by the end of the year, as would the redundancy exercise.

October's Task Force meeting reported the exit of workers at both yards who'd opted for voluntary redundancy. There had also been further progress made on re-training and relocation bringing the number of jobs at risk of compulsory redundancy at that time down to just over six hundred. We were continuing to make slow but definite progress.

Simon Kirby reported that the ALSL contract talks were still ongoing and that they would be concluded shortly. Our patience was being stretched to the limit on this issue and we were at pains to emphasise to him that although we did not doubt his word, those contract talks were complex and detailed and with every passing day the workforce were becoming more exasperated at the seemingly endless delays.

I raised the subject of the PSV contract and I sensed a degree of evasiveness from both Simon Kirby and the politicians. From past experience that spelt business sensitivity with a big S. Although I continued to prod on this matter suffice it to say that Kirby's response was brief and guarded as he stated,

"Talks are ongoing between interested parties and it is commercially sensitive."

Personally I was satisfied that talks were still ongoing and remained optimistic that we could secure the contract. Several days later, the company informed us that there would be no compulsory redundancies in November. Even more importantly they now intended to review the current workload. It would appear once again that my view expressed several weeks earlier on this matter had proved to be accurate.

The Task Force meeting on 9 November revealed that the number of possible compulsory redundancies continued to decrease and was now down to five hundred and twenty. Again, progress was being made with the current number almost half the original number of a thousand.

I was bleary eyed during that meeting, having been awake until the early hours of the morning, awaiting word on the birth of my third grandchild. The arrival of James was a personal high tinged with sadness at what we, as a family, had lost during the turbulent three years of the campaign. The death of Isabel's mum and dad had resulted in a traumatic time for us all. Yet the birth of two grandchildren in the same period had helped ease some of the pain. Following a couple of days of 'granddad' leave, it was back to the grindstone.

On 15 November following a further review of the workload the company announced there would now be no compulsory redundancies in 2001. Over the next few days rumours were rife that the formal signing for the ALSL contract was imminent.

The previous week had seen the commencement of a major investment in Govan. Significantly it had always been indicated to us that the investment would not be rubber stamped until the ALSL contract was concluded.

Monday 19 November was another red-letter day for us. The ALSL contract was signed at last. A flurry of early morning activity from the media had alerted us to the fact that the contract would be completed that day. By mid-morning, BAE Systems Marine Communications Manager John Bonnick indicated that a press conference would be held at 1 p.m. for the official signing.

Wendy Alexander was accompanied by George Foulkes, Minister of State at the Scottish Office and a senior executive from the Defence Procurement Agency.

Obviously, both Foulkes and Alexander set out to get maximum political gain for the government with Govan securing the ALSL contract. I didn't begrudge them their moment of 'spin'.

We had received significant support and assistance from many Labour politicians and to not acknowledge that would have been unappreciative and unfair. Indeed, in the broadest political arena involving all parties we had received a high level of support. When the press conference opened up for the question and answer session a reporter from *The Herald* questioned Alexander if the securing of the ALSL contract had indeed been such good news in light of the ongoing redundancy programme on the Clyde. Wendy Alexander was not slow to remind everyone that it was a good news day for the Clyde and that the media should not present a negative slant to it.

I was also determined to put the record straight on what the ALSL contract meant to Govan and the Clyde. I asked George Foulkes if I could make a statement.

"For anybody here today that has any doubt that this is a good day for Govan, let me remind them of this. In July 1999 this yard was within forty-eight hours of closure. Today, more than two years later we are now signing a contract that will provide work on the Clyde until 2005. This contract provides a strong base to take us through until work commences on the Type 45 contract in 2003. Jointly these contracts bring a decade's work into Govan and Scotstoun. From where I am standing this is a memorable day for Govan and I can assure you that it will be regarded as such by all the workers in Govan.

"Should any section of the media decide to portray it as anything other than a good news day, they will have done the yard and the workers a great disservice. Despite my total confidence for the future at Govan shipyard, the trade unions fully accept the difficulty and disappointment that the redundancy announcement has presented to us. We have been working and will continue to work with BAE and the Scottish Executive to reduce the number of redundancies. We will face that challenge with the same commitment and conviction that we have displayed over the last three years. Nobody should be in any doubt this is a good day for shipbuilding on the Clyde."

I knew instantly that as they all reflected on my words, they realised I spoke the truth.

January 2002 arrived with the disappointing announcement that we had lost out to Turkey for the PSV contract. It was now apparent that the company would shortly implement the compulsory redundancy programme. The concerted efforts of the unions, company and the Task Force had reduced the number of compulsory redundancies to a final total of four hundred and fifty from the original number of a thousand. That number was very close to what I had predicted several months previously.

The hopes and expectations expressed by some full time officials of zero compulsory redundancies had sadly never been a realistic objective. These job losses at Govan and Scotstoun would be a bitter pill to swallow especially as work had now commenced on the ALSL contract. Sadly this work had started too late to secure all the jobs. The redundancy programme would be another painful exercise to go through between January and April.

In the harsh light of day the workers at both yards realised that with a temporary shortage of work it would have been futile to oppose some redundancies. Instead the unions continued to make concerted efforts later in the year to bring many of the workers back when the ALSL contract was in full flow.

I have often reflected on our change of fortunes over the last three years looking back to February 1999 when we faced having no owner, no work and, many said, no hope. Many days, weeks and months of stress, frustration and disappointment had been put behind us and we were now witnessing the dawn of a new era with a decade of work ahead. Who was it that said dreams do not come true? Send them to me and I will tell them, "they do in Govan."

On a further personal note the campaign had opened my eyes in many ways and enabled me to find out a lot about myself. I realised how important my family was to me and how fortunate I was to have them around me when I needed their support. I also learned that you often need to be single-minded if you wish to achieve your goal. There were numerous occasions throughout the campaign when I was pressurised to alter my personal style and also to change the campaign strategy. This I only did if I believed it would help the fight to save the yard.

Looking back I believe it was necessary on occasions to remain single-minded or risk losing sight of our objective. I also realised that the margin between success and failure is often a hairs breadth. Throughout our campaign had we at any time allowed our resolve to waver, lost the media profile or slackened the pressure in the political arena Govan shipyard would surely have closed. These factors allied to good fortune resulted in us achieving our goal.

Consistently over the previous three years I had told all those that were prepared to listen that, God willing, I would retire out of Govan in fourteen years. I also stated that the day I walked out of the yard for the last time, having spent virtually my whole working life in there since leaving school, youngsters would be entering the yard to start their working life. I would hope that it gives as much to them as it has given to me.

An unknown Clydeside orator once stated,

'We don't just build ships on the Clyde, we turn boys into men.'

I have had the privilege not only to work with such men, but to represent them. A countless number of people have asked me how our campaign succeeded where others had failed. Political and public support, a sympathetic media and simple luck have been put forward by many as the principal factors for our success.

They were indeed all contributory factors but the real driving force behind us was the human factor. Simple attributes such as determination, commitment and resilience drove our campaign. However, the ultimate attribute was belief. The belief that we could succeed against the odds but most importantly the belief we had in our industry and ourselves. We proved that in a world that is becoming increasingly materialistic, there is still room for human endeavour.

EPILOGUE
2002–PRESENT

We can't take our eyes off the ball…

25

IN TERMS of jobs the three yards now have the following core workforce.

Barrow has three thousand, and Govan and Scotstoun each have about fifteen hundred. Barrow has had a lot of redundancies. Govan has gained with about 2000 in Govan now including sub-contract workers.

Our workforce has increased significantly, including the transfers from Scotstoun as well as a lot of new starts plus apprentices. In eight years we've brought in about five hundred apprentices to Govan and Scotstoun.

No matter what else has happened the Clyde yards are much bigger in terms of numbers than they were in 1999.

In the early days policy was dictated to by the hierarchy at Barrow and there was frustration at Govan as many complained that our unique culture was being eroded.

Initially we were to be taken over by GEC and GEC owned Barrow and Scotstoun. So if you're a big establishment with, at that time, five thousand people and you also have a yard with two and a half thousand and suddenly this small, relatively insignificant and not particularly wanted yard appears on the horizon what's the natural reaction? You're not going to welcome them, you're going to dictate, and you're going to dominate them. It's like armies, like powers of influence. It was quite clear that GEC weren't listening to Gunnar or our board of directors. They were minor pawns in the game, almost certainly to be dismissed at some point.

All philosophies and dogma came from Barrow. And of course we were about to experience what Scotstoun had already experienced, that Barrow were the heavyweights. Scotstoun went up the pecking order, because Govan were the new kids on the block.

In early meetings with the BAE bosses, July and August 1999 I was asked how long it would take for the Clyde to develop as a cultural mirror image at the two yards. I told them ten years and they were taken aback as they'd heard I came from the optimistic school of thinking.

I told them I came from the realistic school of thinking and that cultures evolve and they would not change overnight. Eight years down the line that prediction has proved decidedly accurate.

The ten years was a calculated guess. What we had were three shipyards all completely different with different cultures. Barrow, down in England, built submarines, was massive and used to calling the tune. Scotstoun, heavily steeped in naval work with an expertise for Royal Navy vessels. And us, basically innocents abroad.

In my view we are now seventy to eighty per cent towards that change in culture. To understand where we are now, you need to understand where we were in 2000. Govan and Scotstoun were a mile apart geographically, but we were a million light years apart culturally. There was a gigantic task to bring us together.

We had a tome, not a book, of different wages, conditions, flexibility agreements, working practices. At that time all three yards believed they were superior.

So what has happened? There was a massive amount of horse-trading over a long period of time, initially between the yards. Meetings were attended by bosses at BAE and the union officials.

It was a minefield. All the yards had different wages, working hours and practices. So, tradesmen at the three yards, all doing basically the same job, were being paid different wages to do it.

On average, wages were marginally higher at Govan, then Barrow, then Scotstoun. The differences were up to seven or eight pounds a week. We're not talking huge amounts, but they were enough to ensure there would be ill-feeling among the workforces.

Other differences included shift allowances, management structures, pension schemes, flexibility agreements. I think the wages were slightly better at Govan because the merchant yards tended to have higher wages than their naval counterparts.

The task of harmonising these issues was horrendous because each yard didn't want to concede rights they'd fought long and hard for which were better than the other two. It was a long struggle.

But in actual fact, the real change turned out to be cultural. Scotstoun was absolutely steeped in naval history, building a wide range of frigates, destroyers, patrol vessels etc., very much the old Ministry of Defence where you thought in terms of cost plus profit. Govan was the opposite. Commercial contracts meant you quoted a price and if the project overran it was too bad for the yard.

Bringing those two potential strengths together, the knowledge of the customer from Scotstoun with the commercial sharpness of Govan, was a nightmare.

Some conditions we had to give up in order to achieve harmony with Scotstoun and Barrow. At the first wage negotiations for example we got a smaller increase than the other yards to reflect the differentials between the three of us. Eventually we would all be paid the same amount for the same job. What Govan began to get was better holidays, very importantly, full sick pay when you were off and that made a big difference and medical leave to attend hospital.

When I evaluate everything over the yards in terms of who gained most from the changes to working conditions then it was Govan, most certainly. Who lost most, or stood still most? Barrow. Remember, big brother would always have the best conditions because big brother was big brother so obviously the workforce there had negotiated strongly around conditions. So although we appeared to do badly out of the wage negotiations, I and the other stewards at Govan realised that would be our big dose of medicine. Once we took that dose there would be a lot of sugar to disguise the taste in terms of our improved working practices.

So how did this go down with the workforce at Govan? Right from the start, they had displayed their usual pragmatism. They had also been generally very trusting of the way the convenors ran the campaign and conducted union business. If you take someone through a war and your territory is safe after it then generally you have a trusting mentality that if you come through periods of adversity and you face another challenge then you'll come through that too.

Add to that the fact that everyone in Govan knew we had two much larger groups of workers to contend with at Scotstoun and Barrow and ultimately had we opposed the deal on wages it would simply have been imposed upon us and we'd have been left vulnerable.

We had a new owner and knew that we had to get security and stability, and that if we had been reckless then it might have given BAE Systems the excuse to concentrate their efforts on the other two yards and hang us out to dry. I also felt that in the longer term when there was more harmony and the dust had settled, Govan would come out of the deal in good shape and with an enhanced reputation.

The real acid test though was how the convenors and I would be able to persuade workers coming to Govan from Scotstoun in large numbers that managing and adapting to change was vital. We were moving towards a singular 'Clyde culture' across the two yards north of the border but in the early years it was horrendous. I would say even more stressful than the actual campaign to save Govan.

Some who moved were quite happy to come over and settled in very well. Others came over with a bit of apprehension which was understandable and there were some who came with varying degrees of resentment. Although both yards worked a thirty-seven hour week, shifts at Govan started earlier and finished earlier. And, Scotstoun's dinner breaks were longer. We worked later on a Friday.

Shift patterns had to change. Govan had a back shift and Scotstoun didn't. That would prove to be one of the most contentious issues. Flexibility was sometimes interpreted differently on both sites with some of the employees from Scotstoun regarding Govan's structure as too expansive and concessionary. Some at Scotstoun thought we'd 'sold the jerseys.'

I often heard the quote,

"We don't do that at Scotstoun."

How burning were those words? Ferociously burning, because they made me realise how tough it was going to be to deliver integration and harmony of thought and purpose on the Clyde.

In the early days, the pressure of this and my natural defensive instinct led me to say,

"You're no' at Scotstoun noo."

Looking back I could cringe at using such a thoughtless response, but in those early, hectic days it seemed the obvious reaction.

Workers had no say in who was transferred. BAE simply told them to swap from one yard to the other. In the early days we had a negotiated allowance but these were phased out within the first two years of unification.

That migration of workers from Govan to Scotstoun was less than a hundred and half of them were office staff who tended to adapt more easily. Fewer than fifty production workers were moved and that's a small number compared to the several hundred who transferred to Govan.

There were massive numbers for steelwork, engineering, pipe work, electricals. So the scale of adjustment was very difficult and I used to despair and become utterly frustrated at having to repeat that wearisome phrase,

"You're no' at Scotstoun noo."

Those words always sounded confrontational. They weren't meant to, but they had to be said. The big challenge was to make people understand that in time there wouldn't be any differentials. The hours would be the same, the dinner breaks would be the same, the shifts would be the same, and the pensions would be the same.

Culture governs everything. How we work, how we think. So the first three years of that migration were a nightmare. Endless attempts to make people from Scotstoun feel welcome and to justify how we did things at Govan. A lot of them did adapt, but there are still small pockets to this day who refuse to adapt and who I dare say will never settle down because they don't want to. I always knew it would it would be a gigantic task.

But, on the other hand, migration between the yards has now been accepted by the vast majority of both workforces as the norm. There was a lot of movement in the first few years, but it's become more spasmodic now and I think people have got used to it.

It's important to remember that in the early days, post-takeover, there were plenty of Doubting Thomases that thought that Govan would be used to build a couple of minor orders and then would be shut down. If you remember, John Reid had told me in July 1999 that getting a new owner would be the easier part of the mission. The real test would be to build a long term future.

In November 2003, there was a welcome, if unexpected, diversion from the day-to-day running of union business at the yard. I arrived in London to attend a routine union meeting and Isabel phoned me to say a letter from Tony Blair had dropped onto the mat. My initial reaction was tongue in cheek; what have I done wrong now, because some of my communications with politicians ended up with me getting some sort of rebuke. But, Isabel was adamant, she said, "No, you're getting the MBE." I told her to stop the wind up and I forgot all about it because I thought it was a joke. It was only later in the afternoon when I called her back that she convinced me she was serious. She read me out the contents and I knew then she couldn't have made it up.

I could hardly believe it. It was a major shock to my system. I thought those kind of honours only went to people who fitted the establishment profile. It had never remotely crossed my mind. A union convenor at Govan getting the MBE!

Isabel, Julie, Amanda and my eldest grand-daughter Emma travelled down to London for the big day in July 2004 where we linked up with my son Fraser who's in the Metropolitan Police.. We went the night before the big event to have dinner at the invitation of MP Mohammad Sarwar who was his usual convivial self. He did his best to calm my nerves but I could feel the butterflies in my stomach as we all woke up the following morning.

You couldn't make up what happened next. It was 8 a.m. and I went to my luggage to take out the suit I was going to wear. I wasn't the slightest bit worried as I looked through the bags, but I got considerably more agitated as I realised, disaster! No suit!

There was no point in blaming anybody. I just had to get another suit. We asked some of the staff in the hotel where there was a men's shop on the way to the Palace and they directed us to Marks & Spencer in Oxford Street. We all piled into a taxi, explained the situation and he drove like the clappers. While he waited for us on Oxford Street, I legged it into the shop. It was now 9.20 a.m. and we had to be at the Palace for 10 a.m.

I was sweating profusely as I bolted up to the men's dept. The sales assistant must have thought I was daft when I barked at him,

"I need a dark suit, now."

He started the usual sales patter asking me what size I was, what colour I wanted, what style. I barked at him again,

"Look, I'm getting the MBE at Buckingham Palace in forty minutes and I haven't got a suit. I don't care what colour it is so long as it's dark and it fits me."

He got the message! The assistant lifted a suit off the rail. I grabbed it and ran into the fitting room. Thank goodness it looked okay. About two minutes later I came out wearing the suit with my jeans in a small bag. I couldn't have found one that fitted me better if I'd looked for an hour and a half.

It cost £150, but it was worth it. We made it to the Palace by the skin of our teeth. We entered by the front gates with our passes and I was directed under a main arch into a holding area with about thirty people who were also getting an MBE. Opulent doesn't do it justice. You actually sank into the carpets because the pile was so thick.

Because I was limited on the numbers of people who could actually come into the Palace, Amanda and wee Emma went to the London Eye and said they meet us later for the official photos. Isabel, Julie and Fraser were ushered away to the Grand Hall where the presentations were to be made.

When they start the ceremony you're lined up in alphabetical order which put me almost at the end of the queue. We there then ushered along a corridor with oak panels and paintings. When you look into the hall you can see the Queen standing on a small podium. One of the flunkies briefs you to go forward and make a slight bow of your head.

As the equerry handed over the medal, the Queen told me she visited Govan ten years previously to launch a ship. I remembered the event. She said she was aware of the recent difficulties Govan had been having and that she was delighted we appeared to have overcome those problems.

The actual wording of the award was interesting since it wasn't for services to trade unionism. I was still seen as a grass roots minion and the union hierarchy would have viewed it with a degree of resentment since the MBE hadn't been given to someone from their elevated ranks. I received it for services to industrial relations and I've never looked on it as a reward for me. I was proud to accept it on behalf of the workers who'd given their all during those six months we fought so hard to keep Govan open. It was an acknowledgment of the ordinary people in our industry of whom I was just one.

I received congratulation messages from all over the place, including a letter from the First Minister at the time, Jack McConnell. In it he said I'd made an "... important contribution to Scottish shipbuilding and industrial relations. Your approach is constructive, seeking to work with a wide range of partners, and taking a view beyond purely sectoral interests. But you have also been a real champion for the interests of your members and the need to bring young people into the industry."

Many of the full time union officials I had crossed swords with, and still do to this day, would do well to read those words. Not one of them has ever said well done. I do think that it's a deliberate snub to me, but it's more of a kick in the teeth to all of their colleagues at Govan.

Between 2000 and 2004 there was constant change at the head of the company with BAE gradually removing most of the old GEC directors. My old sparring partner Rigby and Simon Kirby are both away along with Leggater.

But, we are now engaging a new generation of shipbuilders. Central to our long term future was winning the battle to take on apprentices.

BAE always accepted we had to employ some, around thirty or forty a year was their projection. But, we told them they were kidding themselves. With those numbers we had no long term future. We argued long and hard with them and convinced the then Trade Minister Wendy Alexander that we need more than double that just to be able to cope with what work we already had and more importantly what we were expecting.

The result is that on Clyde we did take on around a hundred apprentices a year from 2003. This batch became qualified tradesmen and tradeswomen by 2006. I'm delighted we've maintained that recruitment level up to the present day augmented by an annual intake of around a dozen graduates who'll eventually work in a variety of departments like finance, human resources, operations and procurement.

The first business plan for the Type 45 Destroyers in 2003 proposed that Govan would build steel units, Scotstoun would then put them together as blocks and finally they'd be assembled at Barrow for launching. This idea was absolutely bonkers and totally irrational, however, at that time in Govan we were in no position to influence a change in strategy. I was convinced though that the plan was seriously flawed and would be altered.

The Barrow influence began to wane from 2004 with the gradual removal of the old GEC management, and BAE systems produced business plan number two which removed them from involvement in the Type 45 programme. Govan would continue to build steel sections and Scotstoun would assemble and launch the six destroyers. However, in 2004 the company made their third and most radical change to the build strategy announcing that the first of class would be launched at Scotstoun while ships two to six would be assembled and launched at Govan. Final outfitting and commissioning (making sure everything works, from engines to generators to radar and armaments) in conjunction with some manufacturing work would be undertaken at Scotstoun.

Unsurprisingly, this decision was not well received in Scotstoun as they were the yard with the long-standing naval tradition. Looking back I believe the company was playing a very astute game because I find it hard to believe they changed their strategy three times. It's more likely that the final position was their underlying plan from the start.

By now, we'd got over the worst of the confrontations between the yard cultures and there was beginning to be a realisation that some things were irreversible. The word 'Clyde' was beginning to be used a lot more when talking about Govan and Scotstoun. Workers who'd moved to Govan, and vice versa were starting to take a more realistic view, appreciating that job security for all 'Clyde' workers was the main objective.

It was a fundamental change of thinking and a very important change of thinking. As long as the Clyde maintained a healthy order book what site you were on became a secondary consideration. Although not everybody subscribed to that view, and some still don't, the vast majority were seeing the advantages of a joined up approach.

You still got comments from some workers at Scotstoun like,

"Those were our ships, the Type 45s."

"We're the naval shipbuilders, how come Govan have got the destroyers?"

"We helped save Govan and this is the thanks we get."

These were all natural reactions, but most people realised it was Clyde and you had a secure job plus with all the movement between the yards the real heat had been taken out of the situation. So, I maintain that BAE played a very clever game and knew precisely what their strategy was from day one.

Talk of new aircraft carriers began to emerge in 2003 and BAE were determined to become prime contractor. However, they faced serious opposition from the French-based company Thales.

Those who know their ancient history will remember Thales as a pre-Socratic Greek philosopher and one of the Seven Sages of Greece. Many people regard him as the first philosopher in the Greek tradition as well as the father of science. Well, science plays a big part in the modern-day Thales.

According to its website profile;

Thales is a leading international electronics and systems group, serving defence, aerospace and security markets worldwide, supported by a comprehensive services offering. The group's civil and military businesses develop in parallel to serve a single objective: the security of people, property and nations. Leveraging a global network of more than 25,000 high-level researchers, Thales offers a capability unmatched in Europe to develop and deploy critical information systems. Thales employs 68,000 people in 50 countries and generates annual revenues of €12.6bn. (Thales Group 2007).

This was a serious, serious player who coincidentally has a manufacturing base in Glasgow two hundred yards from the Govan yard.

BAE are not popular in certain circles of the political arena or with the DTI because of their domination of the UK defence market. Despite knowing this, they were our employers so we lobbied far and wide on their behalf to get the work for the carriers.

During this period we tried to persuade the trades unions at Rosyth to join our bandwagon to become prime contractor. We had a meeting with them to get them to align themselves to BAE but they declined the offer preferring to sit on the fence to see who emerged victorious.

I don't want to gloat at what has happened since then. But, reflect on this. Thales was allocated as prime contractor and BAE Systems were very resentful of that as you can imagine. Later Kellogg Brown and Root were brought in as project managers. KBR are owned by Halliburton who were found to have links with the former American vice-president Dick Chaney.

Gordon Brown announced the full details of the Carrier Project in the first week of July 2007, after Tony Blair stepped down. Watch the shape of that project, because it will be heavily influenced by BAE Systems. Where is Thales? Bit part players, from what I can see, neutralized by the political lobbying of BAE. Baffled, bewildered and bemused by the political muscle of BAE Systems.

And what about KBR? They appear to have almost vanished into the horizon from what I can see.

And what's the reason for BAE's dominance? In my opinion it's because they are a well primed beast who excel in political lobbying and have the industrial muscle to outdo most other companies. They are also led by some seriously hard nosed businessmen, like Chief Executive Mike Turner. When British Aerospace plc and Marconi Electronic Systems merged in 1999 to create BAE Systems, Turner became Chief Operating Officer and then in March 2002, CEO.

Throughout my considerable dealings with Turner I always found him very direct, certainly someone who didn't suffer fools gladly, but who was very approachable. On one occasion in winter, he came to Govan and some of our senior management who were meeting the CEO for the first time were surprised at the light hearted and informal banter and winding up between us. I joked with him that his employees in the huge aerospace division were used to working in a warm and pleasant environment and were 'pussies' while Clydeside shipyard workers were hardy men of steel. Despite the fact he

302   BACK FROM THE BRINK

was blowing on his hands in the icy conditions, he laughed it off, adamant that he was no pussy!

So, who will be the biggest winner in the Carrier contract? There are no doubts in my mind that Clyde will be BIG in Carrier. VT Group will be relatively significant as will Barrow. Rosyth will get one of the carrier blocks and are scheduled to be the base for final assembly of these vast vessels. I would envisage during the final stages of assembly large numbers of employees from Clyde will be temporarily transferred to Rosyth to assist them in this complex task.

Three aircraft carriers have been commissioned; two for Britain and one for France. It was mooted for a period of time that the possibility existed for collaboration between the countries in the building of these vessels and we could end up building bits and pieces of each others carriers. This was a view I never subscribed to if only because Britain and France seldom sustain agreement on anything.

The French trade unions are also traditionally more reactionary than ours and if proposals like this had gathered momentum I have no doubts they would have scuppered them, strongly resisting any attempt to take work away from their own shipyards.

And then you have the last part of the jigsaw; BAE's proposed joint venture with the VT Group. There is an inevitability that within three years BAE will buy out VT and when this happens BAE will, astonishingly, control about ninety per cent of the shipbuilding capability in the UK. The government has not only signed off on this virtual monopoly, but has also agreed a fifteen year partnering deal with BAE that is proposed to deliver work into the 2020s.

At the heart of this, I believe, will be the much heralded Military Afloat Reach and Sustainability (MARS) programme. According to *Hansard*:

MARS will form an essential part of the UK's versatile maritime force, providing a suite of vessels to supply UK and allied vessels with fuel, food, ordnance and other support they need to sustain operations. MARS will also introduce a new capability, providing joint sea-based logistics for those operations where host-nation support is absent or limited or where we would wish to reduce our footprint ashore.

The MARS vessels will have some military features while being technically similar to specialist merchant ships. We therefore want the build of the MARS ships to harness the efficiency of specialist commercial shipbuilding practice. As indicated in the Defence Industrial Strategy, we expect the competition for the shipbuilding element of this project to be wide-ranging. UK yards and other suppliers will be given every opportunity to compete for this shipbuilding work and should see it as both a challenge and an opportunity to demonstrate world-class performance. With the high planned workload on CVF and Type 45, the complex warship design and integration capabilities that we intend to sustain in the UK will remain healthy for some years.

The key phrase there is,

'…we expect the competition for the shipbuilding element of this project to be wide-ranging. UK yards and other suppliers will be given every opportunity to compete for this shipbuilding work…'

The worry was much of the work would go to foreign yards, including some in Poland. There are twelve to fourteen vessels to be built including oilers, hospital ships and non-combatant boats. We have been actively campaigning to keep that work in the UK. We've put our case to Tony Blair, Gordon Brown and the Scottish Executive and in the first few months of 2007 we started to hear some positive noises from them.

But, since then, it's become apparent influential civil servants within the Defence Procurement Agency, were still vigorously pursuing the philosophy of what I call the 'Europeanisation' of the MARS contract. By which I mean opening it up to bidders from the low cost base eastern European shipyards.

If this happens, the bean-counters will win brownie-points for short term savings. However, the consequences would be dire for shipbuilding in the UK and we'd most certainly witness the virtual obliteration of our home-based industry.

You wouldn't need to be psychic to predict that once this happened those same yards who offered us bargain basement ships would hold us to ransom and charge inflated prices for building up our navy.

Britain historically has always maintained a strong naval capability to defend both its shores and its trade routes and this is still relevant today. Past governments have always recognised the need for a strong navy and the ability to build it on home shores and never rely on external sources. This long standing philosophy is now in serious jeopardy.

It is far from inconceivable that some of those countries who are now considered friendly trade partners could in an extremely volatile world become at best fair-weather friends and at worst, our enemies. We must not find ourselves in a position where we have given up the capability to construct our own fleet for the Royal Navy and are left exposed in potential conflicts around the world.

A few years ago I challenged the former Defence Secretary Geoff Hoon about whether or not we should be allowing other countries to build our naval ships. He told me he didn't personally subscribe to that view but some members of the chiefs-of-staff might do so. I asked him if he thought the public would agree with that view, because I thought most people would say that policy could be seen as a dereliction of duty in the defence of the country. He didn't give me an answer.

This eventuality could, however, to some degree happen within the context of the MARS programme. If all of the UK's shipbuilding resources are being utilised during the construction of the two carriers yards in the likes of Poland and Romania could secure some work. But, if this happens, I believe they will be the less complex ships like oil tankers.

As work on the carriers progressively winds down from 2012 onwards, it is imperative that the remaining part of this contract, approximately eight ships, is built in the UK.

There will be implications for the workforce on the Clyde as well. The yards are continuing to recruit, and it's envisaged that between 2010 and 2012 we will need several hundred extra workers. Where will they come from? Some will be Scottish, and inevitably because of our skills shortage and the free labour market, a percentage will also be from other European shipbuilding nations.

It's amazing to see how the pendulum of fate has swung and less than a decade after the Govan yard was days from total closure we could have a recruitment challenge.

We must never become complacent about our future or think about how good we were yesterday. The challenge is always tomorrow.

1.   An inspirational Jimmy Reid leading the '70s UCS work-in

2.   Govan Shipyard, 1977

3.   Portrait of the Author as a Young Man

4.   Kvaerner MD Gunnar Skjellbred, Task Force leader Sir Gavin Laird,
        and Industry Minister Lord Gus Macdonald tour the yard on the
                        day Kvaerner swung the axe

5. Kjell Almskog
   CEO Kvaerner

6. The unopened redundancy
   letters *en route* to Kvaerner HQ,
   London

7.   Celebrate good times, come on!

8.   Our proudest moment. Our jobs were safe… or so we thought

9. Celebrating our success with Lord Macdonald

10. Joe Brown, Jamie's oldest friend in the yard

11.   All smiles: Jamie with Secretary of State for Scotland, John Reid and
Govan MP Mohammad Sarwar

12.   Happy days. Jamie's grand-daughter Robyn arrived the same
day as the official take-over of the yard by BAE Systems

13.   The Webster family:
Left to right: Isabel, Emma, Amanda, Jamie, Robyn, Julie, Fraser, and Gizmo the dug!

14.   Jamie and 'My Rock', Isabel

15.   Jamie Webster MBE

"I received it for services to industrial relations and I've never looked on it as a reward for me. I was proud to accept it on behalf of the workers who'd given their all during those six months we fought so hard to keep Govan open. It was an acknowledgment of the ordinary people in our industry of whom I was just one."

APPENDICES

APPENDIX 1:

These are exact transcripts from taped interviews carried out by Russell Walker in 1999 when he was chief reporter with *Radio Clyde*. They help show how the story developed from March of that year through to the announcement that the yard was saved in July. Much of the material has never before been broadcast or published.

4 MARCH 1999: BILL SPIERS
GENERAL SECRETARY OF THE STUC

RW: What was the mood in that meeting this morning?

BS: Well, clearly it's very sombre in that the yard is facing a very difficult position. But it was considerably more positive than was the case around three weeks ago in that we have had movement in the timetable for the Ro-Ro orders and also the company were quite clear that they are reasonably confident that if the MoD orders are coming forward they can find work to fill the gap. The other thing that came through from everyone – the politicians, the shop stewards, the full time officials, everyone was that this is a strategically important industry. Not just for the city of Glasgow or for Scotland but for the UK. We're talking here about some of the last remaining parts of a high quality shipbuilding industry, so it has to be maintained. And the other issue that came out is the growing concern and anger about the fact that we're not operating on a level playing field when it comes to world shipbuilding. There are other parts of the world where there are hidden subsidies and our shipbuilders are operating at a disadvantage.

RW: How active have the STUC and yourself been in the bid to save this yard?

BS: Our job is to be supportive of the unions who are directly involved and in particular of the shop stewards along with the management. We've assisted in the facilitating of meetings with the politicians, we've made representations to the company and in many ways our job is to raise the strategic question of the need for a level playing field for our shipbuilding industry. It's the shop stewards at the yard and their union officials who are taking the main bulk of the campaign and we're doing everything they ask of us to the best of our ability.

RW: And yet Bill in the past when we've had industrial disputes and we've had manufacturing industries going down the plug hole, big union officials and general secretary's have been omnipresent. Why have you been so low in your profile?

BS: I don't think we have been low in our profile. If you recall the great battle of twenty- odd years ago in the ship-building in the Clyde, the UCS, was led from within the yards by the shop stewards. These are the people who build the ships, these are the people who know the industry, these are the people who better than anyone else understand what has to be done. It's our job to be there with them and we are doing everything we possibly can to be there with them, to put the pressure on the politicians in Britain and overseas to get a level playing field and that's what we will continue to do. It's not for us to impose on the workers of Kvaerner. These are people who have fought before. These are people who are fighting now and will again and we have every confidence in their ability.

4 MARCH 1999: JAMIE WEBSTER
KVAERNER GOVAN YARD CONVENOR

RW: Jamie what was the mood at that meeting?

JW: I think the mood was very upbeat. Obviously we had the unions there, the MPs cross party and the company. And it's quite clear that the local management in there and the MPs and the trade unionists are all of one mind, to keep the yard going. And, I'm very confident the MPs present there will take back to the hierarchy in the party that the case for continuing to support us is very good.

RW: We're hearing that March the 22nd is the date on which the decision on this review is going to be announced. It doesn't give you a lot of time does it?

JW: The reality of the situation is that we are on schedule within weeks of the Chief Executive's decision. It depends on whether you want to be an optimist or a pessimist. But we're still going on the view that the local management as well as the unions will be putting a strong case to keep the yard open. I emphasise the local management will be putting a strong case and we're totally confident that's exactly what they're doing.

RW: I spoke to Harland and Wolff and the categorically deny that there is any sub-contracting work coming here or even fifty workers going over there.

JW: It's a very strange world. Watch this space. What I can say from this end is that there's never been any comments come from within this company, the trade unions which are anything other than the truth as we know it. We stand by that. We never ever get caught playing silly bugger games.

RW: Clearly you're waiting for this Ro-Ro ferry order. Is there any indication from management that they are going to do everything in their power to try and bridge the work gap?

JW: We have absolutely no doubt whatsoever that the company are working very hard to secure competitive commercial tender for the Ro-Ro ferries and that they are working very hard to close that gap. If there's a failing, that is not one of them.

4 MARCH 1999: IAN DAVIDSON MP
LABOUR, GLASGOW POLLOK

RW: Ian you've been in that meeting. It's really the first time you've had discussions with what I'd call the full management team here. What's your impression?

ID: I think we're very pleased with the way in which the regional managers are making it clear that they are seeking to bring work into the yard to bridge the gap until any Ro-Ro orders arrive. We obviously do have a shortfall and I think that's why Kvaerner internationally are thinking about maybe having to close it. If they hadn't been serious about maybe keeping it open they wouldn't have bothered trying to find work on a short term basis in order to keep the workforce employed. So we are very keen to see them continue that path and we were very happy with the way in which they have obviously been scouring the country looking for work. They're bringing staff in from Harland and Wolff, they're getting work transferred up from VSEL, the Vickers contract that they should have got in the first place, that they were actually unfairly robbed of in my view. So, things are looking much better than they were three or four weeks ago. But of course we can't take anything for granted because the Kvaerner management worldwide have still got some very difficult decisions to take about the future of the company. We've just got to hope that they recognise that the Scottish Office and Lord Gus have made clear commitments about seeking to do everything they can to keep the yard going. George Robertson as Minister of Defence has similarly done as much as he possibly could so far under European competition rules to give a fair wind to the yard. We've got to hope now that Kvaerner management internationally show the same confidence in the yard that the local management already have.

RW: They actually told you at that meeting that they were getting sub-contract work from Harland and Wolff and VSEL?

ID: They gave us clear indications that that was being vigorously pursued. Obviously in terms of commercial confidentiality there are some difficulties about what they can really say on the record. But I think we understood them to be meaning that work will be coming here from both of those shipyards. The scale of it we're not certain about. What degree of technical complexity it will be we're not certain about yet. But of course the more technically complex it is the better because we want to be able to demonstrate that no matter how difficult the work, we here in Kvaerner can actually manage it. And of course if technically complex work has to be transferred from VSEL because they can't do it that is an indication to the British government that they need the skills that there are here in Kvaerner for the future. And there are going to be a large number of very complex orders coming up in the future, the aircraft carriers and so on, and if VSEL demonstrate that they can't cope with that scale of work then it makes it absolutely essential that in the British national strategic interests that Kvaerner is actually retained which is of course a defence argument as to why the Ro-Ro contracts have got to be awarded here.

4 MARCH 1999: GUNNAR SKJELBRED
KVAERNER GOVAN MD

RW: What was it like at that meeting this morning?

GS: Well I would say it was a very positive meeting. We explained our situation in detail and how I look upon the near future and the long future for Kvaerner Govan. So we had an open, meaningful discussion I would say.

RW: You think it (the yard) has a long future?

GS: Very difficult question. I sincerely hope we have a very, very long future and we are pursuing every avenue today and in the near future to make certain that we have a long future at Kvaerner Govan and try to secure work here.

RW: The MPs who were at the meeting tell me that one of those options is getting work from other yards like VSEL or Harland and Wolff. Can you tell me a bit more about that and the progress you're making there?

GS: That is one of the avenues that we are pursuing to see if there is any need for our services. And so far we have had a positive reaction from those two yards that you mention and just before this interview I was sitting in a meeting and preparing a tender for Harland and Wolff. So we will just have to wait and see when we will be able to get some work in from those two yards.

RW: It's ironic that you might be getting some work from VSEL since they, in a lot of people's eyes, pinched the work for the two Wave Runners from under you. Is that really a live prospect?

GS: I won't go in to any depth when it comes to that situation. This was something that happened long before my time here. I look upon it as any other request to put in a tender and that is exactly what we are doing.

RW: So you are actively tendering for work from VSEL and Harland and Wolff?

GS: Yes that is absolutely true. That was said at this morning's meeting. Like I say we are actively pursuing every avenue and those are one of the avenues that we are pursuing, yes.

RW: And what do you think your chances of success are?

GS: Oh, that is not for me to say. We are putting in the best offer we can and hopefully that's good enough. And they also know that we are a good shipbuilder and we are a good shipbuilding company and I am hoping that we will get some work from them.

RW: It is generally believed that March the 22nd is the week that the Kvaerner main board will announce its review and possibly the future of Kvaerner Govan. What are you thinking that that might reveal?

GS: Ah, now again you are looking into the glass bowl and of course I have to leave that up to our new President Mr Almskog to say what he has got to say at the end of March. I hope that of course it is positive, seen with Kvaerner Govan eyes. I know that Mr Almskog is doing a thorough job now to find out what exactly is the situation for each of the many companies in the Kvaerner group. I had the possibility last week to sit down with him and explain to him what Kvaerner Govan is all about and I of course cannot guarantee what is going to be said at the end of the month but I am optimistic.

RW: Time could be running out though, let's be honest. If the review says that Kvaerner Govan is going then the yard shuts I guess when work runs out in June. If it says that Kvaerner Govan is staying open you still require the Ro-Ro order to come through.

GS: Of course we would very much like to see the Ro-Ro order coming our way. We have facilities here at Govan which are excellent when it comes to building these Ro-Ro's which have a size of roughly two hundred metres length and with a steel weight of seven or eight thousand tonnes per ship. Those are ideal ships for Govan to build and I know that we will be very, very competitive when it comes to those kinds of vessels.

RW: What would be the timescale for the work from Harland and Wolff or VSEL?

GS: Well this is work that hopefully we could pick up soon and start on immediately. And of course getting those contracts would be very positive signals to Mr Almskog as well before he makes his decision, that yes we are competitive and can bring in work.

RW: And finally, you're not looking for a new job yet?

GS: No definitely not. I very much enjoy working here at Kvaerner Govan and I know we have the potential and I know that Govan has so far gone a long way in improvement and efficiency. I showed an overhead this morning to the politicians showing the efficiency today compared to what it was a few years back. We have a very good relationship with all the unions and I see Govan as a good yard to work in with a good potential. The problem is now, I would say, is a common problem for all the shipyards in Europe and the world. It's the shipbuilding market as such so it's not a specific Kvaerner Govan problem as such.

APPENDIX 2:

13 APRIL 1999: TASK FORCE ANNOUNCEMENT
NEWS CONFERENCE AT THE SCOTTISH OFFICE IN
MERIDIAN COURT, CADOGAN STREET, GLASGOW

Lord Macdonald: Good Morning. At the Scottish Office we've been in contact with Kvaerner in recent days and last night we had a meeting with the unions, the full time officials, the Confederation of Shipbuilding and Engineering Unions and the convenors both from the Kvaerner Govan and from Kvaerner Energy in Clydebank. We had been working with the trade unions in recent weeks in anticipation of various options emerging and we now know from this morning's news that Kvaerner will be making a total exit from shipbuilding. All thirteen of their yards will be disposed of or closed if no other solution can be found. They are making an exit they say from all loss making business.

Now as well as Kvaerner Govan and Kvaerner Energy Clydebank, we know that Kincaid of Greenock which employs about one hundred people in engineering will also be up for sale. And in metals equipment, Kvaerner Energy, other mechanical engineering and manufacturing activities, including the remaining parts of their pulp and paper activity will be sold. As I say the Kvaerner Energy impact in Scotland will be at Clydebank with about seven hundred and fifty workers there. Now they are talking of a radical downscaling of the engineering operation of Kvaerner Oil and Gas and of course there are workers in Scotland in Aberdeen and in Methil involved with Kvaerner Oil and Gas. However, our anticipation is that in Methil where there are about three hundred employed, in fact the workforce is anticipated to go up to around two thousand in the completion of the fabrication work they have in hand. But we have no further information about what the longer term aims might be for Methil.

So what we have done with the active involvement of the trade unions is to set up a Task Force and that Task Force will have the job of trying to identify potential purchasers for the shipyard in Govan and for the engineering business in Clydebank, and any other facilities such as Kincaid in Greenock that might subsequently be identified for sale in Scotland. I believe that both the Govan shipyard and the Clydebank engineering operations can be viable businesses with considerable potential under new ownership.

So we've therefore set up a Task Force which comprises a small number of very experienced businessmen with a trade union background too in Sir Gavin to identify if possible potential purchasers of the yard and of the engineering operation. Now, Kvaerner have welcomed these initiatives by the Scottish Office and they've offered us their full co-operation in working to secure a positive outcome for the workforce. The shipyard has obviously benefited over the last ten years from the investment that has been put in by Kvaerner. We've had a very positive response over those years from the workforce and we believe that it is now a modern yard with a great deal of potential based on very progressive work practices. That's obviously a progress that's been achieved not without some pain, but we believe that because of the efforts that have been put in we've got to do everything in our power to try and make sure that a purchaser can be found.

We've been engaged, as I've said in recent months, in the anticipation of a radical restructuring of Kvaerner's international operations and we can see today that all thirteen shipyards are up for sale including their half dozen shipyards in their home territory of Norway. We see too that there is talk of potential solutions in terms of how these yards might be sold and what approaches might be made to potential buyers. So we will obviously be asking Sir Gavin with the full support of the Scottish Office to explore urgently every opportunity available and to get as much information as we can from the management of Kvaerner both in Govan and Clydebank and at a corporate level internationally to allow us to find a positive outcome to this.

In the meantime of course we will be using the Scottish Office's resources to ensure that all our various public bodies, whether it's the employment service or local enterprise companies, Scottish Enterprise, again are all mobilised to try to get the right kind of positive outcome here. So, the announcement is of course very unwelcome. It was not unexpected given the speculation there has been about it. We've talked very fully to the unions and the workforce involved and they have welcomed the setting up of the Task Force and Sir Gavin will start work immediately and I'll ask Gavin to make a statement on what his immediate intentions will be for the Task Force.

Sir Gavin Laird: Thank you Minister. I'll obviously not repeat all that you have said. The Task Force subscribe to all that you have said and let me say we've already had our first meeting last night. After our visits to the two facilities this morning we're meeting again this afternoon. What we've promised the workforce and their representatives, and the only promise we're prepared to make at this stage is that it will be a full time job for the Task Force. There'll be no effort spared. We'll spend as much time as is required to do the job. We're under no illusions about the difficulties that we face, but we start off very optimistically. Optimistically on the basis of the facilities that are there.

We're bringing in consultants to begin an in depth audit. We know the quality and skills of the workforce. We know the ability to produce in a highly productive and efficient workforce. So we're going to work very hard at it. We'll apply for a very early meeting with the MoD. There'll be no magic wand there. We're well aware of the six Ro-Ro vessels are not defence and are therefore under different constraints, but nevertheless we're going to explore that avenue and any other avenue and we'll certainly be prepared to work with anyone who is prepared to work with us and we're more than pleased that so far at the reaction of senior management because that's the next task, to work with management to ensure that we have all the cards that are available for producing a viable solution for the two facilities.

APPENDIX 3:

13 APRIL 1999: LORD MACDONALD
POST TASK FORCE ANNOUNCEMENT

RW: Lord Macdonald, what's your reaction to the news from Kvaerner, the formal announcement?

LM: Well of course very disappointing but not entirely unexpected. We've been working with the trade unions in recent months in anticipation of a number of options. We've now seen that it is an international problem for Kvaerner. They're coming out of shipbuilding entirely. That means they've put up for sale thirteen shipyards which stretch from Russia through Scandinavia through Germany to American, to Singapore and of course to Govan. So, we were working with the trade unions. We saw them last night. They agreed that the most positive thing that we could do at present was to set up a Task Force that will be led by Gavin Laird, a Clydesider with a great deal of experience right across engineering and shipbuilding. He'll be supported by three other Clydesiders. I'm delighted to say they've all volunteered to work virtually full time on this in a pro bono basis and we'll give them full support from the Scottish Office. We've been promised co-operation from Kvaerner and we want to act as a matter of urgency to find out just whether a buyer can be found, not just for Govan but for the operations in Clydebank as well where seven hundred and fifty people are employed. And we're looking in Greenock, at the Kincaid works there, there's a for sale sign over that too so they won't be neglected by the Task Force. So we're dealing in different markets, we're looking I think for different purchasers but we've got to treat that as a matter of urgency. We're taking a very positive approach as the workforce are so we'll be working closely in the weeks ahead to try and get a positive outcome here.

RW: Certainly in the case of Govan they haven't got much time have they, because the MoD contract for the ferries is going to be announced in the autumn?

LM: They're one of four bidders there. They're part of a consortium in fact that is bidding for this contract. It's not a warship contract; it's actually for commercial ferries. It's not the kind of thing the government can direct to any yard otherwise we'd be in breach of very strict European rules, indeed World Trade Organisation rules. But clearly we'll be asking Kvaerner what their intentions are towards this bid, towards this consortium. If they do manage to find with our help a buyer for the yard, will that work if it is won, still go to Govan and obviously I would very much hope that it would.

RW: And finally, the government was pleased to announce thirteen hundred jobs last week. It's not very good news for the election campaign this though is it?

(The election for the first Scottish Parliament was less than a month away).

LM: What we've said is that these jobs must not become a political football. I'm echoing the words of the Scottish Trade Union Congress and I am sure that the workers in the yard feel the same. At present we're in an election period and I'm dealing with this as the Minister responsible along with my civil servants. We're involved in crisis management; we're not involved in electioneering. So I will make sure as far as I can that this issue is not exploited by any party because it's an enduring problem, we've faced these problems in Clydeside before and I just hope that we can get a positive result this time.

13 APRIL 1999: SIR GAVIN LAIRD
POST TASK FORCE ANNOUNCEMENT

RW: What's the purpose of this Task Force?

GL: It's to identify opportunities. I want to emphasise that. We are sure we can do something positive. Our primary task at this juncture is to identify opportunities and then to exploit those opportunities. And hence the Task Force has already decided to bring in consultants to do a very in depth audit of both Clydebank and Govan. Once we establish the full potential there then we'll start trying to get alternative opportunities.

RW: To be honest, your backs are against the wall time wise.

GL: It's going to be very difficult. Fortunately the company have said to us they'll co-operate with us and equally fortunately they've not given us a time scale. We have no particular time constraint, but on the other hand we're not going to allow any time to slip by us. Hence, as I've said already we've already met once, last night, we're meeting again today and we'll be in virtually permanent session for as long as need be.

RW: You say the company hasn't put a time scale on you, but there is a time scale on you certainly for the Govan yard because the Ro-Ro ferry order is going to be announced in the autumn.

GL: Yes, but we're going to try and do things before then to be frank with you. We hope to have some positive steps before then. Although there is no time scale, we want to do the job as quickly and as efficiently as possible.

13 APRIL 1999: JAMIE WEBSTER
POST TASK FORCE ANNOUNCEMENT

RW: How did you hear the news this morning, the con-firmation?

JW: The managing director sent for us at half past eight.

RW: And what did he say to you?

JW: Basically we're withdrawing from shipbuilding worldwide, including Kvaerner Govan and that we were up for sale.

RW: Now what does that mean in terms of you and the workforce?

JW: Well it means now that Kvaerner Govan are clearing the decks for potentially getting a new buyer for the shipyard. That's the arena we're in now. We're now into a joint venture with the unions, Kvaerner and the government to secure a buyer. And obviously with Lord Macdonald now having put in place the Task Force of four people who I know, two of them very well, they are a body of people who are very well acquainted with shipbuilding and it's now in their arena. The commitment that they have is that we are going to work hand in hand with them

RW: That said, today it must be difficult to remain as optimistic as you normally are.

JW: Absolutely not. I was at the mass meeting and addressed the workforce. Let me assure you once again, we're coming out of this. We raised the profile in the political arena, they have responded. The workforce are totally committed to a man and a woman in here that we are keeping this yard open. Our purpose is exactly the same. We are hoping to secure further sub-contract work to take us through the short term. The Ro-Ro ferries is still ongoing and we're looking for a new buyer.

RW: With the Ro-Ro ferry contact, if Kvaerner is pulling out of shipbuilding, they're still in the Sealion consortium, but their commitment to that must be minimal. What assurance have you been given that any new buyer will be given as much information as is required to take their place?

JW: The commitment towards securing the Ro-Ro's has diminished not one iota. The consortium were in yesterday. It's full steam ahead with the commitment towards that. That's an assurance. It's full steam ahead in getting sub-contract work in. There's total commitment. There's no drop off from the company in here. I make that quite clear, or the workforce. That's a fact.

RW: Any chance of a management buy out or a workers buy out? Has that been discussed?

JW: It hasn't been discussed. It was very interesting when we got into detailed discussion this morning with Lord Macdonald and Gavin Laird and the other interested parties what transpires over the next few weeks. We're moving forward, cautiously forward. I told you that's what we're doing. The workforce accepted that. There's no guarantees. The only guarantee is if you throw the towel in you're dead in the water. We're moving forward. The workforce totally accepted that this morning. They're fine. The workforce are fine. They're carrying on launching that ship on Friday, that's what they're doing short term. The strategy is laid out in front of us, no difference of opinion whatsoever. The political response is there, that was the concern. They've got a great responsibility now and knowing a couple of the people I have the greatest confidence in them.

RW: So, not as many long faces at that mass meeting as you thought?

JW: No. Apprehension soon lifted. The air's cleared now. Kvaerner are leaving. Let's work hard now while the sun shines and secure sub-contract work, Ro-Ro ferries and a new buyer. It's staring in front of us, let's get on with it.

RW: In your heart of hearts is this yard going to survive?

JW: Yes. Absolutely. Yes.

Off microphone to RW:

JW: It was good that meeting this morning. I know these people. It was good. Have no illusion, I'm not kidding you, there's no despondency. Talk to the workers yourself. I've know these men and women all my (working) life. We're going ahead. Let's see what the next few weeks bring. Let's see if we secure work from Harlands on a broad front. Let's watch Gavin Laird's input, right, who knows everybody and shipbuilding people with a lot of experience in here. Let's see. We're talking about people that have got influence now and know the market inside out. Let's see. I've got confidence in them. Okay. The Task Force is full time. From today. That's their remit, to discuss with Kvaerner the implications of selling the yard and to go looking for buyers. I told you before this story has got a lot of twists and turns. It's a long journey. I told the workforce that. I don't care how many twists and turns as long as we end up with this yard staying open. Resilience will not be a problem for us. Right. We're going with it.

RW: And what's your impression of the Task Force, the team?

JW: I was delighted. I know two of them personally and they're shipbuilding people through and through. And they have contacts and they know people and they're well respected. Right. If they brought out some obscure people, businessmen nobody knew. Two people, lifetime in shipbuilding, Gavin Laird, very influential, very well respected, well in in the MoD circles, I couldn't have put together a better package myself. The other gentleman (Malcolm Clark) I don't know. I believe he's a financier. But that's it. They've got a grave responsibility and I spoke to them and they know that and we'll start talking more details at half past ten today, get down to the real nitty-gritty. The assurance they've got from us, and they spoke to us last night relating to that, is positive thinking Jamie. Absolutely. You wanted the political arena, you've got it. Fine. That's why I raised it etc. Now it's into battle with them not against them.

13 APRIL 1999: VOX POPS WITH WORKERS

John Brown (welder).

JB: The meeting was positive, determined and it was also dogged in its determination to keep this yard open. The joint shop stewards committee have the full backing of the full workforce to use every and all means to maintain employment in this yard.

RW: So your heads aren't down?

JB: Our heads are definitely not down. We're going forward and we're going forward together. We feel that force of circumstances in exploiting the present situation we can keep this yard open.

Ewan Cameron (welder).

EC: Some people are a wee bit worried obviously that with Kvaerner pulling out the yard's dead, but the majority are optimistic that we'll actually get taken over by somebody else. And we're going to carry on working as normal and hopefully someone will come in and take us over, you know.

RW: You think there's a future?

EC: Yeah, well I think there is. I think someone will come in and take us over so it's just a case of carrying on and doing our best you know, and make sure that somebody does come in.

Russell Stanley (welder).

RS: I thought it was more optimistic than what I thought it would be. So I'm happy about that. At the end of the day we've just got to get on with it no matter what happens. That's just the way it's got to be you know.

RW: A sad day for shipbuilding though.

RS: Oh definitely. But we've just got to get on with it like I said. I'm optimistic, put it that way.

RW: You think a buyer can be found?

RS: Well put it this way. I think you've got a committed workforce that wants to prove a point to say the least.

13 APRIL 1999: MOHAMMAD SARWAR MP
LABOUR, GLASGOW GOVAN (AT GOVAN YARD)

RW: You're the local MP. What sort of effect do you think this is going to have on the community, on Govan?

MS: At this moment we are trying our best, the government is doing its best to keep the jobs alive for the workers in Govan. These people have shown their commitment, working through Easter holidays. What we are aiming for is that if the management of Kvaerner Govan can wait until the decision by the Ministry of Defence on these Roll-on/Roll-off ferries then it's easy to find a buyer and we will be able to keep the jobs.

RW: You think it's a simple as that? It comes down to winning that contract.

MS: It's not simple, but we will do everything we can to get that contract so that will give us at least five years with jobs for these workers. And it's easy to find a buyer with an order book.

RW: What do you think this does for your MSPs election chances?

MS: I think the government is doing her best to keep the jobs and to convince the Kvaerner management and Lord Macdonald has set up the Task Force and he is visiting this morning. That shows a Labour government commitment to the workers.

RW: So you're not going to lose this (seat) to the SNP on the back of this decision?

MS: I think it is not one party problem. I think we should all get behind the workers of Kvaerner at this time and try to keep the jobs.

13 APRIL 1999: LORD MACDONALD
SPEAKING AFTER A MEETING IN KVAERNER GOVAN

LM: We've had a very constructive meeting this morning with Kvaerner management and with the local workforce. And I have with me here, Gavin Laird who will be leading the Scottish Office Task Force which is made up of people with a very wide experience of engineering and shipbuilding. We've just come back from a visit to Clydebank where Kvaerner Energy say that they take a very positive approach to the ability to sell the plant over in Clydebank and we've then come over to Govan here. We've got no illusions that shipbuilding is in a difficult state at the moment as we can see from the fact that Kvaerner has decided to sell its thirteen shipyards worldwide. So we'll be talking very closely with Kvaerner at the local level here in Govan, we'll be talking to Kvaerner Corporate, internationally to see what the various options are. The Task Force will be in exploring all the possible avenues for the sale of the yard and we'll put the full resources of the Scottish Office and their enterprise agencies behind them. I wonder if I could ask Gavin Laird to say a few words now just about the role of the Task Force.

GL: I would emphasise the fact that there will be no effort spared here. We've been reassured and you've heard Gus, full support from the Scottish Office. It's an extremely difficult task but I am hopeful. I am positive. They are two discrete *(means distinct)* businesses, the shipbuilding and the energy and we'll deal with it and we'll have consultants to assist us in the very near future. But in the meantime we're going to walk hand in hand both with management and the workforce to make sure that we can spread a very positive message that there is hope. It's difficult but we can spread a positive message that we're not going to give up in any sense of that word.

LM: And we've had a promise from Kvaerner that there will be full co-operation between the Task Force, the Scottish Office and the company in our attempts to try and sell what we believe is a great asset with a lot of potential. Gunnar would you like to step forward and say something on behalf of Kvaerner?

Gunnar Skjelbred – Managing Director of Kvaerner Govan.

GS: First of all I would like to say that this is a sad day for all of us working at Kvaerner Govan. But when that is said I am a little bit optimistic that we will try to find a solution so that we can preserve the workforce at Govan for the future. Because we have a fairly good facility and we have a very good workforce so we have something that we absolutely can sell in the market. So I am still a little bit optimistic that we will still have an operation here in the future years to come as well.

LM: Jamie?

Jamie Webster, Kvaerner Govan yard convenor:

JW: Yes, a very good meeting this morning and we've always remained optimistic. We've got a tri-partite agreement here. The trade unions will give total co-operation to the Task Force. It's very good, a lot of experience in shipbuilding. They'll get every co-operation and we'll continue to work with Gunnar who has the highest respect from the workforce, and collectively, total commitment is all we ask for. That's what we're giving and we're totally confident we can come out of this. There's no negativity from the workforce at all, ask any of them. We're going ahead with the Task Force and with Gunnar at Kvaerner Govan to keep this yard open.

RW: Do you think it can still be saved?

JW: Absolutely. Totally. Right. No negativity. Total commitment. Best shot. Absolutely. No guarantees. Total commitment from everybody that's what we're going to get that's what we guaranteed each other this morning.

BACK FROM THE BRINK

Reporter: Have you still got hopes of the MoD order?

JW: Yes we've got hopes of the MoD order. And I'm sure that Gavin and the rest of the committee will move into every area that they can and give it maximum effort to persuade everybody. Everybody's giving it total, total focus in keeping the yard open. We're very happy today. We've never been pessimistic nor never will we be.

Reporter: *(to Lord Macdonald)* Lord Macdonald are there precedents recently for a yard like this to be rescued by another buyer?

LM: Well we'll certainly be looking very closely at the situation across shipbuilding. We've seen Swan Hunter as a shipyard come back from what people thought was the graveyard of shipbuilding in the north east of England. So we believe that the most positive asset here is the workforce. It embodies traditions of course going back generations with the skills involved in that so I back Jamie in here in saying that whatever the difficulties, we don't underestimate the difficulties in the world market for shipbuilding, we'll try to be as positive as possible. The Task Force will try to market Govan on the basis of the positive attitude of both the workforce and the achievements of management.

13 APRIL 1999: GUNNAR SKJELBRED
MANAGING DIRECTOR KVAERNER GOVAN

RW: What's your reaction to the announcement?

GS: Well first of all I was, it made me a little bit sad to see the heading on the information I got this morning that Kvaerner is to exit from shipbuilding. So I would say I was surprised, a little bit sorry. Then I, after a few minutes, I realise, I understand why. So now we have to make the best out of the situation to see, or to try to preserve as many as possible the working places here at Govan and also help this Task Force from Scottish Office to find someone else to operate the yard.

RW: What's your impression of that Task Force, the calibre of it?

GS: Well I haven't really got all the details, but my first impression is very positive that we have capable persons in that committee and we will work very closely with them and I am fairly optimistic that we will find some solution together with them.

RW: Presumably that solution can only be found if the workers and yourself co-operate with the Task Force. What's the mood between management and unions now?

GS: There's no disagreement between management and unions and all the employees. I mean we're in the same boat, all of us. But we have got this message from the board and we just have to accept that and just make the best out of the prevailing situation.

RW: Clearly any potential buyer is going to want to know that there's a very good chance of landing the Ro-Ro orders. What can you tell me about the status of that in terms of Kvaerner's commitment?

GS: The situation is that it is business as usual. We are pursuing other contracts, smaller and bigger contracts as well and when it comes to the Ro-Ro order, the potential order from the MoD, we are actively pursuing that. There was a full day meeting in here yesterday in connection with that.

RW: And are you doing that independently from Kvaerner in Norway from now on?

GS: Eh, well still it is under the Kvaerner umbrella, so we just have to be seeing now how soon we can find somebody who is willing to have a look at the yard and is willing to take over and then we sort out that problem about who is really going to sign for the contract.

RW: It sounds like pursuing this order depends on finding a buyer and quickly.

GS: It depends also on how quickly we can progress. I mean Kvaerner board has made this decision that they want to pull out. So it is a little bit urgent matter that we find first of all some work to fill the gap that we know have or that we can see from mid-June and then start up a dialogue with a potential takeover company. That's very important. But in the meantime we are pursuing the Ro-Ro contract, yes.

RW: But my point is you seem to be doing that now independently of Kvaerner, as Govan shipyard.

GS: Ah yes, but we still got the name Kvaerner Govan *(laughs)* so that's still a fact. So the answer is yes we are pursuing all business opportunities so like I said, business as usual.

RW: And if you don't find a buyer then the contract's lost?

GS: Well in the worst case if we don't find any more work, if we don't find anyone to takeover the yard and we are getting into the autumn and we don't have anything to do then the answer is fairly clearly on the wall. But that's the absolutely, absolutely worst case scenario and we don't believe that will happen at all.

APPENDIX 4:

15 APRIL 1999: JAN FOSSE
MANAGING DIRECTOR OF BRØVIG SHIPOWNERS*
TALKING ON THE LAUNCH DAY OF *CRYSTAL OCEAN*,
A £35 MILLION OFFSHORE OIL-WELL TEST VESSEL

RW: What's been your impression of the jobs that's been done here?

JF: Excellent. The quality of the ship, the workmanship on the ship is excellent. We are getting a first class product and we are very happy that we placed the order with Kvaerner Govan and I hope we will be able to place future orders with Kvaerner. They deserve to go on.

RW: And you'll be glad you placed the order when you placed it.

JF: Well, yes we are happy with that of course but of course it's not the ideal situation to be the last ship out of the shipyard and I hope that's not going to be the case. I hope they get new orders soon and that they will continue.

RW: And if the yard continues you think it's likely you will be a future customer?

JF: Yes. Of course we live in a competitive world, but if they continue to be competitive I have no reason for not ordering ships here.

RW: And the situation this shipyard finds itself in, how do you feel about that?

JF: Yes, I think it's a shame. We need shipbuilding capability in Europe, in northern Europe and it's about to disappear. Particularly for high technology vessels like the *Crystal Ocean* that's just been launched. It's a very complex vessel and yards far away from here don't have the same ability, the same qualifications as these shipyards in northern Europe, with their long history, have. So, we need them and I hope they will stay on for a long time.

---

* A Norwegian company which was established in 1889. The parent company for the group is Gezina AS, which is a diversified company with shipping and venture as the main activities. Gezina AS is owned by Tharald Brøvig and his daughters.

APPENDIX 5:

16 APRIL 1999: GUNNAR SKJELBRED

RW: Mr Skjellbred, are Swan Hunters about to buy you?

GS: *(Laughs)* I think that question is a little bit premature. We next week will be full steam ahead when it comes to getting in contact with potential buyers, persons, parties whatever and then after a relatively short time we will try to sort out who is the best new entity to takeover this facility. That's very important to find the very very best company to takeover.

RW: The management from Swan Hunter is in Glasgow today as you know meeting the Task Force and Sir Gavin Laird. That shows that they are very keen. What's your view on that?

GS: Yes that's fine. That's positive. But like I said we and my interest is to find the best solution. It might be that that's the best solution. I today don't know. But that remains to be seen because I feel it's a great responsibility for Kvaerner for the management and for the unions to find the best solution for this facility and for the workforce for the future.

RW: Swan's owner is quoted as saying that if a takeover did take place there would be radical changes and he'd probably only employ about five hundred workers here. That can't be ideal?

GS: No I cannot really comment on that. I'm not aware of his business strategy so that would be purely speculation. So that's going to be a later stage too…

(interrupted).

RW: But if there were job losses that wouldn't be ideal.

GS: Of course it's never an easy situation when you are talking about job losses but that has to be discussed and looked into down the road.

RW: Any other interested parties that have been in contact, seriously?

GS: Well as I say we feel that we have serious requests from parties asking at least to come up for meetings and we just have to take it from there. Like I said it's too early to comment on that and the good thing is that there are parties showing interest. If the market had been completely dead of course then I would be much more worried than I am. And I am still optimistic that we will find a solution.

RW: The company which owns the ship you've just launched today, why do you think they choose this yard to do that?

GS: Initially it was a combination of price and quality. Today they told me that they were very, very happy that they chose Kvaerner Govan to build the ship and they also expressed interest in building number two once they got a charter for this ship. So they were very impressed with the product that we launched today. That's the best marketing that you can have as a shipbuilder, to have really happy and satisfied clients and these clients they are experienced clients. They have long been in the shipping business so they know what they are talking about.

16 APRIL 1999: JAMIE WEBSTER
AFTER LAUNCH OF *CRYSTAL OCEAN*

RW: Good news today Jamie with the launch.

JW: Yes, obviously the boat's in the water successfully, it's in the basin ready to get fitted out, be completed in August and it was a good day. The owner, the customer is happy. The customer is always happy on the Clyde. I think some people seem to forget that in amongst it. Show me a customer that's dissatisfied, they don't exist.

RW: We're hearing today that the Energy business in Clydebank will probably have a deal for a new owner within the next three months. What's your view on that?

JW: I'm really happy for them. Really happy about that and so will everybody in here. We're of the same ilk. I'm delighted. That's one down and two to go, us and Kincaid's and we'll have a hat-trick of success and that'll be really good for the rest of Scotland and the economy. And I'm, sure everybody will join in hoping that's what's achieved.

RW: You're meeting Gavin Laird, I think the STUC and various other people. What do you expect to come out of that Jamie?

JW: Well obviously I'm expecting to hear from Gavin Laird what progress has been made and give us an update because we will be keeping in constant touch with him to see where we are going together and obviously any views that he wants from the trade unions to keep us involved in how things are developing. He knows he'll get total support so I'm beginning to see, as I've said before, continual progress. I don't bother if it's slow as long as we keep making progress towards securing the future of this yard. We'll stay the course no matter how long it takes.

16 APRIL 1999: SIR GAVIN LAIRD
LEAVING THE SCOTTISH OFFICE IN CADOGAN STREET

RW: I've been waiting an hour to see you, if I could just have two minutes of your time?

GL: No, I've got a plane to catch.

RW: *(Pursuing).* I know but I can talk as you're walking to your car. A hard day at the office?

GL: A hard day, but useful. Not a waste of time.

RW: What about the Swan Hunter talks?

GL: The Swan Hunter talks were constructive and I can say no more than that.

RW: And from a union point of view, how are they feeling about today?

GL: Well the union are, they could not be more constructive and helpful than they are and the meeting continues in that vein.

RW: And finally, what's your programme for next week?

GL: Oh, we're at the yard on Monday morning, we're in Clydebank in the afternoon. I'm down in London with the Minister meeting a variety of ministerial colleagues on Wednesday. That continues. A whole range of things to do next week. I have to go!

16 APRIL 1999: JAMIE WEBSTER
AFTER MEETING THE TASK FORCE

RW: We've just heard from Sir Gavin Laird that the meeting was constructive as far as he was concerned. What was the outcome of your meeting with him there?

JW: Well obviously he's been giving us an update on the situation. It's obvious that the Task Force are now fully at work. I'm totally one hundred percent convinced that we are going to get a good deal with the Task Force. I have no problem with their commitment whatsoever. They're coming into the yard on Monday. They've already been in to speak to the company. I'm so happy now because I'm totally convinced that we have the company, the management at Kvaerner Govan and the Task Force and the unions all in one. That's so important.

RW: If a buyer is found quickly what does that tell you? Does it tell you that someone has been circling before the announcement was made?

JW: Very possibly someone's been circling before the announcement was made. I really don't know that situation. I believe that as every week goes we will see continual twists and turns in the tale but I'm quite sure they are going for the better. I am confident that the Task Force are going about their job in a professional manner. I'm sure there's interested parties and it's a matter of bringing together all the various parties. We're there to play our role and try and play our part in getting a new owner.

RW: What did Gavin Laird tell you about the talks with Swan Hunter?

JW: That they were serious. That they were serious players. You do get frivolous people in this arena but they were serious. But they were initial (talks) and if that was to be followed up it would have to be followed up in much more detail. But it's certain that they are serious runners. A lot of discussions are to take place, a lot of water under the bridge.

RW: Do you know of any other players that might be coming in?

JW: I don't know anything specific but I think it's fair to say that there are other players and obviously as they appear the Task Force will go through the usual procedure of speaking to them, linking up with the company. It's a very, very complex issue obviously and it takes very delicate handling. Obviously on the business side we have to trust the expertise of the Task Force in that area and we'll be there to reassure them that what we are always saying that whoever comes forward will get the total co-operation of the unions with the new owners to let them see that we are a potential asset. We've no problem doing that whatsoever.

APPENDIX 6:

4 JUNE 1999: JAMIE WEBSTER

This was the main interview for a Radio Clyde *documentary charting the success or failure of the campaign. In it Jamie was willing to speculate that the GEC deal would finally happen on the basis that if it didn't those parts of the interview wouldn't be used.*

RW: Jamie as the campaign wore on how did you feel the political support developed?

JW: The political support started to gain momentum. The principal driver for the yard was Ian Davidson who originally was the MP for Govan but who is now Pollok. He co-ordinated many of the things and basically guided us through the intricacies in the political thing. It was quite clear that when we did begin to move we began to get our message across about the campaign and awaken the politicians to the fact that one, it was their job to support us, but two, that we actually had a good case. So things began to become much more positive and that initial bad feeling in some areas began to diminish somewhat and that was absolutely necessary. But then we had a positive case to put.

RW: Were you surprised at any point about how some members of the political arena changed their tack? In other words made themselves more positive towards the campaign. Did it surprise you?

JW: Well I believe that originally they were negative to the campaign. I spoke originally about the fact that I felt there was a defeatism, a legacy from the Conservative government, to say they had contracted that disease. But certainly when we began to put pressure on and to contact them, and actually put our case and the objectivity and necessity of the need to support us they began to come round so I wasn't surprised really. We were determined that was the way it was going to be. If they remained negative we weren't going to allow that to happen. I mean they had a responsibility and an accountability. They had to face up to it the same way I had to face my accountability so it was certainly a lot easier because at the end of the day you don't want to keep banging the drum and nobody hearing you all the time. So it was certainly heartening to realise we're finally getting the message through. So that was good because it was less stress. You realise that you were gathering allies.

RW: Did you ever feel at any point that you, the campaign was actually an embarrassment to Labour or the unions or that you were a thorn in their side and they thought 'Jamie I wish you'd just pipe down and go away and just let it all happen naturally'?

JW: Oh I think in the early stages we were regarded as 'Ooooh, that's a bit of loose cannons flying about there,' certainly because our methods were somewhat unorthodox and not tested as such. I'm quite sure that originally in the political arena there was great disquiet at 'that's not the proper way to go about things', both in the union hierarchy to a degree and certainly in the political arena because we were new kids on the block and I agree that our methods were unorthodox but they were absolutely sort of truthful and we were committed to a cause and it was a desperate situation that required desperate measures. So, yes, absolutely true.

RW: So given that did you ever feel that there was an attempt to gag you?

JW: There's two ways you can look at it. Gag; to actually attempt to stop you speaking or gag; in an attempt to actually take your viewpoints in another perspective and from a different angle. Yeah I would say definitely, most definitely regarding the direction we were going there would be efforts and pressure to control what you were saying and what you were actually doing, because other people know best. But do they? If you're committed to a cause and you are elected by your members they put the responsibility on you and of course I've already told you we've continually reappraised our campaign and never once have they (the workers) ever said that's the wrong direction. We would change nothing. That's very important if I had to do it again. Nothing,

RW: Where did that pressure come from?

JW: Well obviously there is a link to the trade unions and the Labour Party. That works in a positive manner sometimes there's no doubt about that. But at the end of the day individuals can sometimes feel that pressure when they're pursuing a course of action which doesn't quite fit the script and I don't think we fitted the script. So collectively it would come from maybe the politicians who I say would have thought 'Oh that's not the way you go about things', and possibly some senior members of the unions would think 'That's not the way you go about things', right. So, yeah it would probably come from both directions in the early days, because as I say what we did was, eh, well okay it was rather controversial, like naming the MPs but I'll go back to that again, it was the truth.

RW: That must have depressed you. Here you are fighting to save twelve hundred jobs and one of the most famous shipyards in the world from closure and you're lacking the support you thought you deserved and was actually duty bound to come to you.

JW: It depressed me, it disillusioned me, it frustrated me, but most of all it surprised me that that was the situation. Maybe I was a bit naïve to think that everyone would have come on board and rallied round the flag and there was a total affinity to workers in the Labour government and all the MPs. So yeah there was a lot of disappointments at that initial thing. Bearing in mind, I mean, that more than half (of the Scottish Labour MPs) did reply, that's the fact, but yes maybe I was being naïve. We were maybe naïve to think that everybody automatically would have rallied round the flag you know. And that wasn't there initially.

RW: What did you feel the role of Kvaerner bosses, and I mean at national level, main board level. What do you feel their role in all of this has been?

JW: The Executives? I believe that we have been treated very shabbily by them. Mr Alsmkog who is the Chief Executive I think throughout the whole campaign, the situation, has shown most certainly, and sadly, a total lack of sensitivity to the employees. Probably not just at Kvaerner Govan because it's a corporate plan. But the communications situation, the consideration and the accountability of his workers left, putting it mildly, a lot to be desired. Indeed it would be hard not to objectively say that as our principal employer we were treated less than poorly.

RW: What examples can you give me of that?

JW: Well in the early days it was quite clear that shareholders were the be all and end all of it you know. The employees and their contribution whether it was over a long time or whether it was committed would mean ultimately absolutely nothing. I find that an alarming concept for a company that is trimming down but is still remaining. And they've made it quite clear for the employees remaining in such a company I would be seriously concerned. But, throughout the campaign in trying to keep the yard open and bearing in mind we were working away normally and trying to do our best there was never any approach of appreciation or understanding of the distress to the workers. I do not believe that's progressive thinking from a company. So I would have to say having only seen Mr Alsmkog a couple of times, but watching what happened from afar, is that (he's) very cold and dispassionate and one could question, does that kind of company to any degree, should they be entitled to commitment and loyalty? The answer would probably be no.

RW: It's business Jamie.

JW: It's business of course, right. But it's what kind of business you want to run and what direction you want to take your employees forward in. I would not move from the concept, which is shared by a lot of companies believe it or not in business that you treat employees with dignity and you win their hearts and souls and you get the best out of them. I've never believed in actual fact the stick over the back actually gets people's best. I just believe the workers, I believe passionately and I believe the evidence is there, that the workers at Kvaerner Govan come out of this with much more dignity than Kvaerner main board, not the local management, but the main board. We come out of it with much more dignity. I think time will show that to have been the case.

RW: What about local management. You said initially that when the news broke they were numbed and basically your committee and you had to pull them along to try and shake them basically. As the days and months and weeks went by how did their attitude change? What was their input?

JW: Well as I say initially we were all numb, myself included. But it was quite clear that they were shattered by that news and more importantly what direction they would take to try and rectify it. Were we all going to sit back and just fade away into oblivion or was there going to be some sort of structured campaign? Certainly the trade unions in here took the bull by the horns and set that rolling. And after a while they began to come round to realising this company can be saved. We can all have our jobs including the directors and let's go for it. So from a *(word muffled)* of them going from a point of yes definitely numbed they gradually came on board. A second factor was that fact that initially they did appear and were indeed playing no profile with the media and that caused friction in as much as, well the unions in the yard are putting a continuing positive note, but what are the company saying? And of course at some stage I had to approach that with the unions and say there will have to be a response from the company to convince the public and the media that indeed we are in this as one. That was a major turning point when they finally realised it will have to be done. You cannot have two parties assuming they are saying the same thing but only one party actually saying it.

RW: And how tough was it to get them to agree that that was actually the right thing to do?

JW: It wasn't so much tough as approaching them at the right time to do it. Initially we got carried away with ourselves, the trade unions and the workers obviously pushing the campaign with the politicians etc. and we were probably focused too much into ourselves. But eventually the media quite rightly so eventually began to say 'Is what you are saying actually reflecting the company's viewpoint'? And I would always assure them yes. They would say well we would like to hear them say that and it was at that stage that we had to say to the company you will have to speak. Bearing in mind that they were always in a slightly difficult situation of being directors that, what would the chief executive say. They had to be more careful. But they should never have been careful of the fact is did they want the yard to stay open. It was all of our jobs from top to bottom.

RW: What sort of media attention did you get UK and world-wide?

JW: A lot more than I envisaged as a matter of fact. That was one of the things that actually took me right off my feet. As the campaign built up, we still hear about it. I mean obviously the day of the announcement that they were selling off the whole group, the fact is we saw *Sky TV* over there and they wanted to beam over messages to Scandinavia. That took me greatly by surprise and indeed when someone told me there was an article in a paper in Australia about the yard I said my goodness that's really stretched it. And apart from that we had various interviews in papers in Norway and Germany and such so I was astonished quite honestly that it had gathered so much although the indications were that there was a common factor and that was the fact that from the establishment which wasn't a gigantic sized company, twelve hundred workers, that there was such a high profile politically to it, that was the main factor that all the European countries and Australia were interested in the political rumpus and attention that it had drawn. So that was really astonishing and totally unforeseen.

RW: Who would you single out for praise in the way that they have supported you throughout the campaign?

JW: That's something on reflection that I've given a lot of consideration to for when we finally get a result on this. And it's actually a longer list than you would imagine. But certainly top of the tree is most certainly Lord Macdonald and the much maligned I believe civil servants at the Scottish Office. I've had the conviction for several months and I'm sure it's shared by the workforce now that they did an exceptionally good job for us and indeed sold us well in the industrial arena. The Task Force have done an extremely good job, bearing in mind that I'd have been the first to criticise them and the worst criticism of them when they were elected or put in place was that they would be there as a smokescreen until the election and that has not been the case and I never felt that that was the case. That group I believe are the main players in it and I believe we owe a lot of praise and appreciation. Ian Davidson, in the political arena. There are others, but too many (to name), but they'll know themselves, MPs did help us. Maria Fyfe my own MP, not to give her too much of a plug. But, Ian Davidson principally in the political arena. The media was the other delightful surprise, bearing in mind that the media are, and I will say this, a complex beast as people know and can make or break issues and that's a fact that everyone in the country knows. Not only do we believe that we've had very fair coverage from them but much to my pleasant surprise, maybe this is unprofessional for the media to actually say it, is that indeed a great amount of sympathy. That was a bonus point most certainly. A lot of appreciation for that to the media. And the local community, the people you walk about with you know. So in actual fact surrounded by a lot of goodwill. That's what kept us going, believe it or not when you're in an arena like that, seeing where your allies are coming from. But again, I would go back to... I believe the driving force of lifting us out of our own capabilities was Lord Macdonald and the civil servants at the Scottish Office. That would have to be said.

RW: If Lord Macdonald hadn't been there, how much harder would the fight have been? Would you have been able to succeed?

JW: It's a hypothetical question but what I will say is if we succeed their contribution will have been significant. If they had not been there the fight would have been much, much harder. And would we have done it? Possibly not. I would not have like to have travelled that road without them. I'm glad they were there. Very glad.

RW: How much of a handicap was it that the news of the sell off came when it did - at the start to the run up to the Scottish Parliamentary elections?

JW: Obviously when the announcement came, bearing mind we must always remember that the corporate plan affected

BACK FROM THE BRINK

more people than us, but from a personal point of view, the review was expected. It came weeks before, I believe, the Scottish election and principally I believe that the election at that time and the difficulties probably actually helped us because it gave a vital kick at that particular time in the fact that the politicians would have had to be seen to be doing something. But there was that other contradictory thing in as much as some people did indicate you'll be humoured until the 6th of May and then they'll do a runner. I never believed that, not at that stage because I believed the politicians had come round to a much more positive frame of mind. I believe we'd convinced them and I believe some of them after they'd listened to us totally supported us. And then when I saw the Task Force going in place and I knew the integrity of the men I never shared that view that they would do a runner. But at that particular time when you go through a phase it was a good phase that it came that we might lose our jobs and were the politicians actually going to do something coming to an election, or the media and obviously the public might have said they are being less than positive in that campaign for jobs. So, a bit of luck there I think.

RW: Looking at the campaign and the way certain politicians allied themselves to you, or didn't ally themselves to you, I didn't feel that Donald Dewar used his particularly high position when it came to the yard for example. Did that disappoint you?

JW: Yes. But what you actually see and what actually happens turns out to be not the same thing. Certainly we know the situation, at the time we were going through a very difficult time and we had the situation that I've explained before that Tony Blair came and visited Yarrows and there was no problem with that but I made the point that it would have been nice to come to Govan and give us support and let the community see that he was interested in a yard that was in difficulties. Donald Dewar for the First Minister, bearing in mind and not to play a political card here, but I mean Alex Salmond visited the yard on a couple of occasions and gave us his total support. We were disappointed Donald Dewar never appeared. However, hindsight's a wonderful thing and although he never came here, and I was critical of that, I make no bones about it I was critical because to be visible to people is what people notice if you actually seen that. There would be indications that in actual fact and people did warn me to this effect to be honest that behind the scenes he indeed was supportive. So perhaps I was rather harsh and perhaps he didn't sell himself as well as he could have and didn't maybe get the credit for some of the work he did behind the scenes. So I could not certainly say he did not support us because there are indications that that's not true, but his presence there seemed to have contradicted that so maybe the First Minister should look that sometimes best to do both things, be there and help.

Author's note – this interview was recorded on 4 June 1999 five weeks before that fateful Task Force meeting at which Donald Dewar, in Jamie's view, threw in the towel in terms of saving the yard.

RW: He did take a very high profile trip to New York to sort out the cashmere industry when the Americans put an embargo on cashmere goods. Would something like that, that high profile image of him visibly being seen to be doing something for you, be something you'd have been looking for?

JW: Yes, I think most people would have accepted that visible presence. Possibly of course the fact that you go over to America and you're speaking to the businessmen etc., slightly different territory if you're coming into a shipyard to face maybe a whole workforce as such. Maybe slightly more, let's say, controversial, the climate's slightly more hot, maybe he was a bit apprehensive as such. But we were certainly disappointed and I do still believe that he should have come. But I would not say that the indications are that he was not supportive behind the scenes or did not help us because the indications are indeed that he did. So maybe Mr Dewar should look at his PR and actually get maximum benefit out of it as such.

RW: You've already touched on it, but what were your first thoughts when the Task Force was appointed?

JW: My first thoughts were, that's a step forward. Ehhh, I wonder who's on it and I hope they're good at their job. That was my first thought.

RW: And your assessment of the people involved?

JW: First class. Absolutely first class. And I can say no more than that. From day one to when I'm speaking to you right now. When I saw who they were I could not ask for a better team to be put together. And when I saw them working and in my dealings with them, high respect for them. Simple as that.

RW: What's your assessment of Sir Gavin Laird and his contribution to getting this sorted out?

JW: Sir Gavin Laird, obviously as the Chairman and the main driver, trade unionist, senior leader, knows the ropes, knows people. Calls a spade a spade and so do I. So that's a good combination. I knew that we wouldn't be given any false promises but I knew we'd get total commitment. And we would get the truth. That's a good start. And the other people had a lot of knowledge and background to shipbuilding etc. right. And that common cliché, that we're all Clydesiders and if I were in their position, hypothetically in years to come, if I was, I'd like to think I'd have showed that same commitment because I'd grown up in that culture and that's what they showed so, I mean we owe them, we owe them a great deal. There's no doubt about that.

RW: On a personal level, did you get on with Gavin Laird?

JW: Yes. Yes, absolutely. And you always worry about that because I can be regarded as somewhat abrasive and outspoken at times. And some folk like that and respect that. Other folk get frightened by it and don't like it. So, I was wondering how I would come across as such but I'd like to think we had, well I'm sure we had a good relationship. You get vibes about people and our points of view were quite pointed to each other, we didn't always agree on everything in terms of that. But we'd the one aim and that was what was important and we had a mutual respect. And of course I find it hard to work with people I don't respect. I can be very uneasy and narky.

RW: Paint me a picture of those meetings with Gavin Laird, Jamie. What was the tone of them? How were they structured?

JW: Obviously myself and the convenor from Clydebank Energy would be there, a couple of the full time officials and the Task Force. The meetings were very informal. We'd continually get an update on what was happening and obviously they would always ask me how the situation was in the yard. Because it was important we were working normally and the morale was good and the information flow was good etc. And they were progressive and, obviously, informative. They were absolutely vital. I often ran by this other hypothetical situation which alarmed me if it had ever happened. No Task Force, right, possibly negotiations between GEC and Kvaerner themselves; that would have been a problem, because Kvaerner would have told us absolutely nothing. That's not conjecture, that's a fact. No information, more tension on the shop floor, more apprehension, more pressure on us. Erratic decisions might be taken sometimes. So those meetings were absolutely vital to take us through this all the time. Plus you're listening to four people that know what they're talking about so, I mean, I used to live for they meetings because they were my food to feed on and take back to the workforce to keep their heads up and say "It's going well, it's going well, we're moving. Here's an update all the time..." You can't go into a limbo land for information. Pressures from the workforce will crush you and rightly so. You must keep them informed. You must be positive. You must be up to date and accurate.

RW: How did you feel when you found out that the work at VSEL was so far behind schedule? Bearing in mind that they'd pinched it from under your noses basically.

JW: How did I feel? Angry initially, I suppose and eh, angry. Angry at the fact that that situation had ever been allowed to arise. But I was not surprised you know. I was angry, but I wasn't too resentful because it was done you know, but, initially it was anger because the circumstances of losing that order should never have arisen and here we were and it was having an effect on us maybe closing and such. So a lot of difficult and complicated emotions went through, not just myself but the whole workforce relating to that you know. But once we realised it was late, it was, let's do something about it you know.

RW: And when the work came up to the yard how did that make you feel emotionally and mentally?

JW: When the VSEL work came up? Almost as if justice had been done. That sounds too simplified, but yeah, justice. A miscarriage had been done and what goes around comes around. And relieved of course that the work came because we needed it. It was vital work to us you know.

RW: And what did the workforce feel about that? Was it a morale booster?

JW: Yeah. I think they felt the exact same as me because we're all as one. *(Words muffled)...* it should never have happened. More important what had come up. Very important. A commitment to do the business on that ship. No problems, no late deliveries, first class quality.

So that people would say, yeah, that ship should have come to Govan.

RW: Swan Hunter were going to buy the place. Ferguson's were touted to buy the place. There was even a Cuban order supposed to be coming in. There was even a guy in Renfrew above a bakery shop who had three hundred and seventy-five million quids worth of American shipping orders coming in to save the yard. There was all of those things. How do you cope with that coming in on a daily basis and assessing and assimilating which is good and which is bad?

JW: How do you assess them? Ehh. Principally with gut reaction. Some of them were laughable in reality and didn't take too much assessing. Other ones were certainly more serious in content but had possible repercussions relating to how this yard would be under them as such. Some of them were serious intentions but the practicalities of them actually taking over the yard were unlikely. But the most serious in my view was keeping the courtesy, the civility and don't be rude. But be selfish and aim for the owners who'd be best for you. That may be pragmatic to the situation but...

RW: And looking at the people who made the bid, was there ever any doubt in your mind as to who the front runner should be?

JW: Well on the surface obviously it was GEC. I'd a lot of time for Ferguson's because they're a Clyde shipyard and a good wee company. I don't mean that patronisingly, but the thought is that David beating Goliath again seemed somewhat unlikely. But, eh a lot of respect for them as such, but I doubted their capabilities to actually manifest themselves to take us over. Swan Hunters I always treated with, unfortunately, suspicion because they changed their tune too often, changed their perspective too much and I was worried. But nevertheless it wasn't my company.

Kvaerner were dealing with them and I'd have to let that go
through its motions. But I have to say I was always uneasy
with that situation. GEC always had the combination of
all the factors. Big company, reputable, had muscle behind
them. Had work short term and almost certainly long
term and so they had the ingredients and so they had to
be the logical choice.

RW: I defy you to convince me otherwise. There must have
been times when that mask of Webster optimism slipped
either privately or in front of your stewards. What was
going through your mind in those moments? You must
have had dark moments.

JW: Are you right on that? I'm not quite sure. If I was always
at the same high then that would be wrong because
I had peaks and troughs just like everybody else, but I
was always optimistic. Always. It's just that something
would happen on a day that would take me down a notch.
But you didn't lose your optimism but it got you down a
bit. But the word that keeps coming back, not just saying
this about myself, it's everybody right, is resilience right.
The ability to bounce back in times of adversity. So yeah,
I had my highs and my lows etc., but you go to you bed
at night and you come in the next day and the wee blip
the day before, go for it again. Because, oh by the way,
often two steps forward and one back all the time, but it's
a resilience and a belief in what you're doing. That's what
keeps you going all the time. But I certainly won't accept
the fact that I put on a show of optimism, no no no no. I
was always optimistic. I think I'm an optimistic sort of
guy. But I saw a lot to be optimistic about. It's conveying
that optimism to other people and taking them on board.
Nae good Jamie Webster being optimistic if you cannae
get the workforce to go with you, you know. So that was
it, some days down a wee bit and a problem, and... there's
a problem, but is that problem going to stop you? Are you

going start going back the way, the head going down?
The answer's always NO! No, it's not getting you down.
Solve it and move on. And that's exactly what we did.

RW: You've obviously never run a campaign like this before
because you've never been in a situation where you had
to. What particular stresses and strains did it put on you
particularly as an individual?

JW: Every kind, every kind. I thing the most telling thing, and
I say this continually to people, and they laugh but they
believe me, when this is over, when it's over, I'll look back
on January, February, March, April, May and June and
say, where did they go in my life basically and I know
where they went, into this campaign. Because I find it
difficult to differentiate between an hour, a day to a week.
Just flew by. My whole life was wrapped in the campaign.
People told me to unwind a wee bit. It put a lot of stress on
the family, obviously and such and I mean their patience
has been exemplary as well, I mean it would have been
impossible if they hadn't supported me and backed me
and left me to it. It's a stress in as much as it was hard
to concentrate sometimes. And, eh, the biggest pressure,
the accountability of no' letting the workforce down.
Even more than your own personal thing, the no' letting
them down. They'd put so much faith in the stewards and
myself to take them through it and always saying am I
up to it? Have I made the right decisions? Am I guiding
them in the right way? Yeah, lots of stress. But overcoming
the stress was that commitment and belief. Is it worth
going through it? Yeah.

RW: At home, what were your family saying to you? Were they
saying you're doing too much? Can you keep going?

JW: Oh, they never said are you doing too much? They did
things like answer the phone and leave me alone when I
wanted to be quiet and let me talk when I wanted to. And,
eh, they were just, they were just with you. They were

just with you. I mean they believe in what you're doing. My wife knows her husband, my children know their father. If I take something on board, if I say I'm going to do it, I may not do it but it's not going to be through lack of effort. So, and I try to instill that in them as well that you give it your best shot. You must maximise the potential in your life and give it your very best, so they knew me and they were with me. And that was absolutely vital. You could not have distractions and pressure in the house and in here (the yard). I mean it would bring I think anybody to their knees.

RW: Did you have much of a private life? Were you able to do things that you were able to do previously to January?

JW: I had to give a lot of it up obviously. *(Word muffled)...* there's a meeting, go to that meeting. There's a phone call, there's the media. So, they were all distractions as well. Even at the weekends which is your relaxation times, you're still thinking about it, thinking about Monday, what strategy do we have as such, so I've not been the same person as I am for these six months and it's not been pleasant. But I know why I did it and I don't regret why I did it. And the stewards as well, they've obviously had their pressures as such. But when you're the leader and that's what you are, you've been appointed to do it, the biggest pressure's on you. If you don't like the heat get out the kitchen.

RW: And you got a mobile phone.

JW: I got a mobile phone. Something that I said I'd never get. Yuppie style, but I had to get it. Which at the end of the campaign will be returned, when I get back to normal life

(nearly 10 years on Jamie still has a mobile phone. Life has never returned to normal).

So yeah, found a lot out about myself. That's a thing as well that when I sit back and try and reappraise myself in a few months time, I found a lot out about myself you know. Found in the last six months more about myself and life than I have in my lifetime. I'm serious about that you know. About everything. About what I really believe myself, what I'm capable of. Dealing with people, the best side of people, the worst side of people. How to deal with good times, bad times. Everything. I just know that a new me's come out in the last few months to cope with a really difficult situation.

RW: Are you a more rounded person now do you think? Are you a better leader?

JW: Yes. I would think a more rounded person because when you're in a situation like this no matter what your personality is people *(words muffled)...* and they'll influence you in a way and you must listen to other people's opinions and such like. But not too much, because if you listen to other people's opinions too much then you lose your own. And whether you like it or not only time will tell good leader, bad leader and such like. You must be your own person sometimes because you're there to lead and lead you must, inspire and have your own viewpoints and sometimes in actual fact, force them on other people. But then again because you're into so many meetings with so many different people it makes you a much fuller person. You learn a lot, you must learn a lot. You go through experiences you never envisaged going through.

RW: Did you ever consider backing away? Allowing the big union boys to take over and run the campaign the way they wanted to do it. Did it ever cross your mind?

JW: Never. Not for one single second did I ever consider that. Never. We said early days, we're running the campaign. They elected us to do it (the workforce). Let's hope we're good enough and competent enough. Let's be honest. Let's be committed and determined in our belief that we're running it. Let our fate principally be in our own doings. I think time will prove that to have been absolutely right. That's not against other *(word muffled)...* it's just a conviction and a belief in ourselves. No bad thing.

RW: And, looking back, anything you'd have done differently?

JW: There's nothing that I'd have done differently. That sounds arrogant. No. And by the way it's a thing that we often reflect, we reappraise weekly in the shop. Is there something we could have done differently? Absolutely nothing would have changed. And, there was a lot of luck along the way, but not all luck. It's a commitment and a belief and maybe you find out you actually have a bit of ability, you and your colleagues have that ability so, nothing would have changed.

APPENDIX 7:

10 JUNE 1999:
SHOP STEWARDS MEETING AT KVAERNER GOVAN
Present; Jamie Webster, Jim McFall, Johnny Johnson,
Joe Brown, Alan Curran, Davie Torrance, Ian Cameron

JW: We move on to the main item on the agenda which is
the current situation relating to the yard and securing
an owner. Well we had a broad discussion last week but
the position is that we are obviously conscious of the
time factor and the HR1 running. We know what that is.
Five weeks from now it activates itself and three weeks
from now the company would start in actual fact not
only indicating the numbers specifically but individuals
as such. So we're aware of the apprehension on the shop
floor, that's quite obvious. Today, I think it has to be said
is most certainly a big day, because we have VSEL in here
today and right now they're meeting the directors. That's
obviously about the oilers and even more importantly
I've just been told this morning that in London right now
is probably the most important meeting of all. Almskog
is meeting GEC this morning and that meeting is vital.
You link those two things together and there has to be an
expectation that when we meet the Task Force tomorrow
something is actually going to be happening. It must be.
We've all agreed quite conclusively that in going back to
the mass meeting next week and obviously we'll discuss
that later, there must be a definitive position. To maintain
at this particular time, still waiting, still waiting I think
you'd agree would be virtually impossible and I would
certainly be fearful of going back to a mass meeting on
the basis of that. So there has to be high expectations for
tomorrow and we believe there's a good possibility that
that will materialise. I'm aware of the situation. I spoke to
the convenors this morning and in relating to that meeting

tomorrow which should last about an hour, I'm convinced there'll be quite a media presence there tomorrow because they're perfectly well aware that something big could be happening tomorrow and also the fact is that the HR1 is still running and the two of them go hand in hand at this stage. I'll phone the yard in between half eleven and twelve o'clock to tell you exactly how that meeting went. The talks today are obviously about the oilers. They appear to be going quite well and they're obviously linked as well. We also know that the Yarrow's convenors are going down to Barrow tomorrow and having a meeting with the VSEL convenors and the GEC board. We are on that agenda. We are not THE agenda, but we're on the agenda and indications would be if we're on the agenda there can only be two things that are being covered. One, GEC's position relating to us and two, the position regarding the oilers. So, that's the position. I'll phone the yard in tomorrow. We have our joint shop stewards meeting at eight o'clock on Monday and subject to whatever happened in that we'll decide on the mass meeting. We'll keep an open mind on when it'll be, whether it's Tuesday, Wednesday or Thursday because factors might determine that. Because ideally we hope, and we set this out, that the next meeting would be between Gunnar, the joint shop stewards and the workforce. That's wur ideal scenario and that's what we're aiming for so we're really into the nitty-gritty, a tense time. I'm personally still supremely confident but I'd be lying if I didn't say that the apprehension's getting to us, but then I'm sure that's the case with everybody. So, on that aspect of it there's one other thing; Gunnar, although he's on holiday this week, he did during the week, was having a meeting with Pankakoski and I think with all the directors of the shipyards in the Kvaerner group and obviously that would be a meeting giving an update on what was happening in each yard. For example we know the *(word muffled)*... yard's been bought back by the *(word muffled)*... brothers. Alan, is that right?

AC: Aye. It was hingmied yesterday on the internet that the *(word unclear)*... brothers had bought back Kvaerner *(word unclear)*... but it doesn't take into account Kvaerner *(word unclear)*... Kvaerner *(word unclear)*... is still part of the Kvaerner group. But, *(word unclear)*... I think it's from a fortnight's time becomes part of... they go back into their own autonomy again as the *(word unclear)*... brothers.

JW: Right so, no doubt there's some questions, points. But we're certainly moving into what I think you know is one of the most important time factors and it's go to start coming together. It must. Does anyone want to raise any points or discuss anything?

Anon: We discussed about the oilers. What time scale are we talking for steel coming in? Do we know is it gonnae be before the Fair, *(the Glasgow Fair; a two to three week holiday in July traditionally taken by manufacturing workers)* or after?

JW: Alan do you want to...

AC: The earliest they're talking about getting the steel in for us is in August. And that would tie in with what we've got at the present moment. The Harland and Wolff stuff, the 320, 319 and by the time we get rid of they three, then by the time the steel comes in for the oilers then we're talking sometime in August for the steel coming in which would work in all right for steelworkers.

JW: It was indicated to me that we'd be starting it right after the Fair. No great delay, but obviously, I mean, we must keep addressing the situation. Despite things looking good we are now on that run, that run of work. The stockyard's finished, the prep's finished, the back shift's coming off. The workers see this. There is no way back on this run *(words muffled)*... The signs are we're moving into a reverse mode and the fact is that GEC and the oiler work will come together but it must and that's why the timescale cos the workers are getting dodgy. So if it's pulled together for next week then regardless of the wee blips of work, as you say Alan two or three weeks we've...

(someone talks over Jamie)

... We'll ride that.

JB: Jamie, I find it strange that we're talking now about possibly August because I can recall earlier on when we talked about this Gunnar the managing director said that once we finally have that ship we can have steel in here in ten days.

DT: What you've got to remember as well John is that VSEL have got fifty units built down there at the present moment in time for the oiler. Now, depending on what agreement they come to today and dependent on what happens in London today they could possibly ship they units anytime. They units could start coming into the yard at anytime. Within a week to a fortnight they units that they've already built down there could start coming in here.

Anon: That doesn't in actual fact help the situation directly in the shed. They'd be put about the yard until that berth is ready for us.

JW: But, see the situation right, for when the work's coming in or what, I don't mean it's not important, but if we get a position where it's quite clear that GEC are taking us over and we're getting the oiler work then there's nothing going to stop this workforce remaining intact. I mean we've been to that moving about different sections and interchangeability right and in an ideal world we'd like the work in next week. Bear in mind we're off in five weeks time for three weeks and if it's the beginning of August that'll not be a problem. If it's the beginning of July that'll not be a problem. We'll live with that, that's the technicalities.

AC: I think it all boils down to the fact that what goes on the day in the boardroom within Kvaerner and what happens down in England or down in London. It all depends on that. They, as Davie's already said, at Yarrow's have already cut fifty, I mean there's nothing to stop it. I mean it could happen, it could start from this Friday. And it could just be a continuation of steelwork coming into the yard. It could happen at any point in time.

Anon: Tommy Long asked me yesterday to identify essential maintenance tasks and any pre-work work we could do, particularly for platers and caulkers in the plater's shed. He didn't anticipate having the necessity to put any of them on the boat cos for all he thinks there will be hiatus in work he doesn't think it'll be that long, so I think they maybe have some idea of the plan lead times. But we don't know what that is.

JW: On the assumption, okay let's not get carried away but, on the assumption that things are going to go well. If the GEC thing comes together and the VSEL work comes together then we'll sit down with the company and we'll do what we always do. We'll co-operate for any lull there is with the interchangeability and doing all the requisite jobs until we get into full flow with the oilers. That will be a minor problem to solve. So really let's hope talks go well today with the company. I've every expectation. And let's hope they talks in London are fruitful. They must be good today, they must be, and get a good answer from the Task Force tomorrow.

IC: In the meantime are we still trying to get sub-contract work in here?

AC: I personally think that would be a no-no. That depends on what happens today in both places, here and London. I would imagine that Kvaerner, if there's any indication from GEC that they're going to take over in here, any work that we've actually tendered for, sub-contract work,

I think will just stop. I think it'll just die Ian. Because they'll no' want to commit themselves.

IC: You mean they'd rather do maintenance work than contract work?

AC: I'm only surmising Ian that they'll stop any contract from coming in from outside. If GEC are making a statement today that they're going to take over Kvaerner Govan, then any work that Kvaerner Govan has tendered for in the past I think will just drop. I know for a fact that we won't be looking for any more steel work for Harlands.

JW: On that, Ian, to be quite clear that may well be a positive aspect. Remember, there was a situation at Harlands we believe that they were indicating that they wished us possibly to tender for more work. And it looks as if we're not actually doing it. Now on a bad day you could worry about that, not tendering for more work, but on a good day you could actually be happy because the block's been put on Kvaerner taking on any more work because there's not going to be any more Kvaerner. At the end of the day there's only one commitment to Kvaerner right now, linked to GEC if they take us over. Completing the current contracts. Now they'll not put more work in if they're going to be moving out. They'll want the work completed, right. If GEC are taking over they'll be starting with 'a new broom sweeps clean'. At the end of the day our only concern is if we're doing maintenance work under GEC before we do the oilers that's exactly what we'll do. And we'll move on that. That shouldn't be a problem.

IC: I'll go back to a point that got made on Saturday. There's every possibility Harlands will be interested in this yard. Because it was mooted that we had a working relationship. I don't know if there's any truth in that but it was said on Saturday.

JW: But Ian, there has been a good working relationship between Harlands and Kvaerner (Ian; I'm only saying), but if Kvaerner are in the throes of moving out then they will not be masters of their destiny in here. It'll transfer to GEC. Now GEC might have a relationship with Harlands in bringing work in.

AC: You get a funny sensation with GEC. If GEC put work into Harlands and get Harlands to build all their units for them, for GEC, for Barrow-in-Furness and then Harlands had to sub-contract work to us because they couldn't handle their own work, so it's a weird situation Ian, but you're right. You cannae take away from the fact that Swan Hunters are still in the ball game as well. I mean everyone's concentrating on GEC, but you can't dismiss this Swan Hunter thing. GEC are in today. GEC are talking to Almskog today as well. Fine, that's all right. But you still cannae take away from the fact that Swan Hunter are there and this Dutch guy's still there. So you don't know. There might be something come out of that, but nothing could come out of it.

JW: Alan, we can only go on indications. We know we'd Swan Hunters in here and everybody knows my views on Swan Hunter, the situation with them visiting the yard. They're there. What deals they have with Kvaerner we've no control over. But the indications *(interrupted)...* the indications that we get are, and there's nothing to change the indications, are that GEC are well to the front and well to the fore and at an advanced stage. Well we'll soon find out if that's correct. Come today, come tomorrow. Because we're looking for a deal to be concluded. Are we absolutely certain? No because as Alan says, we do not know what Kvaerner are saying to Swan Hunter. We know what we'd like them to be saying, ultimately and we know who we'd prefer to be taking over, but we'll just have to wait and see.

APPENDIX 8:

24 JUNE 1999: SIR GAVIN LAIRD
TASK FORCE CHAIRMAN

RW: Sir Gavin there had been an expectation that a deal to save the yard was actually going to be announced this week. How damaging is it to morale, to the campaign to save the yard that that has not happened?

GL: It's both worrying and extremely disappointing. I'd hoped that by now, certainly by today that I'd have been able to tell the shop stewards that we had done a deal. But it's proving more difficult than I imagined. It's harder work that I could possibly imagine. That's not to say that there will not ultimately be a deal. I am still reasonably optimistic but it's got to be understood that there are a whole range of parties involved here. There's the MoD involved, there's Kvaerner, obviously, there's GEC Marconi Marine. On the one hand Kvaerner want to maximise the return they get for their investment. On the other hand GEC are not prepared to pick up the liabilities that they would inherit should they move in to the yard, should they take over the assets. So, it's bridging that very difficult gap that's proving tougher than I imagined.

RW: Would it be fair to say that Kvaerner were being difficult?

GL: I've said from the beginning that it would be commercially driven, it would be a business driven deal. I'm under no illusions. Despite the fact Kvaerner have made a very hefty provision for writing off cash and redundancy payments and all that goes with it, nevertheless they want to sell their assets and maximise their return. I mean that's perfectly natural. Not that I welcome it. I want a deal done as quickly as possible. The workforce are entitled to know their future. And I'm particularly concerned that redundancy HR1 notices have been issued and come into effect the day that the guys, the men and women, go on holiday. Now the last thing I want is this continuing uncertainty. But all I can do is work and work and work at it and that I am currently doing.

(Tape is switched off, then back on again).

RW: When were you first aware that you were going to be called in to try and solve this problem?

GL: I was involved and informed a week before the announcement was made publicly that Kvaerner were opting out of shipbuilding. I had initially a telephone call from Lord Macdonald who asked me to come and see him and I had a lengthy discussion with him about how we would go about forming a Task Force, the type of person who would be appropriate for a Task Force and were there people who would be prepared to join it and of course events subsequently proved that was the case. And was there the possibility of selling a shipyard in today's climate? So all of these things did take time, but as I say that was the week before the public announcement.

RW: When that phone call came in was it a phone call to ask you to become part of the Task Force or was it a phone call initially to ask your advice on whether or not it was a good idea and subsequently you were invited?

GL: I think the truth of the matter is that the minister had made his mind up, that he had to tackle it in some fashion and it's not the first time there's been Task Forces established. So the principle had basically been agreed before I was involved. My involvement came as a; a member and b; would I chair it, to take the ultimate responsibility as Chairman? Of course to which I agreed. I underestimated just how much work would be associated with it, but there you are.

RW: How hard a task has this been?

GL: It's been extremely difficult. What's made it even more difficult is the obvious fact, but one has to state it, that we the Task Force own none of the assets whatsoever. All we have been told to do, our brief has been and remains to be facilitators and bring interested parties together. Normally trying to sell a facility like a shipyard or the gas turbine plant in Clydebank the first thing you've got to do is get a prospectus together. You've got to do due diligence. These things take weeks and months. We're trying to compress months and months of work literally into weeks. As I've said before at different times to try and eliminate the uncertainty as quickly as possible and do a successful deal. That's been the task but it's been immensely difficult. We've had to see a whole range of ministers. We've had to meet corporate management of Kvaerner. We've had to meet the Chairman and senior management of GEC. We've had interviews and discussions with Swan Hunters. The same applies to Ferguson's. We've had to be down to the yard, we've had to go to Clydebank. All of those things to do and to be seen to be doing because it's important that people knew we were working as hard as we could to resolve the issue.

RW: You mentioned the three principle players there, GEC Marconi, Swan Hunter and Ferguson's. What was your own personal assessment of the merits of each of those bids?

GL: Well I had no doubt that from the beginning GEC Marconi Marine was certainly the most probable purchaser of the yard. For the obvious reason that they own Yarrows just across the river. For the equally obvious reason that they own Barrow-in-Furness, the VSEL shipyard down in Barrow-in-Furness. We were well aware that Barrow had orders which were falling behind and therefore there was the possibility of transferring some of the work that was slipping off in Barrow up to Govan. So it was a rather obvious target from the beginning. Allied to which was one of the very first things the Task Force sat down and did which was to identify companies and people in companies. I happened to know Lord Simpson, I happened to know a range of senior industrialists and one of the reasons why Lord Macdonald, Gus, asked me to participate in the fashion I did, was because I'd made literally dozens of business contacts during a long, active life in industry. So, to come back to your question, GEC were clearly the front runner but at the same time we made it known as widely as we possibly could that we would welcome interest from anyone else. Hence the Swan Hunter involvement. Hence the Ferguson involvement.

RW: What was your assessment of Swan Hunter and Ferguson?

GL: Extremely interesting. In fact, the operation in Holland, Centrestaal, I had made an arrangement with the senior civil servant John Mason to go across and visit it. In the end I had to call off because of developments that demanded my attentions here in Glasgow, but the fact of the matter is that they do have an extremely efficient operation. Not in shipbuilding, that's a misunderstanding. They don't build ships. What they do is they cut and form steel for shipbuilders for no fewer than twenty in Holland And they do it very efficiently. And that's why the Dutch are so successful in tendering for ship orders. And if we can apply some of that technique, and indeed they do apply some of the same techniques at Govan at the moment, that's one of the things going for them. But if we can apply them in the sense they do and to the scale they do in Holland it would dramatically reduce prices of ships and the tender process would be more effective.

RW: Did you ever feel Swan Hunter was right for Kvaerner Govan?

GL: It certainly would not be my first preference. We're talking about shipbuilding. It would be a poor second best. But the target was could we get a GEC Marconi

Marine shipbuilder and could we also bring in Swan Hunter stroke Centrestaal. So it became a dual target. Then it would be a bonus. From a dreadful prospect of no merchant shipbuilding on the Clyde to where we continue with shipbuilding and add to it a facility that would help the shipbuilding process in other yards throughout the UK. That's very exciting.

RW: And how about Ferguson? Was that just a whim from the owner?

GL: No, I don't think so. It was a genuine interest. I mean they're senior business people out to make a buck and they're quite right and they devoted some time to actively examine what the prospects were for a purchase. I think it was too big a task for them frankly, the Govan facility, but it was a genuine interest and I welcomed that.

RW: So what made Kvaerner Govan saleable in your opinion? What did it have going for it?

GL: A whole range of things going for it. The first of course I have to say, only because I mean it, the quality of the workforce. Their flexibility. The quality of their product. The excellent industrial relations they've had over a number of years. The mixture of skills. Allied to the substantial investment which has taken place in capital equipment, the new processes and techniques that they've been able to implement. And they've been delivering ships in budget and on time. The record in recent years from Govan has been tremendous. The great tragedy of all of this, if Kvaerner had not taken their eye off the ball when they bought over Trafalgar (House), that shipyard was profitable. They had turned it around, they'd invested, the workforce had responded tremendously and just at the time when it went in to profit building ships, on time, excellent quality, lo and behold Kvaerner pull the plug. So all of these things were going for Govan. But first and foremost was the quality of the workforce and that includes the management. That includes a whole range of people, eh, that build ships. Everybody.

RW: One thing that I thought was very interesting when the Task Force was appointed was that it was appointed by Gus Macdonald, an ex-shipyard worker. You were on it, a Clydesider, I think the rest of the Task Force have Clydeside roots. It seemed they were all from the same team. How important was that and what part did that play in your understanding of the overall picture?

GL: I think that the people who decided to establish the Task Force gave it considerable thought. Three quality, prestigious business people with great contacts within the shipbuilding industry, well certainly two in the shipbuilding industry, the third, Malcolm (Clark) he has more expertise in gas turbine, which of course is Kvaerner Energy in Clydebank, so you had that mixture. Inviting me to participate in the fashion that I have, with my many, many contacts in the industrial world that I've referred to already. In addition to that, we have been and I have been involved in ships all my life, one way or the other. When I was a kid at school I had two uncles working in the shipyards and a cousin. My young brother worked in ships most of his life. I was in the Merchant Navy for six years and I've worked in ship repair. And it, it sounds trite I know it, in the blood stuff, but I really am part of this community. My nephew works at Govan right now. So I think it was immensely important that there wasn't any window dressing. It was people who had a genuine interest, it was people who were prepared to work hard and work for nothing, who really, really, really wanted a solution to the problem. Who were really, really interested in the continuation of shipbuilding on the Clyde, a wonderful tradition that we've let slip for so many years. So I think it was a well thought out decision to involve the kind of persons that they did involve.

RW: And I suppose it's like all heavy industries and traditional industries, there is a certain emotion about shipbuilding, about coal mining, steel.

GL: I can't understand it. I went to a launch at Yarrows just a couple of weeks ago. There is something unique about a ship being launched. And many, many people to whom I spoke at the launch and after it said exactly the same thing. Some people in this very office (the Scottish Office in Meridian Court, Cadogan Street, Glasgow), who'd never been to a launch in their life said there's an emotional thing. I can't understand it, despite having sailed in ships all those years. Of course there's an emotional element to it, but it's bread and butter that matters and of course what people perhaps don't appreciate is that a ship nowadays is extremely sophisticated, particularly a naval ship. There's high, high added value, sophisticated equipment and machinery. It's not just big chunks of steel welded together. They are very sophisticated vessels and platforms for other equipment and it's important that on the Clyde we retain those skills.

APPENDIX 9:

6 JULY 1999: JAMIE WEBSTER
INTERVIEW AFTER THE FIRST ANNOUNCEMENT THAT GEC HAD PUT IN A FORMAL BID FOR KVAERNER GOVAN

RW: Well, I don't want to say 'At last!', but at least a formal bid is now on the table. What's your reaction to that initially?

JW: Absolutely ecstatic. I could jump over a tenement building I think. The first absolute, definite, positive step forward to I'm sure success in this.

RW: There's not a bit of you that's maybe urging a wee bit of caution, because I know you're always optimistic but it's not been accepted yet?

JW: Yeah there's a bit of caution, but I'm trying not to be cautious because this is the first absolutely positive step. We must now get a deal. We must. GEC and Kvaerner surely, surely must work out a deal.

RW: What would you say to the workers that are listening to this?

JW: Eh, what would I say? This is the first night in six months we've actually had good news. And, I think tomorrow will be an even better day and what we said, "we're gonnae do it, we're gonnae get there," we must, we can't go back the way, we must go forward. We absolutely must go forward.

RW: What do you reckon about your trip to London tomorrow? Do you think that's on or not? *(To take the unopened HR1 redundancy letters to Kvaerner HQ).*

JW: I think a trip to the moon's better for me than down to London actually. We'll take tomorrow as it comes, if I can sleep at all.

6 JULY 1999: JAMIE WEBSTER
SECOND INTERVIEW A FEW MINUTES AFTER THE FIRST

RW: Are you going to go down to London with the redundancy notices?

JW: I would like to think no'. I'd like to think we could just dispose of them in another way. Redundancy notices, I'd like to think we're putting them behind us.

RW: But clearly you've got to hear from Kvaerner. What would your message to them be?

JW: Lift the redundancy notices and let's get on with the business to everybody's satisfaction.

RW: Now on a more general level, you've had five or ten minutes to consider this now, has the euphoria diminished a little bit? Have you got your cautious but optimistic head back on?

JW: No, I haven't got my cautious but optimistic head back on. I've got my hyper head back on. Eh... I'm just happy in the yard with everyone that's supported us right. I'm where I want to be, where we want to be. You cannae be in a better place.

RW: And again, a word maybe for, okay it's not a done deal yet let's not say it is, but a word perhaps for the role the politicians and the Task Force have played in all of this to get us to this point?

JW: I'm appreciative of everyone that's helped us and tomorrow I will set about communicating with every single individual and every group that's helped us and there are many, and they will not be forgotten, because it was a team effort. That's why I think when it's all revealed who did help this will be a good message for people in Scotland. I'm sure of that. Ultimately this was driven by human endeavour, there's no doubt about that. Human endeavour.

APPENDIX 10:

7 JULY 1999: JAMIE WEBSTER
SHORTLY BEFORE HE FLEW TO LONDON TO HAND IN THE REDUNDANCY NOTICES TO KVAERNER HQ. HE'D FOUND OUT THE PREVIOUS EVENING THAT KVAERNER HAD REJECTED GEC'S OFFER FOR THE YARD

RW: Did you have any conversation with the workforce this morning and, if so, what happened?

JW: No, no actual conversation. The workers did what we agreed yesterday and returned all their redundancy notices because this affair will not and should not be allowed to break their dignity and self-respect, and respect for each other. The rest of them can do what they want. They're not taking that away from us. The letters are going down to London to Kvaerner headquarters as agreed.

RW: Now what are you going to be saying to the bosses down at Kvaerner today, because clearly you're going to say something? You're not just going to dump the letters on the doorstep.

JW: What I'm saying to them if they want to listen is; – Let's forget GEC for a second. They currently employ us, they have a responsibility to us. If this cesspit of negotiations, right, is allowed to continue in the same terms of absolutely no respect *(word inaudible)...* of those companies, I believe they should actually be saying to GEC, no more. GEC may not have a responsibility to us, but Kvaerner, if there's any humanity, they most certainly do.

RW: So make their position clear. Not a woolly, well, it might happen or it might not.

JW: Absolutely not. I never thought I'd say this, and I've certainly not been saying it, but I'm saying it now because this workforce I am sure expect me to say it. If they cannot

384   BACK FROM THE BRINK

today, at this hour, say to themselves we are going to get into serious discussions and show each other respect and give the workforce respect walk away from each other right now and let us carry on our lives.

RW: What would the consequences of that be do you think?

JW: The consequences of that will be that that yard may close. We are now in a situation that it's not a question of actually being stripped of our jobs. Right. The effect is now that with they two companies by eventualities or by design are now actually trying to strip us of our self-respect and dignity. They should not be allowed to do that. Nobody should.

RW: You're going to see John Reid as well today. What's the message to him?

JW: The message with all due respect to the Secretary of State for Scotland is a line must be drawn today and with the greatest respect to the Secretary of State for Scotland if this government today cannot get those companies to show decency in their talks, if he is incapable of getting them to make a statement, Tony Blair the prime minister surely is. The Prime Minister who came to Glasgow in March, across the river (to Scotstoun) at a time when we were going through a trauma, would not come (to Govan). See today, he must come and spend five minutes of his time looking at what's happening to twelve hundred people in Scotland and their families and if he truly leads this country he will not allow two multi-national companies to destroy our minds and souls. If he's half the man I think he is and is a true leader he will stand beside us and put this absolute mental torture to an end.

APPENDIX 11:

8 JULY (LUNCHTIME) 1999: JAMIE WEBSTER
FOLLOWING HIS RETURN FROM MEETING KVAERNER BOSSES AND SCOTTISH OFFICE MINISTERS. HE'D ALSO ADDRESSED A MASS MEETING IN THE YARD

RW: Jamie first of all, that mass meeting this morning, how did it go? What was the temperature?

JW: Oh the meeting went very well. That was me giving a report back from meeting the chief executive of Kvaerner, Almskog and obviously John Reid, the Secretary of State for Scotland and Lord Macdonald. Giving them an update on that. And from that meeting down in London I was able to tell the workforce that I came back quite chirpy from London yesterday and when they see me chirpy, they're chirpy.

RW: But, we're Thursday now and the naming of names (redundancies) was supposed to start today. It's been delayed until Monday now. In the overall programme of events, how crucial are the next two or three days?

JW: Absolutely crucial. I have to be honest and of course the workforce are realistic. We really do not want to travel into the Monday situation where people are actually identified for compulsory redundancy within four days. That's a really high temperature situation and one I pray we don't face.

RW: So from what you're saying you're really wanting a result on this obviously as soon as possible, but by no later than Sunday?

JW: Yes, I mean really if we have to take the temperature down, I don't think it can get much hotter, but between now and Sunday I really do think we have to break that barrier.

RW: What do you think happens on Monday if that barrier isn't broken?

JW: Well there is a concern, the fact is, we've stuck together so hard but there's something very emotional about actually being identified, you're being identified for redundancy four days later. And it would be fair to say that with all the best will in the world those individuals would have a right to possibly disregard me at that stage because they personally have a problem which could be seen that I've failed to deliver and save their job at that time.

RW: So, talking generally, you think you might have a job holding them on Monday if that situation arose?

JW: Yes, because that's human nature and the people know that. I may be wrong on that, but I'm a human being and I work with the people and it'll be a very, very difficult time. I seriously, seriously hope that situation doesn't arise. That's why obviously I'm concerned about it, but nevertheless, balanced against that is that I'm very confident, very confident. London will be a busy place today with activity relating to us I'm sure with GEC, Kvaerner and government bodies. So, eh, we went from one hour on Tuesday from ecstasy to actual desperation. I'm looking for a reverse trend on that and it's quite possible.

RW: I was speaking to Kvaerner this morning and they were saying that yes there is still the way open for a deal to be done and in their minds they're not actually talking to GEC physically face to face at the moment but they're talking through the government. Is that your understanding from your meeting with John Reid yesterday? He's a broker basically.

JW: Absolutely that is the situation. They are working as a broker and at some stage once that part of the negotiations is finished the two bodies will come physically together. I know the government are working very hard at that and I'm fairly confident that if the situation is that both parties actually want to be brought together, and I think the indications are they are wanting to get together, then I think that's a progressive step. Today, tomorrow, let's see what both of those days bring.

RW: Speaking again to sources I have in government, there is an indication although not a guarantee, that in some way, and I don't know whether it would be in redundancy payments or in grants or whatever, there might be some cash from the government to help sweeten the pot as it were. What's your impression of that scenario?

JW: Well on the basis that the difficulty is the liabilities relating to the redundancies, and that bridge has to be breached somehow, the gap has to be filled and I believe the government are looking at various options to try and bring them closer together on that. It's not an enormous sum of money by business standards so there would be something sadly wrong if that problem couldn't be solved, because as I say it's not significant money in business terms. So between the three parties I can't see that not happening.

JULY 8 (EVENING) 1999: THE WEBSTER FAMILY
AT THEIR HOME IN SUMMERSTON, GLASGOW
PRESENT: JAMIE, WIFE ISABEL AND DAUGHTER AMANDA

AW: Dad, you never told us what happened at the mass meeting.

JW: It went okay. I mean obviously we're all getting edgy about the time factor and such like. But that's to be expected. You cannae expect people to go into the last few days and keep the same sort of temperament you know. But I mean the vast majority absolutely still positive but obviously they're beginning to say, "Jamie, oh you know this is a' next week." We're into only four or five days away. But you know what the really sad thing is, it's right next to the holidays. People are going away next Friday. And, this guy comes up to me and he says, "Jamie I'm going away on holiday this Friday, early, for a fortnight." You know he was frantic, he says, "What happens? A letter could be behind my door when I'm away on holiday." I says, "Whoa, I've not figured that situation out." I says, "Leave that one with me." I says, "Look, see at the end of the day I'm telling you we're coming out of this so don't panic. Let's just keep a sort of logic to it." But you can see some of them getting a bit *(to barking dog;* Gizmo stop it...), you can some of them getting a bit edgier and there's nae doubt about that. *(To Isabel)* That's what the woman in Asda was saying to you. You were saying the woman in Asda was saying it was looking really terrible.

IW: Aye.

JW: Who was she?

IW: Someone worked with me with years ago.

JW: What, do you know her?

IW: No I just saw her.

JW: And that's what she was saying, she's watching it? What was her man saying? Is he saying it looks okay or what does he think?

IW: No. He says it's looking bad.

JW: I'll give you the laugh today. On the Govan road at dinner time this old man came up to me, right, and he obviously recognised me. I mean it's nice, just somebody in the street. And he says how's it going? He was really genuinely concerned. Just a wee sort of man about seventy etc. He says that's a terrible thing, I hope it's okay. Are they still going to meetings? I says aye, so it just shows you how people follow it.

IW: How did London go, you've hardly told me anything about it?

JW: Well I didn't get in 'til quarter to eleven last night. Seriously I was absolutely dog tired. It was good, but you know I hate London. I absolutely hate London, you know that. I wouldn't live there for a king's ransom. I don't like it. It's all hustle bustle. In actual fact I almost bust my foot there was that much walking. By the way, I took some noise up at work today. What was that a tour of London? You were everywhere but the Tower of London and one guy shouts, that's where you should be put the Tower of London *(laughs)* by the way. No, it was good. It's a long day.

AW: You're looking a bit better, a bit more cheerful than you were the other night.

JW: Oh you've noticed! What have you noticed? I've been sleeping okay. I have seriously. You know sometimes you're stressed and you cannae sleep? You know I'm sort of worse when I'm maybe going to a meeting and you've built up an expectation as such you know. But you know eventually I think if you're stressed up that much you know, mentally stressed, you become so physically tired as well you actually have to sleep.

IW: You should be paying me as your secretary for all the calls I'm taking for you.

JW: All what calls? How many?

IW: About twenty-five.

JW: Twenty-five calls? That must have been a quiet night.

IW: No, it was quite a busy night actually.

JW: Well you'll be getting to know them all. They're all getting to know you on first name terms. Hello Isabel.

IW: That's true.

AW: How come I didn't get a bouquet of flowers? I've answered more phone calls!

JW: Well, Isabel, eh that was a nice gesture. Everybody was saying that and they appreciated it. Amanda, have you seen the card? To Isabel for taking all the hassle and stresses. By the way, that's what they're like as well. See the men in there, they actually know when I'm saying I got in last night and Isabel's taken twenty-five calls, cos they were saying that's a lot of calls. And of course I say sweet little pea that you are there's not a lot that would put up with that. Remember last week one night, there was more than twenty-five calls. What time did it start at?

IW: Quarter to five to quarter past eleven.

JW: Tell you one thing, see this morning, they were all laughing about it, but see at the time, it wasnae funny. Look on the bright side. We've never seen so little television.

RW: Isabel, can I ask you a question? Since this whole thing started really back in February, how's your man been? What have you noticed him being like? With the family at home.

IW: He's been quite quiet and very tired and not really speaking a lot. As if his mind's away on something else, you know what I mean, on his work.

RW: What's the routine when he gets in at night?

IW: Well there's no' really a routine because as soon as he gets in the phone goes. So we don't get a meal and it could be nine o'clock, ten o'clock before we get our dinner. And then after that he has his bath and goes to bed. And that's about it. Or, he's away doing interviews somewhere.

RW: And on a personal level in himself, do you notice a change in him?

IW: I try and push him on and make him, make sure he gets up and does it all again the next morning. You know if he'd down a bit I'll say you've got to see it through, get back up and get on with it. And he's got to be there at the end you know what I mean? So, I don't really have time to notice things *(laughs)*.

RW: Do you think realistically to be successful in a campaign like this and to keep going you need your family?

IW: Well, I would say so. And we try to encourage him. I think we do anyway. *(To Jamie)* We all try to encourage you and have our points of view don't we?

RW: And what about you Amanda? What have you made of it all?

AW: I do see a change in my dad's personality. I think he's become a lot quieter. But I definitely think we need to put a great input into it cos I feel as though if it was a person myself they wouldn't have done as much because we're always there to support my dad at the end of the day no matter what he decides. And whether other people support his decisions, we're always there. And it doesnae matter.

RW: Does he seem stressed to you or his he coping with it do you think?

AW: I think at the beginning he was coping really, really well but as the time goes on and the pressure's like advanced he is, the stress does come to a point where he can't control it and he does need us. But he's always been someone who can control his stress and he's always taught us how to do it so I think he's coping actually very well, better than I would myself.

RW: And, Jamie from your own point of view, have you noticed a change in yourself over the last four or five months?

JW: Eh, yes I suppose there has been that. Eh, I mean the family, the family must have been left behind at some stage obviously, the time factor. They've taken the second priority and I know that but months go, weeks go by and you just forget that your leaving them behind you know but occasionally you'll understand and you'll say I haven't spent much time with them this week. That's noticeable, that's not right and then you look and you say, but they know that and they understand it. I mean I say to lots of people in work and it's a fact and everybody knows it, that's one of the things, I couldn't have done what I've done without the family. That would have been impossible. The stress in this campaign is so, is of such a high volume and so, so continuous that if you continued more stress in the house and pressure, I wouldn't be able to do it. But in actual fact when you come back in here you can get relaxed to a degree, you can talk with your family, you can do things. But it's more important than that. You heard the laugh there about the twenty-five phone calls, but that's true. Well a lot of women wouldn't put up with that, I know they wouldn't you know. But I don't want to take it for granted because they know deep down I don't take it for granted. But you don't do favours for you family, you do it because you love them you know. You don't cast up at all etc. you know. But I really you know I'm going on holiday at the Glasgow Fair with them and I want to try and make up for that a wee bit, be together and have a right good week together you know. And then of course, that one, that one night, I came in at the back of eight totally shattered man and my two daughters were there and I just said to them, let's go out, let's go out to a karaoke night. And it was just an absolute urge to get away and I think at that time I switched onto the fact that, one;– how much have they had to put up with me, actually living with stress and two;– how much when I needed them they were there. And we just went out the three of us and it was crazy. It was almost like going back when they were much younger and you were going out and okay it was a pub this time and not the sea shore, but we had a really good night.

RW: Were you surprised at that Amanda?

AW: I was actually quite surprised that my dad took us to the pub, because he usually doesnae do things like that. But it was a good night and it was quite a relaxing night considering the amount of stress he was under and my dad needed it and we needed it because me and my sister Julie we felt we had the communication links that we had with him before all this campaign started and that was a night to renew it and speak about everything we had to and although it was a busy pub we got a lot of things talked about. It had to be talked about.

RW: Isabel, regardless of what happens, the outcome, do you feel that this family can ever be back to normal?

IW: I think so, yes. I think life will just go whether Jamie's in with Kvaerner or not. Cos our family's quite a close family and we will all just pull together. And we've got to think of our family and no just his work and get on with it, it's as simple as that.

APPENDIX 12:

9 JULY 1999: JOHN REID

SECRETARY OF STATE FOR SCOTLAND

AFTER THE TASK FORCE MEETING IN WHICH JAMIE FELT FIRST MINISTER DONALD DEWAR THREW IN THE TOWEL AS FAR AS SAVING THE GOVAN YARD WAS CONCERNED

Alan Saunby, *STV News:* Obviously a very key meeting this morning in what's been a very eventful week.

JR: It has been an eventful week. It's been a disappointing week in many ways because we haven't seen progress. We've seen the highs and lows of an offer and a refusal. This morning's meeting was to discuss with the Task Force some other approaches and avenues that they've been following up and to inform the representatives of the workforce who've been under increasing uncertainty and I do really think they've conducted themselves with dignity. All I can say is that we continue to explore all avenues to try to get the two companies to come together over what I regard as the basis for negotiation. But it isn't easy and I wouldn't like anyone to think it is.

RW: What was the mood of the unions at the end of the meeting?

JR: I think we're all very realistic. We've learned over the last few weeks to avoid the highs of exaltation and the lows of despair because in thirty-five minutes one day this week we went from having no offer, to having an offer, to having it rejected. So, we're realistic. Everything that can be done is being done.

Alan Saunby, *STV News:* It's forty-eight hours isn't it basically before the notices are issued?

JR: Well we're talking about a large number of workers for the rest of their life, so the next forty-eight hours is important. So is the last forty-eight hours and I have said that I will not give this up until I am absolutely convinced that there is no hope left and we're not at that stage and I will still do everything, as will Donald Dewar and others to try and make sure that try to bring the two companies together.

RW: Are we near that stage?

JR: I don't think it's for me to guess at that, it's for the two companies. They know their minds and we're trying to bring them together. We have been for some weeks, indeed months now, looking for someone who could take over the yard. Our aim remains the same which is to make sure this goes on as a viable and continuing operation at that yard. There aren't signs at the moment that there is an end game, but we'll continue to push until we're absolutely convinced there is no hope left.

Alan Saunby, *STV News:* What do you say to people who think, well the government is a big customer of both of them and they can bang heads together?

JR: Well at the end of the day it's for the two companies themselves. The companies themselves know the wider concerns. I hope they want to be good corporate citizens. The government is under no illusion about the importance and they are under no illusions about how important we think it is. Over the last ten years of the order of a hundred million pounds have gone in to this yard so it's not money, Kvaerner have turned down hundreds of millions of dollars to stay in shipbuilding in the United States, so again it's not money. It is the two companies themselves who seem to have a difference over the valuation of the prospects and the assets and the debts of this yard. We are trying to bring them together and I will do everything possible to do that.

9 JULY 1999: JAMIE WEBSTER

RW: Jamie, you certainly sound as if you're not as optimistic as you hoped you were going to be. Why is that? What went on at that meeting that has led you to feel this way?

JW: Because nobody knows what's going on. Nobody. Absolutely nobody. There's efforts being made to get them together but nobody actually knows anything, that can tell us anything.

RW: Who's nobody?

JW: Well, the government are trying to find things out and they appear not to be able to do that. And it's not because of lack of effort. I simply do not know what is going on.

RW: Do you think that GEC and Kvaerner are playing hardball with the government?

JW: I know this sounds very contradictory. I actually do not know what those companies are doing. I'm actually drifting away from what any of them are thinking, saying or doing or what their beliefs are. I simply do not know. It's incomprehensible.

RW: Did you get the feeling that Gavin Laird felt there was any progress made in his talks with the two companies yesterday?

JW: They're still working and they met them etc. and they continuously say that they're open to negotiations but, I mean, in relation to tangible evidence, I don't see any. I just don't see any.

RW: Now presumably you must have said to Gavin Laird, look what the hell do I tell the workers on Monday when they start getting named for compulsory lay-offs. What was his response to that?

JW: Yeah, he realised it's a very difficult situation but we must keep continually trying to bring them together. I believe they've got frustrations as well.

RW: Do you think the government and the Task Force are doing enough at this moment in time?

JW: Yes, as far as I know but, in reality when you're dealing with multi-national companies I actually don't know what enough is. I mean I'm only a convenor you know. I mean their idea of enough and my idea of enough might be different. I don't know the mechanics enough you know. My role is to report back and represent that workforce and try and make people listen to us but the mechanics of what they're doing and what's going on is, I don't know. I just left that meeting bamboozled. I mean I'm telling you the truth, bamboozled you know.

RW: So what do you tell the workers on Monday?

JW: At the present time? That I'm bamboozled, cos I am. Something might change over the weekend. I'm using the word bamboozled because I am. I've not made it up or manufactured it.

9 JULY 1999: JIM MOOHAN
REGIONAL INDUSTRIAL OFFICER, GMB UNION

RW: Jim, people pick up on vibes. I have to tell you the vibes of people coming out of that meeting are not good. What went on?

JM: Well it was laid on the line that there's problems with both sides in getting to the table. At this stage of the game so to speak it's very disappointing. We've got seven days to save the shipyard and stop the first employee leaving and once that sort of train starts running then who knows what can happen then. It's a failure from my point of view once the first employee leaves. I'm hoping that things can happen over the weekend to bring the two parties together and we'll just have to wait and see.

RW: Was there anything out of that meeting that gave you hope that Gavin Laird's meeting with these two companies yesterday was profitable in any way?

JM: Well, the fact that the Task Force travelled down to London to meet the two bodies for the first time gave me hope. And the Task Force have been doing an excellent job up to now and they'll continue to approach these two companies to bring them round the table. The differences between the two I don't think is insurmountable. We're talking about twelve hundred employees and their families. If we put our mind to it then I'm quite sure we can get a deal done here.

RW: Do you or do you think we're heading for closure?

JM: I don't want to think about that. Ehh, I'll not think about that until employees start to leave the yard. And even if that happens I'll continue to fight along with the shop stewards and the employees in order to try and maintain that shipyard as a viable concern.

RW: Now Jim I have to put this to you because I witnessed it with my own eyes. The body language between you and the convenor Jamie Webster was not good when you come out that meeting. Is there a difference in strategy that you two are fighting?

JM: There's no difference at all in strategy. Jamie has carried this flag up to the present time and continues to do so. He's done an excellent job and it's a lesson that should be picked up by people outside. Eh, how an individual's approached and tried to look out for the interests of the membership and the families and there's no difference. Jamie and I are as one in relation to where we're going forward on behalf of the shipyard.

RW: And yet it didn't appear, in fairness, to be like that.

JM: Of course we have discussions and maybe some differences. At the end of the day my aim and Jamie's aim is the same, save the shipyard.

APPENDIX 13:

12 JULY 1999: JAMIE WEBSTER
FOLLOWING A MASS MEETING OF THE WORKERS WHO HAD JUST FOUND OUT THE NAMES OF THE 241 REDUNDANCIES

RW: Jamie, the mood in the place this morning? What did you say to the workers and what response did you get?

JW: Well it was obviously a very emotional meeting. The fact is that we knew two hundred and forty-one people would be identified. There was the usual complete dignity and the one thing no one can break, the respect that we have for each other. That's something that will remain untarnished. Eh, obviously this afternoon, a cauldron of emotions etc. I could have wept this afternoon and that was only watching about six people getting the letters. What they do tonight? Be where they should be, with their families trying to come to terms with this. But, I'm emphasising it, the fat lady has not sang yet. She's not sang yet, and indications are that there are moves in London today still as we depend on the government, and so much is relying on their shoulders just now, to resolve this issue. So that's the workers with us to the end. We can still come out of this, out of this quagmire, this nightmare, we can still come out. And we're still holding fast. But in the homes tonight, just another turbulent time trying to come to terms with what the bloody hell is going on and what we did to deserve this.

RW: And even at this stage, Kvaerner have pulled another stroke it must be seen as by naming fifteen apprentices. What is that all about?

JW: There was a difficulty with the apprentices getting named. We've had a sharp exchange of views with the company on that. Totally, utterly, completely unacceptable and I don't like giving people ultimatums but it's sometimes when we say that's not to be allowed to happen, it's not. Right, there's no way those kids are getting thrown on the street. This company and the unions have a responsibility towards them. If we do get paid off we've got a skill behind us. There's no way they get put on the scrap heap at nineteen or twenty without finishing their apprenticeships. We've been moving heaven and earth and we told the company in no uncertain terms, that is a complete, utter no-no.

RW: What happens if they don't accept that and continue with that?

JW: They will accept it. Let me assure you, they will accept it. They've made a grave, grave miscalculation relating to that, unheard of in the shipbuilding as long as I've been there, thirty-two years. They apprentices will be protected until we get them a job. I mean, they kids are not throwing away three and a half years of their life, no way.

RW: And when do you expect a decision from management on that?

JW: Tomorrow morning. That will be addressed and I am confident will be rectified. It better be.

The following day Kvaerner and GEC reached a heads of agreement deal.